American Poverty
in a New
Era of Reform

American Poverty in a New Era of Reform

Second Edition

Harrell R. Rodgers Jr.

M.E.Sharpe
Armonk, New York
London, England

Library of Congress Cataloging-in-Publication Data

Rodgers, Harrell R.
    American poverty in a new era of reform / Harrell R. Rodgers, Jr. — 2nd ed.
        p. cm.
    Includes bibliographical references and index.
    ISBN 0-7656-1595-9 (hardcover : alk. paper) ISBN 0-7656-1596-7 (pbk. : alk. paper)
    1. Poverty—United States. 2. Poor—United States. 3. Public welfare—United States.
I. Title.

    HC110.P6R638 2005
    362.5'0973—dc22   2005005390

Printed in the United States of America

BM (c)   10   9   8   7   6   5   4   3   2   1
BM (p)   10   9   8   7   6   5   4   3   2   1

Contents

Tables and Figures

Tables

Figures

Preface

The first edition of this book was published less than three years after the passage of the Personal Responsibility and Work Opportunity Reconciliation Act of 1996 (PRWORA), the most significant alteration in America's welfare policy since the Social Security Act of 1935. As with any new public policy, especially one of this magnitude, it will take twenty to thirty years to take full measure of its impact on federal and state welfare systems and the poverty population. While assessment data are still far from optimal, by the early 2000s they were greatly improved, allowing a much more sophisticated analysis of PRWORA and American poverty in this edition.

To accompany the improved analysis of PRWORA, all the data on poverty measurement, the demographics of poverty, causes of poverty, use of welfare and the cost, and design and impact of major social welfare programs have been updated. The chapters have been rearranged to allow an examination of state design and implementation of PRWORA and state characteristics associated with particular choices of policy options. Last, how these changes have impacted the poverty population and the overall welfare system have been analyzed.

The last two chapters of the book analyze the most recent research and data on the impact of the new law. To evaluate program implementation and impacts, they assess data on specific goals of PRWORA. More general data on the work patterns of single mothers and other poor family heads, their use of welfare, and the poverty rates of these households are also used to evaluate some of the broader goals of reform. The last chapter summarizes and analyzes the positive and negative impacts of reform, and discusses possible reforms both in policies and implementation. The last section discusses deficiencies in the evaluation data and the implications of these problems, and suggests ways to rectify them.

To make the often rather complex data easier to understand, the tables and figures have been redesigned to make it much easier to comprehend trends, patterns, and impacts of policies and poverty among individuals and groups over time. An appendix has been added to help readers easily find Internet updates on the topics and data used in the book.

Acknowledgments

I had a great deal of indispensable help in writing this new edition. Given the fast moving subject matter, the new edition took a major rewrite. The burden of starting from scratch in many of the chapters was greatly lightened by my excellent graduate assistants. Juan DiBello, Mohit Manti, and Andrew Rogers helped me find and retrieve information from dozens of federal data bases, research the literature, and design the tables and graphs. Mohit Manti and Juan DiBello designed all the figures and tables. Mohit Manti created numerous versions of each of the figures that we could review in making the final selections. Chandru Swaminthan contributed technical advice when we had problems extracting the files we needed from data bases. Natashia Davis contributed in dozens of ways to the final copy of the book. I am grateful to Larry Mead, Scott Allard, and Paul Rich for reading and critiquing various sections of the text.

As usual, M.E. Sharpe was a delight to work with. Patricia Kolb, Vice President and Editorial Director, has long been a supporter and guide. The political science editor, Niels Aaboe, and editorial coordinator Amanda Allensworth, kept the ball smoothly rolling from signed contract through production. The production editor, Henrietta Toth, made this stage of production amazingly painless and contributed significantly to improvements in the readability and quality of the text.

Gordon Fisher and Elizabeth Lower-Basch with the Department of Health and Human Services came to my aid several times when I could not find needed data and technical information. I am most grateful for their help. I should note that no public officials read the text, therefore they bear no responsibility for the manner in which I have used data, my interpretations, or conclusions. I am solely responsible for the content.

I dedicate this book to my son, Michael James Rodgers, who loves to see his name in daddy's books. You make it all worthwhile, pal. Thank you for everything.

Acronyms

ABAWDs	able-bodied adults without dependents
ADC	Aid to Dependent Children
AFDC	Aid to Families with Dependent Children
CCDF	Child Care and Development Fund
CHIP	Children's Health Insurance Plan
CSE	child support enforcement
CSJs	community service jobs
DHHS	Department of Health and Human Services
EITC	Earned Income Tax Credit
EP	Employment Plan
ESAP	Employment Skills and Advancement Program
FEP	Financial and Employment Planner
FSA	Family Support Act
FTYR	full time year round
IDAs	Individual Development Accounts
IRP	Individual Responsibility Plan
JOBS	Job Opportunities and Basic Skills Training Program
NAS	National Academy of Science
NLSY	National Longitudinal Survey of Youth
OCSE	Office of Child Support Enforcement
OECD	Organization for Economic Co-operation and Development
PRWORA	Personal Responsibility and Work Opportunity Reconciliation Act
QMBs	qualified Medicare beneficiaries
SCHIP	State Children's Health Insurance Program
SSI	Supplemental Security Income

TANF	Temporary Assistance to Needy Children
TMA	Transitional Medicaid Assistance
TOP	Teen Outreach Program
WIC	women, infants, and children
WOTC	Work Opportunity Tax Credit
WPA	Works Progress Administration
WWTC	Welfare to Work Tax Credit

American Poverty
in a New
Era of Reform

1

Introduction

American Poverty

Poverty may well be America's most serious and costly social problem. Each year millions of Americans live in poverty, and hundreds of billions of public and private dollars are spent on efforts to prevent poverty and assist the poor. Poverty is a complex socioeconomic problem that is causally interwoven with other costly societal ills such as unemployment, underemployment, crime, out-of-wedlock births, low educational achievement, mental, emotional, and physical illness, domestic violence, and alcohol and substance abuse. The cause-and-effect relationship between these problems is complex and greatly debated. Cumulatively these problems account for a huge percentage of all government and charitable spending. They are, in short, a major reason for the size and cost of government.

Poverty, of course, is not a new or uniquely American problem. By the standards of modern societies, most of the people who have ever lived on this planet lived and died in poverty. Even today, poverty is a serious problem in every nation, including the most advanced and prosperous societies (Smeeding, 2004). As Figure 1.1 shows, the most modern and advanced nations struggle with poverty, which often involves large numbers of poor.

In less economically developed nations, poverty rates are staggering. Modestly estimated, at least 20 percent of the world's population lives in stark poverty, barely able to avoid starvation (World Bank, 2004, 7). Many nations do not even pretend to the goal of creating a broad middle-income population; and among those nations that do, creating and sharing wealth in some equitable and effective fashion that produces and nurtures a healthy and extensive middle-income population has always been a challenge imperfectly achieved.

3

Figure 1.1   **Poverty in Selected Nations**

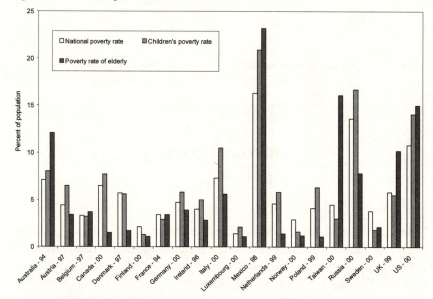

Source: Luxembourg Income Study (LIS), Key Figures, available at www.
lisproject.org/keyfigures.htm.
Note: Poverty is defined as 40 percent of median income for family size.

Despite massive outlays and a network of major antipoverty programs,
the number of poor Americans is enormous. Every year since the mid-
1960s the federal government has tried to identify those Americans living in poverty. In 2003 the federal government estimated that almost 36
million Americans were poor, over 12 percent of the population (Figures 1.2 and 1.3). To put this number in perspective, the collective poverty population in 2003 was almost as large as the total population of
California, twice the size of the population of Florida, and several million larger than the entire population of Canada.

The cost of services to the poor is sobering. In 2003 the major welfare
programs (for example, Temporary Assistance to Needy Families, food
stamps, Medicaid, Supplemental Security Income) involved outlays at the
state and federal levels that substantially exceeded $500 billion (see Fig-
ure 7.2; Howard, 2003). Poverty, of course, is expensive in more ways
than outlays. People idled by poverty lessen the overall productivity of the
workforce, lower tax revenues, reduce the nation's capacity to compete in
the global economy, and may reject mainstream values leading to engage-

Figure 1.2 **U.S. Poverty Count by Race, 2003**

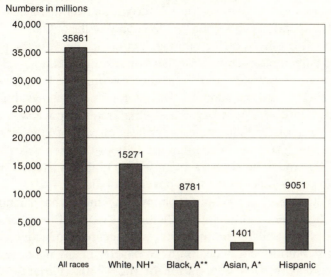

Numbers in millions

Source: Bureau of the Census (2004a), table 4.
Notes: * Non-Hispanic; ** Alone, not in combination with any other race.

Figure 1.3 **Percentage of Population in Poverty**

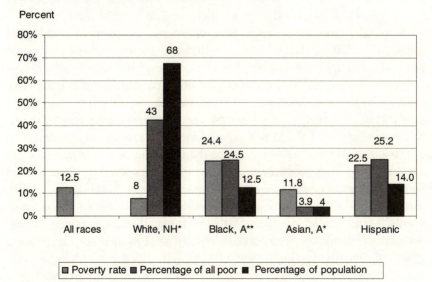

Percent

□ Poverty rate ■ Percentage of all poor ■ Percentage of population

Source: Bureau of the Census (2004a), table 4.
Notes: * Non-Hispanic; ** Alone, not in combination with any other race.

ment in crime, domestic violence, child abandonment, and other antisocial behaviors that burden society. Poverty, in all its manifestations, is extremely expensive and a drain on the vitality of the nation.

Poverty also weighs on the national conscience because the poor are the most vulnerable members of the American population—children, single-parent households (mostly headed by women), the poorly educated, the aged, and the handicapped. As Figure 1.2 shows, black and Hispanic Americans suffer particularly high rates of poverty, and children are particularly vulnerable, regardless of race or ethnicity. From 1990 through 2003, the annual number of poor children was 13.7 million. In 2003 over one-sixth of all American children lived in poverty, comprising 36 percent of the total poverty population.

Given the size, cost, and impact of poverty, America has a major stake in preventing this condition and in helping as many of the poor as possible to become self-reliant, economically secure, productive citizens. America's commitment to dealing with poverty in any major way goes back to the New Deal legislation of the 1930s (Patterson, 1986; Abramovitz, 1988; Allard, 2004). These early, rather modest programs have evolved and matured substantially over time. As welfare expenditures have escalated, especially in the last two decades, skepticism about the cost and effectiveness of these programs has become increasingly widespread both within the government and among the public.

Americans are conservative about the role of government, and highly skeptical of helping the poor in ways that might undermine their sense of responsibility and self-respect. Figure 1.4 shows the results of a recent survey in the United States and twelve other nations. Respondents were asked if they "completely agreed" that it is the responsibility of the government to take care of very poor people who cannot take care of themselves. Notice that only 23 percent of American respondents "completely agreed," by far the lowest rate among the thirteen nations. In seven of the nations more than 60 percent of the respondents were positive, and in three nations the positive rate was 70 or 71 percent. In this same survey, Americans were much less likely than Europeans to believe that government "should provide everyone with a guaranteed income, reduce the differences in income between people with high and low incomes, and provide a decent standard of living for the unemployed." Even less-affluent Americans shared these views (ISSP, 2001). Americans, in short, are much less trustful of government than citizens in many other democracies and very concerned about eroding core values and creating a dependent class.

Figure 1.4   **Public Obligations to the Poor, 2000**

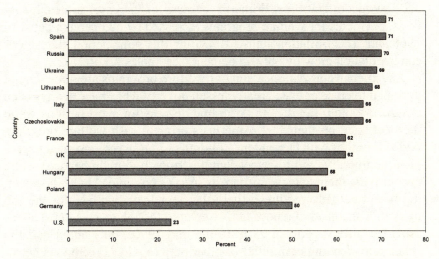

Source: ISSP (2001).
Note: Percent who "completely agreed" that it is the responsibility of the govern-ment to take care of very poor people who cannot take care of themselves.

One reason for this conservatism is that Americans believe there is un-limited opportunity for those who work hard. When respondents in Europe and America are asked if they agree that "the way things are in their coun-try, they and their family have a good chance of improving their standard of living," Americans are the most optimistic. Over 70 percent of Ameri-cans agree, compared to only 40 percent of Germans, 37 percent of the British, and 26 of the Dutch. Minorities are almost as optimistic about opportunity in America as whites (ISSP, 2001). Americans believe that this is a land of great opportunity, and that "failure" cannot be rewarded with-out doing great harm to the most fundamental societal values.

While Americans are conservative and skeptical about welfare, they are often confused about how aid programs are designed and how public dollars are spent (Berinsky, 2002). Welfare is generally thought of in terms of cash aid, but most welfare programs provide services rather than cash. The vast majority of welfare program spending, in fact, is for services. Medicaid, food stamps, child care, housing assistance, Head Start, school lunch programs, and job training programs make up the major costs of welfare. Only about 15 percent of all the poor receive any cash aid (see Table 7.2), and payments to individuals are rather modest. By

far the most expensive programs are those that provide health care to poor
and low-income citizens. Primarily because of increases in health care
costs, payments for welfare programs increased by 523 percent between
1968 and 2002 (inflation adjusted). During this same period, the American population grew by only 43 percent (see Tables 7.1 and 7.2).

As expensive as America's major welfare programs are, they are not
designed to erase or even greatly lessen poverty. They have always been
designed to help families in economic distress for short periods while
they get back on their feet. America's original cash welfare program,
Aid to Families with Dependent Children (AFDC), was designed to provide "temporary" aid to select families (mostly female-headed) while
encouraging them to leave welfare as soon as possible. AFDC, however,
did not effectively require or help the poor leave welfare for the job
market. If the head of a poor family entered the job market, most states
provided little support or cash. In the mid-1990s, only about half the
states provided any cash relief or other help to AFDC recipients working half time. Fewer than a dozen provided any cash support to full-time
workers, regardless of how low their income or the size of the family.
The result was that even among those families who could qualify for
cash assistance, almost all were unemployed and almost all continued
to live in poverty. Only rarely did America's complicated and increasingly expensive programs help the poor escape poverty and become self-
reliant and economically secure. Thus, as the overall costs of welfare
soared during the 1980s and much of the 1990s, the poverty rate actually increased (see Figure 3.1).

As skepticism about the design, expense, and effectiveness of American welfare programs increased, presidents Nixon, Ford, and Carter recommended major welfare reforms to Congress. None was passed.
President Reagan also recommended reforms, and an important but
poorly funded reform plan reflecting some of his proposals was passed
in 1988. Fundamental reform was not adopted until President Clinton's
first term in office. In 1996 a bipartisan coalition in Congress passed the
Personal Responsibility and Work Opportunity Reconciliation Act
(PRWORA). After having vetoed the first two versions of this bill, President Clinton signed the reform plan into law in August 1996.

The new legislation, PRWORA, clearly mirrors America's conservative values. PRWORA is not a mere incremental adjustment in welfare
policy. It is the most comprehensive reform of a major public policy in
recent American history. PRWORA aligns welfare with American phi-

losophy much better than was the case with AFDC. The focus of welfare policy under PRWORA has shifted from providing limited and modest cash aid to programs designed to help recipients or potential recipients become viable members of the workforce. The administration of the new reform approach has been turned over to the states, and they are given considerable discretion in designing and implementing policies to help their poor become employed. To make the transition to employment feasible, the states are given grant dollars to help them provide recipients with such critical support services as transitional child care, health care, transportation aid, and even job preparation loans, education, and training. PRWORA also provides states with funds that can be used to significantly improve the quality of child care, after-school programs, and other supervised activities for millions of children from poor and low-income families.

PRWORA is also designed to reduce future generations of poor by funding programs to lower out-of-wedlock births, particularly among teens. It requires both parents to accept the responsibility of financially supporting their children. Over fifty changes to existing laws were made to improve the chances of identifying the parents of children and to force all absent parents to pay required child support.

The new welfare policy is complex because states are given program flexibility and encouraged to be innovative in the design and implementation of PRWORA. By 1998 all the states had written and implemented new welfare plans. These plans differ in comprehensiveness and imagination, and they are being carried out with varying degrees of creativeness and enthusiasm. The result is that the pace of welfare reform varies a great deal among the states.

Much of this book focuses on the nature and causes of American poverty, the evolution of welfare policy, the passage and implementation of PRWORA, assessing its impact, and identifying the strengths and weaknesses of recent reforms.

Organization of the Book

In Chapter 2 we analyze how the federal government defines poverty and identifies the poor. We evaluate the government's measure of poverty, an evaluation that reveals serious deficiencies. We then use alternative methods to correct some of the most obvious flaws in the official measure and produce a more valid, but still flawed, poverty count. In the final analysis, the data show that regardless of the method used, America has a large poverty population.

When we contrast the American approach of measuring poverty with the approaches used by other nations, we not only see important differences in how nations relate to poverty, but also the underlying goals of the American measure. Developing nations try to identify their poorest citizens chiefly to prevent starvation and acute need. In contrast, the major nations of Western Europe and Scandinavia are mainly concerned with preserving the standards of living that are required for their citizens to be healthy, educated, and productive. Surprisingly, America's goals differ considerably from those of other advanced nations.

Chapter 3 examines the demographics of American poverty. The central question is: Who are the poor? This chapter documents the high rate of poverty among children, racial and ethnic minorities, female-headed families, and the poorly educated. This chapter also explores one of the major patterns identified by our analysis of the demographics of poverty— the growth of single-parent families. Why are single-parent families growing so rapidly and why are they so vulnerable to poverty? The answers to these questions provide insight into both the causes of high poverty rates in single-parent families and the problems that must be ameliorated to lessen that poverty.

Chapter 4 analyzes some of the major theories that try to explain poverty in rich America. There are many theories about the causes of poverty and by analyzing and critiquing the most widely accepted, we gain an understanding of some of the possible cures for American poverty. While there will always be major disagreements about the causes of poverty, reaching some common understanding about some of the reasons why people are poor provides valuable insight into how poverty can be alleviated.

Chapter 5 examines contemporary efforts to reform the American welfare system, efforts that culminated in the passage of PRWORA in 1996. The provisions of this act are surveyed in detail.

Chapter 6 examines the states' efforts to design welfare programs and to implement PRWORA. To better explain the act and the discretion that states have in carrying it out, the approach of one of the states that has led the reform movement is analyzed in some depth. Analyzing Wisconsin's well-designed plan, along with early evidence on its impact, provides insight into the discretion states have in designing and fulfilling reform, along with many of the complexities and challenges of reform. This chapter also examines how the states are choosing to adopt and adapt options allowed by PRWORA.

Chapter 7 provides an overview of the American welfare system. It describes the evolving size, complexity, cost, and impact of our major welfare programs since the adoption of PRWORA.

Chapter 8 examines the evidence on the impact of the 1996 welfare reform bill. It examines the reasons and implications of huge declines in welfare use, the extent to which states have been successful in engaging welfare recipients in work, and how those who have left the rolls are fairing. It examines the quality of support services for those who have left welfare, and the earnings and well-being of former recipients who are trying to become settled in the workforce. It also examines the success in lowering the out-of-wedlock birth rate and the collection of support from absent parents.

The concluding chapter evaluates the strengths and weaknesses of PRWORA, with focus on two questions. How can welfare reform be continued and even improved? And if welfare reform can be made to work, resulting in fewer Americans living in poverty, how should American social policy evolve?

2

How Many Americans Are Poor?

How do we know when someone is poor or what percentage of a nation's population lives in poverty? Is poverty simply an economic issue? Is someone poor only when he or she is unable to afford an adequate diet, reasonable shelter, and other basic needs? Or more drastically, is someone poor only when he or she is so destitute as to be in danger of acute malnutrition or even starvation? A poor nation might have little choice about how poverty is defined. Identifying only those citizens in danger of starvation so that they can be assisted might be the only realistic goal. When poverty is defined only by basic or bare economic resources, the measure is called absolute. An absolute measure is a fixed dollar amount that a person or family requires for some level of basic survival.

An alternative approach is to consider the social or socioeconomic aspects of income. A wealthy nation might be primarily concerned with identifying people who live so far below average income standards that they struggle to obtain basic necessities and cannot develop their abilities or become productive, contributing members of society. When poverty is conceptualized in this fashion, it combines economic and social indicators and is called relative poverty: people are poor in relation to average standards of living in their society. The assumption of a relative standard is that when people live far below average standards, it is harmful not only to the individuals, but to the goals of the larger society. When nations use a relative standard, they must decide how far they are willing to let citizens slip below median living standards.

Basically, then, the poverty measures used by nations are either relative or absolute. Several research organizations, including the European Commission, the Organization for Economic Co-operation and Development (OECD), and the Luxembourg Income Study (Figure 1.1) have developed relative poverty standards by which they periodically estimate the extent of poverty within the highly developed economies of Western Europe, the Scandinavian nations, and increasingly nations of Eastern Europe (Foster, 1993; Hagenaars, DeVos, and Zaidi, 1994; Smeeding et al., 1993; Smeeding, 1992a; Smeeding, Rainwater, and O'Higgins, 1990; Smeeding, Rainwater, and Burtless, 2001). These measures are based on the theoretical work of two notable scholars, Sen (1992) and Townsend (1979). Major industrial and postindustrial nations such as France, Germany, Belgium, Austria, Norway, Sweden, and Finland use these relative measures as their official estimates of poverty. Sen (1992) has also used this methodology to calculate poverty rates in many other nations.

Relative poverty measures are usually designed to identify individuals and families with incomes below 50 to 60 percent of the national median for households of similar size. If the median income for the average household of four is $40,000, for example, any four-person household with an annual income below sixty percent of that amount might be considered poor. This socioeconomic measure is designed to identify the level at which individuals and households have adequate resources to enjoy the blessings of their nation, develop their potential, and be contributing members of society. In 1985 the European Union adopted a relative measure of poverty for its member nations: "The poor shall be taken to mean persons, families, and groups of persons whose resources (material, cultural, and societal) are so limited as to exclude them from the minimum acceptable way of life in the member state in which they live" (European Commission, 1985).

A very different approach is used by the World Bank, which is primarily interested in determining the percentage of the world's population living on extremely marginal incomes, incomes that are so low that people may be in danger of starvation. In 2001 the World Bank calculated that 2.8 billion people lived on less than $2 dollars a day (World Bank, 2004). Almost all were in developing nations. Given an estimated population of about 6.2 billion people in 2001, this meant that about 45 percent of the earth's total population lived in stark poverty in 2001.

The American approach to measuring poverty differs from the socioeconomic methodology employed by the other prosperous industrial and postindustrial nations. Rather than the relative standards employed by the other developed nations, the United States government annually estimates poverty using an economic or absolute standard. The absolute standard employed sets a specific dollar amount that a family of a particular size and composition must have to avoid poverty. The dollar levels set by this absolute standard are not related to the median income of similar American families. The dollar levels, in fact, are considerably below the median income of similar families.

The absolute standard used is concerned only with a dollar amount that has been assumed to be adequate to move a person or family out of poverty. The American measure is focused on determining when a person or family does not have enough money for food, shelter, and other necessities. As such, the American approach is more like the methodologies used by developing nations—and by the World Bank—than the approach employed by the other advanced economies of the world. The federal government wants to keep the annual count of American poor as low as possible.

The data used to estimate how many Americans live in poverty each year are collected by the U.S. Bureau of the Census (Fisher, 1998, 1997, 1992; Orshansky, 1988, 1995). The data are drawn from interviews conducted nationwide in March each year with roughly 60,000 households. The Census Bureau collects data on the before-tax cash income of families and households, excluding noncash benefits such as food stamps, medical services, and housing subsidies. These income data are compared to fixed dollar standards for families of varying sizes and composition to calculate how many people are poor. The fixed dollar standards are called thresholds. An individual's or family's income is either above or below the threshold. The income thresholds are based on the estimated cost of an adequate diet for individuals and various types of families. The Department of Agriculture annually estimates the cost of adequate diets for individuals and families of various types. The cost of the diet is then multiplied by three to obtain a poverty threshold for various sizes and types of families.

Table 2.1 provides an overview of the poverty thresholds for all households for 2003. Notice that the thresholds vary by the size of the family and the number of related children under eighteen years of age, and are adjusted for age when the householder is sixty-five years of age or older. Single people younger than sixty-five with no children would be judged to be poor if their income fell one dollar below $9,573, or $797.75 a month. Since an absolute standard is being used, these same people would be classified as nonpoor if their income rose as much as one dollar above the poverty threshold. At the opposite extreme, a family of nine or more with six children under eighteen would be judged to be poor if its income fell one dollar below $37,229.

As an example of how the thresholds are calculated, we can analyze how the standard is calculated for a family of four. In 2003 the poverty threshold for a family of four with two adults and two children under eighteen was $18,660 (see Table 2.1). This standard is based on a Department of Agriculture estimate that a family of this size and composition required $6,220 in 2003 to purchase enough food to support an adequate diet on a temporary basis. It is also assumed that the food budget constitutes one-third of all the family's income needs for a year. Thus, the food budget is multiplied by three to compute the yearly income needs of the family. Although it is not part of the government's actual calculation, for purposes of illustration, we can analyze the various components of this family budget to demonstrate how much money it allows for food and other types of expenditures.

Poverty Threshold for Family of Four (Two Children), 2003: $18,660

Food budget (one-third): $6,220
  $119.61 per week
   $17.08 per day
    $5.70 per meal
    $1.42 per meal per person

Shelter budget (one-third): $6,220
  $518.33 per month

Essentials budget (one-third): $6,220—utilities, clothing, furniture, transportation
  $518.33 per month
  $129.58 per month per person

Examining this budget suggests some serious problems. First, the food budget is modest. It assumes that the family of four can obtain an adequate level of nutrition for about $17.00 a day for all four family members. This allows less than $6.00 per meal for all four family members. Not many people would consider this realistic. Second, the family's income for shelter and other necessities is extremely modest. It is highly unlikely that adequate shelter could be obtained for a little over $500 a month, especially in major urban areas. Similarly, there is little chance that the rest of the budget could make up for the deficiencies of the food and shelter budget and leave any funds for utilities, transportation, out-

Table 2.1

Federal Poverty Thresholds, 2003

Size of family unit	None	One	Two	Three	Four	Five	Six	Seven	Eight or more
One person (unrelated individual):									
Under 65 years	9,573								
65 years and older	8,825								
Two people									
Householder under 65 years	12,321	12,682							
Householder 65 years and older	11,122	12,634							
Three people	14,393	14,810	14,284						
Four people	18,979	19,289	18,660	18,725					
Five people	22,887	23,220	22,509	21,959	21,623				
Six people	26,324	26,429	25,884	25,362	24,586	24,126			
Seven people	30,289	30,479	29,827	29,372	28,526	27,538	26,454		
Eight people	33,876	34,175	33,560	33,021	32,256	31,286	30,275	30,019	
Nine people or more	40,751	40,948	40,404	39,947	39,196	38,162	37,229	36,998	35,572

Source: Bureau of the Census (2004a), p. 39.

of-pocket medical costs, and other necessities. A reasonable conclusion is not only that the income standard is conservative, but, in fact, artificially low, resulting in a serious underestimation of poverty.

As noted above, the thresholds are not related to median income levels for the various types of families, and thus they do not reflect changes in living standards over time (Fisher, 1999; Orshansky, 1965). The only annual adjustment of the thresholds is the inflationary changes in the cost of the food budget. Among the prosperous nations of the world, America is the only nation that does not adjust its poverty measure to incorporate rising standards of living (Rainwater and Smeeding, 2003, 8). As Gordon Fisher (1995, 76) notes: "When the current official poverty line—the only poverty line that more and more people had ever been aware of—was made absolute and remained so, it became more difficult for many people to realize (and less likely that they would investigate history to find out) that the basis pattern both in this country and in other countries is for poverty lines to rise in real terms as the real income of the general population rises."

Adjusting for rising standards of living would result in major alterations in the poverty thresholds and significantly raise the poverty count. In 2002, for example, the median income for households of four with two children under eighteen was $52,362 (Bureau of the Census, 2006, Historical Tables, table 4-1). The poverty threshold of $18,244 for this type of family is only about 35 percent of the median. If the threshold were set at half the median, the poverty threshold for a family of four would have been $26,181, an increase of over 40 percent.

Applying the absolute dollar thresholds, the Census Bureau concluded that 35.9 million Americans, or 12.5 percent of the population, lived in poverty in 2003 (Figure 2.1; see also Figure 1.2 and Figure 3.1). Figure 2.1 shows the yearly percentage of the American population identified as poor since 1959. Examining the annual percentage rates since 1959 shows both progress and reversals in reducing poverty since the late 1950s. The poverty rate dropped from the 22 percent range in the early 1960s to below 12 percent during several years in the 1970s, but then rose again to exceed 14 and 15 percent in some years since the early 1980s. Rates declined in the late 1990s and 2000, but increased in 2001, 2002, and 2003. The government's very conservative measure of poverty, therefore, shows a high level of continuing poverty in America, with rather disappointing results in reducing the number of poor since the 1980s. A more sophisticated measure would show even less progress in combating poverty.

Figure 2.1   **Percentage of Population Below the Poverty Line, 1959–2003**

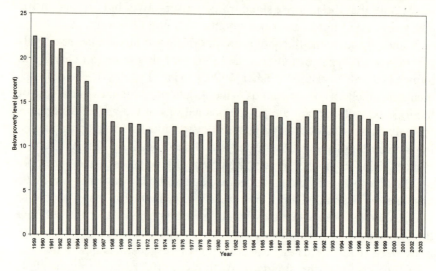

Source: Bureau of the Census (2004a), table 8-2.

Although the threshold levels are generally considered to be extremely low and flawed since they are not adjusted for rising standards of living, there are other major problems with the official government measure. While critics point to a rather large number of problems, some flaws are consistently cited.

Flaws in the Official Measure of Poverty

Lack of Regional Cost Adjustments

The poverty thresholds for various family sizes and types are uniform across the nation, although there are significant variations in regional costs of living, especially for shelter. It is hardly logical, for example, to use exactly the same threshold for a family of four with two children when one family lives in New York City and the other in rural Mississippi.

Failure to Include Taxes and the Value of In-Kind Benefits

Because the current measure defines family resources as gross money income, it does not include the value of government programs, such as food stamps, subsidized housing, or school meal programs. These government programs significantly improve the disposable income of millions of families and, hence, their poverty status, but they are not reflected in the government measure. On the other hand, taxes such as Social Security reduce disposable income, but are not included in the calculations either.

Employed Versus Unemployed Families

The measure does not distinguish between the needs of families in which the parents work outside the home. There are significant costs associated with employment, including transportation, uniforms, perhaps equipment, and often child care. Child care is generally the most complex and expensive problem. Since more mothers work and since more parents are single, there are more working families who must pay child care now than when the poverty thresholds were designed.

Variations in Health Care Costs

The health care costs of families vary considerably. Some families may enjoy good health and have no costs; others may require expensive care. Of those who need care, some may suffer significant out-of-pocket expenses, while others may have excellent private coverage or be covered by government programs. The current measure does not take health care costs into consideration.

Family Size Adjustment

There are many problems with the family size adjustments, including the fact that family sizes have been declining, and more families are headed by single parents. Yet, the thresholds have not been adjusted since their original formulation.

The Food Budget Base

As the figures above show, the food budget base that forms the core of the thresholds is anything but generous. A family of four with two children is allowed less than $6.00 per meal. While it might not be impossible to buy adequate food on this budget, it would be a continuing challenge and probably cannot be done in many high-cost cities. The original author of the poverty thresholds, Mollie Orshansky, formulated two versions, one based on an economy food plan and another based on a more generous low-cost food plan. The government chose to adopt the version based on the economy food plan, acknowledged by the Department of Agriculture as for "temporary or emergency use when funds are low" (Fisher, 1999, 26). In other words, even the Department of Agriculture does not claim that any family could purchase an adequate diet for any significant period with the funds allowed by the economy budget.

Additionally, there is reason to doubt the logic of basing the thresholds only on the food base and inflationary changes in that base. Why should food costs be considered one-third of the income required by a family? As Ruggles (1990) has concluded, neither changes in lifestyles nor consumption standards are reflected in such a restrictive approach. In 1969 the Interagency Poverty Level Review Committee decided against making measurement adjustments to reflect changes in the general standard of living. In 1970, the original author of the standard, Mollie Orshansky, wrote that the 1969 decision "tend[ed] to freeze the poverty line despite changes in buying habits and changes in acceptable living standards" (Fisher, 1999, 28). As detailed below, there is considerable evidence that if changing living standards were taken into consideration, poverty thresholds would require significantly higher income standards than the current measure (Citro and Michael, 1995).

The restrictiveness of the official standard actually makes it a better measure of income inadequacy than adequacy. In a 1965 article, Orshansky (1965) made this argument. "If it is not possible to state unequivocally how much is enough, it should be possible to assert with confidence how much, on average, is too little." As Fisher (1999, 27) notes: "To the best of my knowledge, there is no analysis-based federal policy document that has presented the poverty thresholds as representing the total amount of money required for minimum basic necessities for a family, or has presented them as being enough for a family to live on." Thought of this way, the poverty measures tell us how many individuals have too little income, but not how much money they need to live decently.

The Missing Poor

There is widespread agreement that the Census Bureau does not find all the poor, primarily because many low-income people live with others or move too frequently to be counted. Additionally, the homeless and those individuals residing in mental hospitals, college dorms, nursing homes, the military, jails, and prisons are not counted. Estimates of the number of people left out of the count vary considerably, but conservatively number several million.

The Severity of Poverty

The official standard makes no distinction between those individuals or families that fall a few dollars below the poverty threshold for their family size and those with incomes far below the standard. Most of the families and individuals who are counted as poor have incomes considerably below the poverty threshold for their family size. In 2002, for example, 4.9 percent of the population had incomes that were under 50 percent of their poverty threshold. This included 6.9 percent of all children (Bureau of the Census, 2003, table 5). The average poor family had a deficit of $7,205 below their poverty threshold. For families headed by a single mother, the deficit was $7,648 (Bureau of the Census, 2003a, table 6).

Why Is the Standard So Flawed?

Why would the federal government use such an obviously flawed methodology to estimate yearly poverty rates? The answer is somewhat complex. When the now official measure was first formulated in the mid-1960s and backdated to 1959, the federal employee who designed it was simply trying to improve upon a very crude standard in use by the Bureau of the Budget. The original poverty standard had been a flat rate of $3,000 in yearly income for any family, regardless of size, composition, or geographic location. The author expected the new standard to be used only as a demonstration of how income and expenditures for families of various types could be used to design a more sophisticated standard (Orshansky, 1988, 1965; Fisher, 1999; Haverman, 1987). Unfortunately, the Bureau of the Budget adopted the new standard but then decided against improving it because it was understood that doing so would produce a higher poverty count, increase program eligibility, and raise annual costs.

As often happens in the political arena, stalemates between critics of the measure have resulted in the 1960s' standard remaining the official

Table 2.2

Poverty, 2002: The Impact of Improving the Measurement of Income and Benefits

	Poor	Rate
Results of official definition in 2002	34,570	12.1
Impact of combined changes		
1. Money income plus realized capital gains (losses), less income and payroll taxes	33,164	11.6
2. Money income plus realized capital gains (losses), less income and payroll taxes, plus value of employer-provided health benefits and all noncash transfers except Medicare and Medicaid	28,166	9.9
3. Money income plus capital gains (losses), less income and payroll taxes, plus value of all noncash transfers	26,750	9.4
4. Money income plus capital gains (losses), less income and payroll taxes, plus value of all noncash transfers, plus imputed return to home equity	24,632	8.6

Source: Bureau of the Census (2003a), table 8.

methodology for estimating yearly poverty rates, warts and all. In recent years the Census Bureau has published data demonstrating the impact of improving the measure by including various taxes, work expenses, and in-kind programs. These data are insightful and they provide a better understanding of poverty in America. However, as we will detail below, they do not correct all the flaws discussed above because the changes are designed to improve measures of income, but basically neglect the costs faced by families.

Table 2.2 shows the changes in the official poverty count for 2002 that would have resulted from some improved measures of income, taxes, and noncash transfers. The table shows the impact of four combinations of improved measures of income and benefits. All of the measures lower the poverty count because they improve on income and benefits without providing a better measure of the costs faced by families of various types by geographic location. The most sophisticated of the measures, #4, includes all money income from any source, capital gains or losses, the value of all noncash transfers, plus the imputed return on home equity. This measure lowers the poverty count in 2002 from 34.6 million (12.1 percent) to 24.6 million (8.6 percent). Of course, these changes produce an inadequate measure because they only address the income/benefit side of the problem.

Table 2.3

Poverty Estimates Based on National Academy of Science Recommendations, 2002

	Number below poverty level (million)	Poverty rate (percent)
Official measure	34.5	12.1
Thresholds adjusted by subtracting out-of-pocket medical expenses from income	35.0	12.3
Threshold adjusted by including out-of-pocket expenses in the thresholds	36.5	12.8
Thresholds adjusted by combining both methods of including out-of-pocket expenses	36.9	12.9

Source: Bureau of the Census (2003a), table 7.
Note: Each estimate includes adjustments for geographic cost variations.

Still, Table 2.2 shows that the measurement of income can be substantially improved. A sophisticated measure of poverty would improve measures of income and include more realistic indicators of family income needs.

In 1995 a research group appointed by the National Research Council recommended that a new poverty standard be based on more accurate calculations of income, noncash benefits, taxes, work-related expenses, and medical costs, along with more realistic estimates of actual needs and consumption patterns of families of various sizes (Citro and Michael, 1995). The committee recommended adjustments be included for geographic differences in costs. Estimates of the median expenditures of families for food, clothing, shelter, utilities, and other needs would compose the base for the new standard. Once median expenditures were determined, some percentage of those costs could be calculated (e.g., 78–83 percent) and then added together. A modest multiplier (e.g., 1.15–1.25) could be used to allow for other unmeasured needs. The committee concluded that this approach would better reflect actual consumption, spending patterns, and lifestyles of families, yielding a conservative but more realistic measure of poverty (Citro and Michael, 1995; Burtless, Corbett, and Primus, 1998).

Table 2.3 shows three Bureau of the Census estimates of poverty in 2002 based on the National Academy of Science (NAS) recommendations. The only difference between the three estimates is the way out-of-pocket medical expenses are included. In the first estimate out-of-pocket expenditures are subtracted from income. In the second, the thresholds are adjusted for out-of-pocket expenditures. In the third, the two methods are combined. The more comprehensive and sophisticated measures recommended by the NAS increase the poverty count in 2002, ranging from an increase of about .5 million to as many as 2.5 million. Depending upon the multipliers used, the NAS measures have the potential to substantially increase the poverty count. The fact that NAS measures increase the government estimate of poverty is the reason they have not been officially adopted as the national standard. No administration wants poverty to increase, even if it is the result of a more sophisticated and accurate measure.

Summary and Conclusions

The federal government's official measure of poverty is extremely flawed. Table 2.2 shows some of the alterations that could be made in the current measure to better calculate individual and family income and benefits, but these changes would not improve estimates of family needs. Table 2.3 demonstrates the impact of a more comprehensive and sophisticated measure proposed by the NAS. The drawback of the NAS measure is that, using even very conservative multipliers, it increases the poverty count, a politically unacceptable outcome. Given the problems with the official government standard, the annual poverty estimates published by the Census Bureau are clearly an undercount. Using a more sophisticated measure like the one proposed by the NAS would not only raise the poverty count, it would alter the demographics of American poverty.

Does the fact that the United States uses an absolute measure of poverty mean that the American poor resemble the poor of the Third World? The answer to this question is clearly no. As a group, the American poor are generally not homeless, and the vast majority is not on the verge of starvation. Most poor families, in fact, report that they have enough to eat. Yet, food insecurity and actual hunger exist in many households (see Figures 8.17 and 8.18). A Tufts University (1995) study found that poor children often have inconsistent food supplies (Cook and Martin, 1995), while a second study found that children who live in poverty long-term are 2.7 times as likely to suffer from stunted growth (Korenman and Miller, 1997). The problem of food insecurity and hunger is addressed in Chapter 8.

Some 40 percent of all poor households own their home. Among poor elderly heads of households the home ownership rate is about 60 percent, while it is about 29 percent for other poor households. These homes, of course, were generally purchased long before these household heads became poor, and most of the homes are in very bad repair (U.S. Department of Housing and Urban Development, 1995). Seventy percent of all poor households own a car; 27 percent own two or more. Without cars poor household heads generally cannot work, or even shop or transport children and family members for purposes of education or health care. Some 97 percent of all poor households report owning a color television (Council of Economic Advisors, 1995). For a poor family, a television is probably the least expensive entertainment option.

Given the possessions of the poor, should we assume that poverty is not really a very serious problem? That would be a serious mistake. First, the evidence suggests that life for the American poor is difficult. Over half of all poor households report: loss of utilities in the past year; food shortages over the last four months; poor quality housing, including plumbing, electricity, and rodent problems; crowded housing; lack of access to a telephone, refrigerator, or stove; and eviction in the past year (Federman et al., 1996).

Second, the evidence is clear that children who grow up in poverty, especially early and long-term poverty, suffer very significant disadvantages (Haverman and Wolfe, 1994; Duncan and Brooks-Gunn, 1998; Corcoran, 2002). Children who grow up in poverty are twice as likely to drop out of school and one and a half times as likely to be unemployed. Poor teenage girls are four times as likely to be unwed mothers (Gottschalk, McLanahan, and Sandefur, 1994, 102), and all poor children are at greater risk of drug and alcohol abuse, mental illness, suicide, and criminality. The data are also clear that early childhood poverty has a highly detrimental impact on the cognitive development of children (Duncan and Brooks-Gunn, 1998; Brown and Pollitt, 1996; Shore, 1997). Not surprisingly, there is a clear link between poverty and lack of educational success.

Some critics (Rector, 1998) argue that poverty does not cause low educational achievement; rather, the problem is the values of the parents. But studies show that when the income of the family increases, so does the achievement level of children in the family (Sherman, 1997; Venti, 1984, table 1). Two major studies also show that when families move in and out of poverty, the educational achievements of the children vary with the prosperity of the family. During improved economic periods, the children do better in school (Duncan et al., 1998; Sandefur and Wells, 1997). There is a clear link, then, between the income of families and the chances that their children will obtain the education they need, not just to escape poverty and many other social problems, but also to be productive, competitive members of American society.

Poverty, therefore, does matter. It is a problem worth careful identification and vigorous remediation. In Chapter 3, we will take a more in-depth look at who are the American poor.

3

The American Poor

Over the last four decades, despite massive expenditures by federal and state governments, poverty rates have fluctuated, but have remained stubbornly high. As Figure 3.1 shows, despite three recessions, the rate of poverty declined significantly during the 1960s and 1970s. Unfortunately, even with substantial inflation-adjusted increases in welfare spending, the trend in poverty reduction did not continue. By the early 1980s the rate of poverty was increasing. Poverty declined modestly after the early 1980s, but then increased quite dramatically in the early 1990s. Poverty rates declined from 1994 through 2000, only to increase in 2001, 2002, and 2003. In 2003 there were 4.3 million more poor people than in 2000. The poverty rate in 2003 was 12.5 percent, a rate higher than in most years in the 1970s. Making significant progress against poverty has clearly been an elusive goal.

This chapter will focus on four major topics relevant to the nation's efforts to ameliorate poverty. First, it will analyze the basic demographic composition of the poverty population. Knowing which are the major poverty groups provides valuable insights into the causes of poverty. Second, it will analyze poverty among American children, the largest single group of poor Americans. Third, it will examine the rapid growth and extreme economic vulnerability of single-mother families. Last, the analysis will allow us to examine some of the major factors that have impeded progress in reducing poverty.

Who Are the Poor?

In 2003 almost 36 million Americans were counted among the poor. As the analysis below will show, the poverty population is not only sizeable, it is quite diverse. A wide range of Americans from all races,

Figure 3.1   **Number in Poverty and Poverty Rates, 1959–2003**

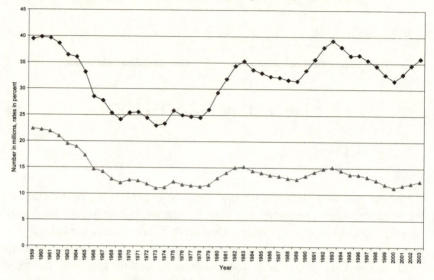

Source: Bureau of the Census (2004a), table 8-1.
Note: The data points are placed at the midpoints of the respective years.

ethnicities, ages, backgrounds, and geographic locations find themselves in poverty. Still, some groups are much more vulnerable to poverty. It is the highly vulnerable groups that make up most of the poverty population and they are of primary interest to us here.

Racial and Ethnic Groups

In 2003 for the first time the Census Bureau allowed respondents to identify themselves in one or more racial groups. For example, a person could identify him/herself as being both white and black, or a person could identify him/herself as being both black and Asian. This change makes year-to-year comparisons among groups more complex. Additionally, the designation Hispanic is an ethnicity, not a racial group. Hispanics may be white, black, Asian, Native American, and so on. Thus, Hispanic identification often overlaps with and includes people of several different races.

To deal with these issues, when the figures are available, we have reported data for non-Hispanic whites, black alone, Asian alone, and Hispanic.

Figure 3.2   **Poverty Rates for Individuals in Selected Demographic Groups, 2003**

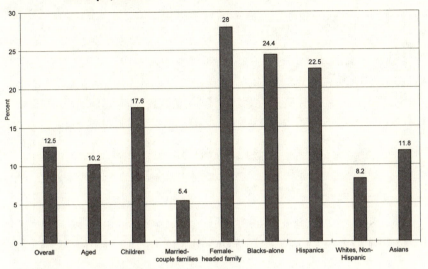

Source: Bureau of the Census (2004a), table 3.

Basic Demographics

Figure 3.2 shows how substantially poverty rates vary by age, family structure, race, and ethnicity. While the overall poverty rate is about 12.5 percent, many identifiable groups have low risks of poverty while others suffer very high rates. Notice first that age is a relevant factor in poverty. Children endure a higher rate of poverty than any other age group (Figure 3.3). In 2003, the poverty rate for children was 17.6 percent, and children comprised about 36 percent of all poor Americans. As Figure 3.3 shows, progress in reducing poverty among children since the late 1950s has been difficult. The poverty rate declined in the 1960s and 1970s, and then increased in much of the 1980s and through the early 1990s. From 1993 to 2000 the rate declined, and then rose modestly in 2001–3. The poverty rate for children in 2003 was as high as the rates in most years in the 1960s and 1970s.

By contrast, the poverty rate for Americans sixty-five years and older has declined appreciably since the 1960s. In the early to mid 1960s about a third of the elderly population lived in poverty. The poverty rate among the elderly has been noticeably reduced over time by increases in Social Security payments. In 2003 the poverty rate of the aged was 10.2 percent. Despite the decline in the poverty rate of the aged, the rate is still

Figure 3.3   **Poverty Rates by Age, 1959–2003**

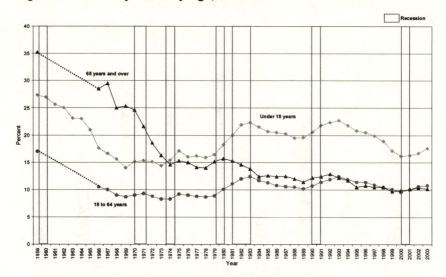

Source: Bureau of the Census (2004a), table B-2.
Notes: The data points are placed at the midpoints of the respective years. Data for people 18 to 64, and 65 and older, are not available from 1960 to 1965.

rather high and Americans sixty-five and older make up a little more than 10 percent of all the poor. When combined with poor children, the youngest and oldest Americans are almost half of all the poor. Notice also in Figure 3.3 that the poverty rate of the eighteen- to sixty-four-year-old population declined significantly from the late 1950s to the 1980s where it has basically stabilized in the 10 to 12 percent range.

About 71 percent of all poor live in families, with some family types being much more vulnerable to poverty. The poverty rate for married-couple families is rather modest. In 2003 only 5.4 percent of all married-couple families were poor. These families, of course, are more economically viable because there is generally at least one full-time worker, and they are better situated to handle and share responsibility for children. By contrast, single parents are often challenged to balance work with child care and all the other responsibilities associated with running a household. Not surprisingly, the poverty rate for female-headed households is high. In 2003, 28 percent of all female-headed families were poor; almost six times the poverty rate of married-couple families. Half of all the poor in 2003 lived in a female-headed family. When we

Table 3.1

Poverty Rates by Race and Ethnicity, 1960–2003

Race and Hispanic origin	1960	1970	1980	2003
White	17.8	9.9	10.2	9.9
White, NH*	NA**	NA**	NA**	8.2
Black	55.9	33.5	32.5	24.4***
Asian	NA**	NA**	17.2	11.8***
Hispanic***	NA	24.3	25.7	22.5

Source: Bureau of the Census (2004a), table 8-1.
Notes: *Non-Hispanic; **Not Available; ***Alone. No other race; ****Hispanics may be of any race.

examine family structure in more detail below, we will see that minority female-headed families endure an even higher rate of poverty.

Race and ethnicity are particularly powerful predictors of poverty. The white non-Hispanic population has the lowest poverty rate of any major racial or ethnic group. In 2003 the poverty rate for white non-Hispanics was 8.2 percent. Because white non-Hispanics make up 68.0 percent of the total population, however, even a low rate of poverty produces a great many poor people. In 2003, some 15.5 million white non-Hispanic Americans were poor. Numerically they are the largest group of poor Americans, accounting for 45 percent of the total poverty population.

The black population is relatively small but has a high poverty rate and contributes significantly to the poverty population. In 2003 the black population was about 35.8 million and constituted about 12.5 percent of the total population. While black Americans have historically accounted for a significant percentage of the poor, since the 1960s some progress has been made. In 1960 over half of all black Americans lived in poverty. After declining steadily for years, in 1995 the poverty rate dropped below 30.0 percent, and has remained below 25.0 percent since 1999. In 2003, 24.4 percent of black Americans were poor, a slightly higher rate than in the preceding four years. Still, even after years of progress followed by modest reversals, almost one in four poor Americans in 2003 was black (see Table 3.1 and Figure 1.2).

The Asian population in 2003 was about 11.8 million, about 4.0 percent of the population. While Asians tend to be well educated and have

Figure 3.4   **Poverty Rates of People in Families by Family Type and Presence of Workers, 2002**

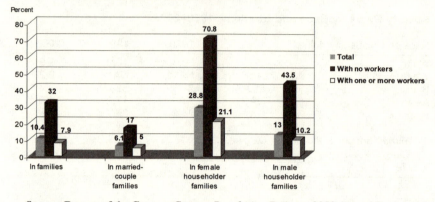

Source: Bureau of the Census, *Current Population Reports*, 2003 Annual Social and Economic Supplements, www.bls.census.gov/cps.

a high median income (Bureau of the Census, 2003b, 3), their poverty rate is rather high. In 2003 some 11.8 percent of all Asians were poor, composing about 3.9 percent of all the poor. Poor Asians tend to be more recent immigrants struggling to gain an economic foothold in America.

The Hispanic population, an ethnic group that may be of any race, was 14.0 percent of the population in 2003. Along with Asians, the Hispanic population is growing significantly. In 1988 the Census Bureau counted about 20 million Hispanics. In 2003 the count had doubled to 40.3 million. Poverty rates among Hispanics are high, but have generally declined since the early 1990s. In 2003 the poverty rate was 22.5 percent, and Hispanics constituted about 25 percent of all the poor. Combined, the black and Hispanic populations make up about 26 percent of the population, but about half of all poor Americans.

Figure 3.4 provides insight into how the combined role of family structure and employment impact poverty. Families without workers, especially if they are headed by a single male or a single female, have very high poverty rates (43.5 percent and 70.8 percent, respectively). Poverty rates drop dramatically when there are one or more workers in a family, but remain high (21.1 percent) for families headed by a single woman. Married-couple families have a high poverty rate when there are no workers in the family (17.0 percent), but the rate drops to 5.0 percent when one or more family members are employed.

Figure 3.5   **Employment of Working-Age Poor, 2002**

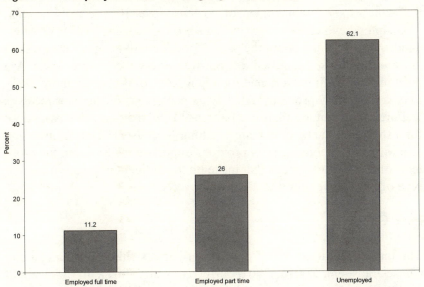

Source: Bureau of the Census (2003a), p. 8.

Figure 3.5 shows the employment record of poor working-age adults (eighteen to sixty-five) in 2002. Slightly more than 11.0 percent were employed full time year round and still could not escape poverty. Another 26.8 percent were employed part time or part of the year, but lived in poverty. The majority (62.1 percent) did not work at any time during the year. Among the non-workers are a large number of single parents who have little chance of working unless they have childcare and often other support services.

Summary

Some Americans are much more likely to suffer poverty. As Figure 3.2 illustrates, single-parent families, especially those headed by women, along with minorities and unemployed or underemployed adults suffer particularly high rates of poverty. If single parents are employed, especially full time, they have a much better chance of escaping poverty, but a significant percentage remains poor despite full employment. Children are the victims of the problems that afflict their parents or guardians. About one-sixth of all American children are poor, and they constitute about 36 percent of all the poor. While the poverty rate for Americans sixty-five and older has declined significantly over the last forty years, individuals sixty-five and older still constitute over 10 percent of the poor.

Chapter 4, which examines the causes of American poverty, provides another way to think about the poor. There we will examine issues such as how long those identified as poor live below the poverty level. Are most of the poor impoverished for a long time, or is poverty more likely to be a temporary problem? Also, what percentage of the poor receives welfare, and what are their use patterns? How many receive assistance for a short period and how many are long-term users? The combination of information about the poor provides important insights into the problems of the various groups that make up the indigent population and the type of policies required to alleviate poverty.

Poor Children

The largest single group of poor Americans is children (Duncan and Chase-Lansdale, 2001a, 2001b; Morris et al., 2001). In 2003 about 12.1 million children, some 11.6 million of whom lived with related family members, were poor. Since preventing and alleviating poverty among children is critical to the long-term goal of improving the economic security and productivity of American citizens, this group of poor Americans deserves particular attention. Figure 3.6 shows the trend in child poverty rates since 1959. What the data show is that during most of the 1960s considerable progress was made in reducing poverty among children. However, the rate of poverty gradually increased during much of the 1970s, and then moved up and down over the next thirty or so years. In 2003, the poverty rate was higher than the rates during much of the 1960s.

Child poverty rates vary considerably by race and ethnicity but are high for all groups. Figure 3.7 shows the poverty rate for children by race and ethnicity in selected years between 1974 and 2003. The data show the rise and decline in child poverty over the last forty years, and the overall decline in child poverty by the early 2000s. The poverty rate has always been lowest for non-Hispanic white children; their poverty rate is less than one-third of the rate for black and Hispanic children. Still, there were over 4 million poor white children in 2003, making them the largest group of poor children. The poverty rate for black and Hispanic children is particularly high, but had been declining until recent years. In 2003 about 32 percent of all black children were poor, and

Figure 3.6   **Poverty Rates of American Children, 1959–2003**

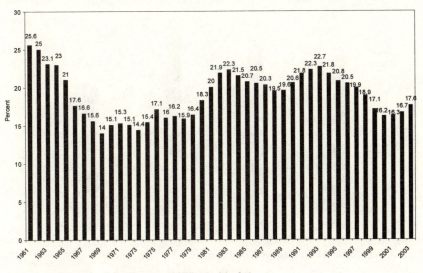

Source: Bureau of the Census (2004a), table 8-1.

they comprised about 30 percent of all poor children. Hispanic children, who may be of any race, had a poverty rate of 29.7 percent in 2003 and were about 32 percent of all poor children.

Just as race and ethnicity are strong predictors of poverty among children, family structure also plays an extremely important role. Figure 3.8 compares the poverty rate for children by whether they live in a married-couple family or in a mother-only family. The differences between the poverty rates for children in these family types are stark for all racial and ethnic groups. Children, regardless of race or ethnicity, suffer very high rates of poverty when they live with a single mother. Almost 40 percent of all children living in mother-only families live in poverty, and the poverty rate for non-Hispanic white, black, and Hispanic children in these families is exceptionally high. In 2002 almost 48 percent of all black and Hispanic children in mother-only families lived in poverty. While lower, over 29 percent of white children living in a mother-only family suffered poverty. When children live in a married-couple family the risk of poverty is significantly lower. Non-Hispanic white children living in married-couple families have a poverty rate that is about one-sixth of the rate for mother-only families. For black children the poverty rate in married-couple families is about one-fourth of the poverty rate of

Figure 3.7 **Poverty Rates of Children by Race and Ethnicity, 1974–2003**

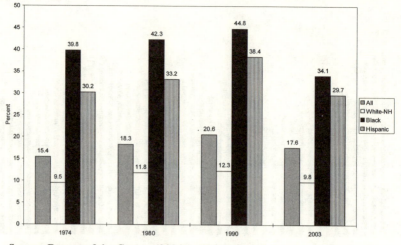

Source: Bureau of the Census (2004a), table 8-1.

Figure 3.8 **Poverty Rates of Children by Family Type and Race, 2002**

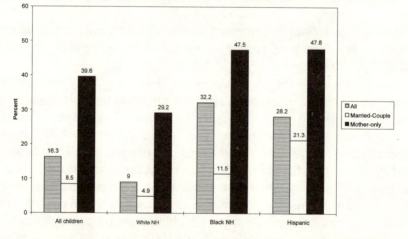

Source: Department of Health and Human Services (2004b), table ES 1.2A.
Note: Figures are for related children in families.

mother-only families. Hispanic children have a much lower rate of poverty when they live in a married-couple family, but at over 21 percent the rate is still very high. Clearly, children living with a single mother are at very high risk of poverty.

Figure 3.9 shows the percentage of all poor children living in mother-

Figure 3.9   **Percentage of Poor Children in Mother-Only Families, 2002**

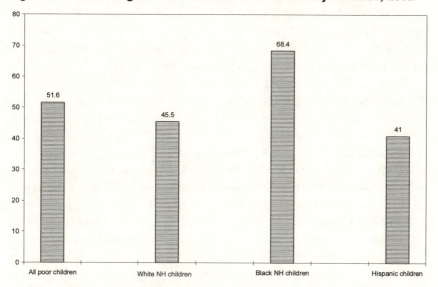

Source: Bureau of the Census (2003c), table C-3.

only families in 2002. Over half of all poor children, regardless of race or ethnicity, live in mother-only families. Over 45 percent of poor white children, 68 percent of poor black children, and 41 percent of poor Hispanic children live in mother-only families. If fewer children lived in mother-only families, or if these family types were more economically viable, poverty among American children would be substantially lower.

The causes of poverty among children vary somewhat by race and ethnicity, but are always complex. Although white non-Hispanic children are poor for a variety of reasons, family structure is extremely important. Rising rates of divorce, separation, and out-of-wedlock births have greatly increased the number of white non-Hispanic children living in high-risk, single-parent families. Many white non-Hispanic children are also in families with low, stagnated earning power and families that have found welfare benefits in decline.

Family structure is also a very important predictor of poverty among black children. The poverty rate for black female-headed families with children exceeded 50 percent in every year between 1970 and 1999. In 2000 the poverty rate declined to 49.4 percent and was 47.5 percent in 2002 (Bureau of the Census, 2003a, 82). By comparison, the poverty rate for black married-couple families with children is much lower and has generally declined over the last twenty years. In 2002 it was 11.5 percent, less than a fourth of the rate for single-mother families. In 2002 the median income of black married-couple families was $51,514, while the median income of black mother-only families was only $20,894 (Bureau of the Census, 2004c, Historical Tables, table F-7B).

The median income of black married-couple families has made progress in catching up with white families. In 1975 the median income of black married couples equaled about 76 percent of the median income of white married-couple families. By 2001 the ratio was 84 percent (Bureau of the Census, 2004c, Historical Tables, F-7A, F-7B). By contrast, black female-headed families had a median income of about 42 percent of black married-couple families in 1975 (table F-7B). In 2002 median incomes for these families had declined to 40.5 percent of the median income of black married-couple families. Significantly reducing poverty among black children, therefore, would seem to depend substantially upon (a) reducing the proportion of families with children headed by single women, and (b) helping more single mothers gain economic independence through education, job training, and supported employment.

How can the high rates of poverty among Hispanic children be explained? There are a number of obvious contributing factors. First, compared to other major racial and ethnic groups, Hispanic adults on average have lower education levels. For example, in 2002 only 57.0 percent of all Hispanics twenty-five and older had a high school degree. As Table 3.2 shows, this is considerably below the level for Asians, non-Hispanic whites, and blacks. Hispanics also compare unfavorably with other major racial and ethnic groups on measures of advanced education. In 2002 only 11.1 percent of all Hispanics twenty-five and older had a college degree. This is less than one-fourth of the rate of Asian Americans, about 30 percent of the rate for white non-Hispanic Americans, and considerably below the rate for black adults. Many Hispanic adults, therefore, would seem to be particularly disadvantaged by recent trends in technology and the employment market's shift toward better-educated workers.

The lower educational achievement of Hispanics is reflected in earnings. In 2002 the median income of Hispanic households was $33,103, compared to $52,626 for Asians, $46,900 for non-Hispanic whites, and $29,028 for black households (Bureau of the Census, 2003b, table 1). The median income of black households suffers from the high rate of

Table 3.2

Educational Attainment of the U.S. Population Age 25 and Over, 2002

| | Percent | |
| | High school graduate | Bachelor's degree |
Race and Hispanic origin	or more	or more
White non-Hispanic	88.7	29.4
Black	78.7	17.0
Asian	87.4	47.2
Hispanic	57.0	11.2

Source: Department of Commerce (2003). CPS, PPL-169, Press release, June 24, 2004.

single-parent households within that group. Compounding these economic problems, divorce and out-of-wedlock births are increasing in the Hispanic population, resulting in a growing proportion of all Hispanic children living in families headed by single females. As noted in Figure 3.8, the poverty rate for Hispanic children in mother-only families was about 48.0 in 2002. One last problem is that many of the poorest Hispanics may be recent immigrants with little formal education and struggling with language barriers.

Summary

Children are the major victims of American poverty. The overall poverty rate of American children is very high, especially compared to poverty rates in many other industrialized nations (Figure 1.1). Only one group of American children has a fairly low rate of poverty—white non-Hispanic children who live in married-couple families. The poverty rate for black and Hispanic children is staggering. All children, regardless of race or ethnicity, have high poverty rates when they live in a mother-only family. In fact, a majority of all poor children live in a mother-only family, including over 40 percent of poor non-Hispanic white and Hispanic children. Almost 70 percent of poor black children live in a mother-only family. The causes of poverty among children vary somewhat by race and ethnicity. Single parenting, especially when combined with unemployment, is a major contributor to poverty among children, leaving them extremely vulnerable to economic insecurity and deprivation. Ameliorating poverty among chil-

Figure 3.10   **Children With Single Parents and Proportions With Cohabiting Single Parent, March 2002**

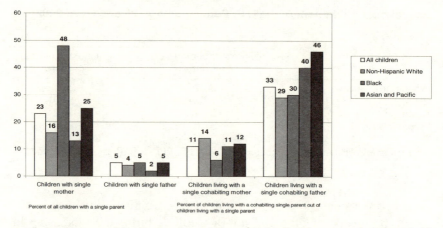

Source: Bureau of the Census, Annual Demographic Supplement to the March 2002 Current Population Survey.

Notes: The parent is the householder or partner, in an unmarried-partner household. Single means the parent has no spouse in the household. People of Hispanic origin may be of any race.

dren will require reducing the number of unplanned and unwanted children to parents who are unprepared to take care of them, while providing opportunities for parents in financial trouble to become economically viable. In later chapters, we will assess the possibilities of the PRWORA of 1996 to accomplish these goals.

Mother-Only Families: Growth and Causes of Poverty

Since the growth of mother-only families has played such a major role in the escalation and persistence of poverty, and especially poverty among children, this demographic trend deserves carefully examination (Gabe, 2001; Primus et al., 1999). Designing policies to reduce poverty among women and children requires insights into why an increasing proportion of families are headed by a single woman, and why these families are so economically vulnerable. There are two major reasons for the dramatic increase in mother-only families. The first is greatly increased rates of divorce and separation over the last several decades. The second is significantly higher rates of out-of-wedlock births.

Figure 3.10 shows the percentage of all children, by race and ethnicity,

Figure 3.11   **Percentage of All Children Born Out of Wedlock**

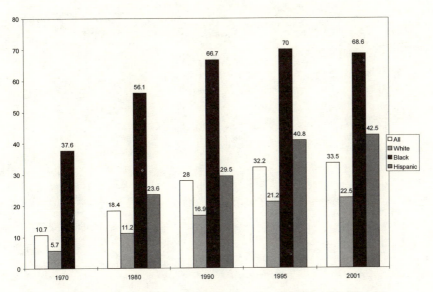

Source: Department of Health and Human Services (2004b), table PF 2.3B.

living in single-parent and cohabiting households in 2002. Almost one-fourth of all children live with a single mother, with another 5 percent living with a single father. Single-parent households are common for children of all races and ethnicities, but the rate is particularly high for black children. Over half of all black children live with either a single mother (48 percent), or a single father (5 percent). As Figure 3.10 shows, 11 percent of all children living with a single mother have a cohabiting adult in the household. The cohabiting adult may be the child's parent. Children living with a single father are even more likely to have a co-habiting adult in the household.

Until very recently, divorce was the number one reason for the for-mation of mother-only families with children. Since the late 1980s divorce rates have stabilized, but out-of-wedlock births to adult women have continued to rise. During the 1950s and 1960s, the yearly divorce rate per 1,000 women ages fifteen and older was about ten. By the mid-1970s the rate had doubled. The rate continued to increase in the late 1970s and early 1980s but has since leveled off. Still, over 40 percent of all marriages end in divorce (Centers for Disease Control, 2003, table A).

Figure 3.12   **Living Arrangements of Poor Children in Mother-Only Families, 2002**

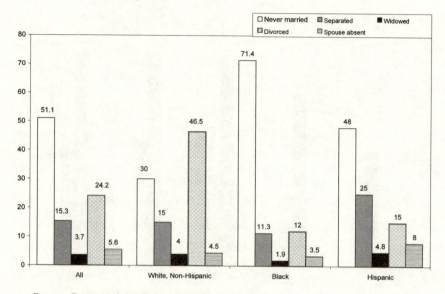

Source: Bureau of the Census (2004b), table C-1.

Out-of-wedlock births also increased quite dramatically over the last several decades, and remain very high. Figure 3.11 shows the rise in out-of-wedlock births since 1970. In 1970 only 11 percent of all children were born out of wedlock. By 2001 the percentage had tripled to 33.5 percent. With the exception of a small decline for black children in 2001, out-of-wedlock births have increased for all racial and ethnic groups. By 2001, almost 69 percent of all black children were born out of wedlock, as were over 40 percent of all Hispanic children and 22.5 percent of all white children.

The events that bring poor children into a single-mother household vary significantly by race and ethnicity. As Figure 3.12 shows, the majority of all poor children find themselves in a mother-only family because their mothers never married. The second major reason is a divorce. A relatively small percentage of all poor children live in a mother-only family because their mother was widowed (3.7 percent), or because their father is absent (5.6 percent). However, the story varies by race and ethnicity. The primary reason that poor white children end up in a mother-only family is divorce (46.5 percent), although

Figure 3.13 **Percentage of All Children Living in Families With a Never-Married Female Head, by Race, 1960–2002**

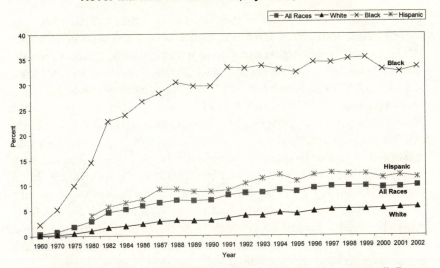

Source: Bureau of the Census, "Marital Status and Living Arrangements," *Current Population Reports*, various years. Data for 1960 from "Persons by Family Characteristics," PC(2), 4B.

birth out of wedlock is another significant reason (30 percent). For black children the overwhelming reason is out-of-wedlock birth (71.4 percent); divorce accounts for only 12 percent. For Hispanic children, the family forms primarily because the mother never married (48 percent), and because of separation (25 percent). Figure 3.13 shows the percentage of all children living with a never-married mother from 1960 through 2002. The trend line increases for all children during this period, and is particularly dramatic for black children.

Why Have Divorce and Unwed Births Increased?

The huge increases in rates of divorce and births to unmarried women over the last several decades constitute two of the most important demographic changes in American families in the last century. These changes have significantly altered life patterns such as sexual roles, parenting, careers, and social interactions. The changes have massive implications for social policy. Why have they occurred? Below we examine the four major reasons most often offered as explanations.

Changing Social Mores

The great social movements of the 1960s have been credited with liberalizing public attitudes toward single parenthood and divorce (Magnet, 1993). Certainly the stigma associated with either phenomenon has declined significantly over recent decades (Garfinkel and McLanahan, 1986, 82), and behavior such as premarital sex is both more common and more accepted (Bane and Ellwood, 1994, 114). Demographic change has also played a role in these changing attitudes. Increasingly mature women of childbearing age are single. Women are entering their first marriage later and divorcing more frequently. In 1950 the average age of first marriage was 20.3, in 1985 it was 23.3, and by 2000 it was 25.1 (Bureau of the Census, 2004d, table 61). In 1950 only about one-fourth of all twenty- to twenty-four-year-old women had never been married. By 2000 the proportion had risen to 72.8 percent (table 62). The growing number of adult, single women, many with careers, therefore, increases the number of women who may decide to have a child out of wedlock.

It is reasonable to assume, then, that changing demographics and a more accepting public have made it easier for adults to make choices about both divorce and out-of-wedlock births. However, as we will detail in Chapter 5, the huge increases in out-of-wedlock births over the last couple of decades, especially among teens, seems to have created a backlash that is reflected in some of the provisions of the welfare reform passed by Congress in 1996. Additionally, the data show some recent declines in out-of-wedlock births among teens, especially black teens.

The Availability of Welfare

Although the public tends to believe that the availability of welfare has had a major impact on divorce, remarriage, and out-of-wedlock births, the best evidence suggests that there is a relationship, but it is modest. Danziger et al. (1982), Ellwood and Bane (1985), and Bassi (1987) all found a link between welfare receipt and divorce. Garfinkel and McLanahan (1986) concluded that although welfare receipt delayed remarriage, the implications for divorce and out-of-wedlock births are limited. They found that the increase in welfare benefits between 1960 and 1975 contributed to about 15 percent of the growth in mother-only families, rising to about 30 percent of the increase among the low-income population (Garfinkel and McLanahan, 1994, 211). Moffit's (1992) review of the empirical literature basically reached the same conclusions.

Acs (1996), in a very comprehensive evaluation, found little relationship between state cash benefit levels and the out-of-wedlock birth rate in the state. States that paid the highest cash benefits did not have higher rates of out-of-wedlock births. In fact, some of the states that paid the lowest cash benefits had the highest rates of out-of-wedlock births. The pattern clearly did not suggest that women were having babies in response to cash incentives. Acs's findings are consistent with the major body of research on this topic (Ellwood and Bane, 1985; Duncan and Hoffman, 1988; Plotnick, 1989).

Some critics, however, have argued that the amount of the state grant is less important than the fact that an out-of-wedlock birth opens the door for impoverished women to enter the welfare system and receive a package of benefits. Additionally, under Aid to Families with Dependent Children (AFDC; replaced by Temporary Assistant to Needy Children in 1996) if a woman on welfare had another child, she received a modest increase in her cash benefits along with medical coverage, food stamps, and perhaps other benefits for the new child. As Chapter 7 will detail, to some extent, the PRWORA of 1996 accepts the validity of the argument that welfare contributes to unwed births. PRWORA allows states the option of denying cash assistance to teenagers who have children out of wedlock. If the state does provide assistance to single teenage mothers, the teen must live at home or under the supervision of an adult, and must stay in school or job training. Additionally, states may cap benefits to welfare families, providing no additional assistance to women who have children while on welfare. About half the states have capped benefits.

Female Employment

Another reason often suggested for increased rates of divorce and births to unmarried women is the independence women increasingly enjoy because of their careers and independent incomes. Over the last thirty years women have greatly increased their percentage of all college graduates and their role in the job market. Over the last two decades particularly, more women have balanced career and family roles (see Figure 8.5). In 2002, women workers were 47 percent of all wage and salary income recipients, up from 32 percent in 1947. While more adult women are employed, they are less likely than men to be full-time year-round employees. In 2002, 73 percent of all men aged fifteen and over worked full time year round. Among women in the same age group, 58.6 percent worked full time year round (Bureau of the Census, 2003b, table 3).

The evidence indicates that when women have employment or other independent sources of income, they are somewhat more inclined to leave bad marriages, take longer to remarry, and are more willing to have children outside of marriage (Groeneveld, Hanna, and Tuma, 1983; Garfinkel and McLanahan, 1986; Ellwood and Bane, 1985; Bassi, 1987; Garfinkel and McLanahan, 1994, 211). The impact of employment is modest but often important (see Cain, 1987; Bane and Ellwood, 1994, 109–13).

Male Employment and Earnings

As will be detailed in Chapter 4, Wilson and Neckerman (1986) and other scholars have argued that marital instability and the epidemic of out-of-wedlock births are in part the result of decreasing job opportunities for men, especially inner-city minority residents with low skills. Wilson and Neckerman's argument is that when young men cannot earn enough to support a family, they avoid the responsibility of marriage, or may be rejected by women as suitable mates. There is some evidence to support their argument. In a recent poll, 77 percent of young women said that a well-paying job was an essential requirement for a husband. There is also a high correlation between male income levels and their rate of marriage. Among men in their thirties, those earning $50,000 a year or more are almost twice as likely to be married as those earning less than $10,000 (Casey Foundation, 1995, 5).

Yet, the median income of many men is quite low, especially when they are minorities. In 2001 the median income for non-Hispanic white men was $31,791; for black men, $21,466; and for Hispanic men, $20,189 (Bureau of the Census, 2004c, Historical Income Tables, table P-2). If men work full time year round, incomes improve significantly, but are still on average rather low for minority men. With full-time, year-around employment, non-Hispanic white men had median earnings of $43,194, black men, $31,921, and Hispanic men, $25,271 (tables P-36 B, C, D, E). Additionally, many men, especially minorities, undergo lengthy periods of unemployment. In 2003, 5.1 percent of all white men were unemployed, along with 10.2 percent of black men, and 7.5 percent of Hispanic men (Bureau of the Census, 2004d, table 621).

The evidence suggests that low median incomes and periods of un-employment for many men are often not directly caused by a shortage of jobs (Jencks, 1992, 127; Blank, 1994, 171). A major problem is a shortage of jobs that pay low-skill workers well and a shortage of entry-level jobs that lead to middle-income employment. This is true regard-less of whether those jobs are in service or manufacturing. In America's increasingly international and technologically sophisticated economy, there are decreasing economic opportunities for low-skilled workers, regardless of race (Gottschalk and Moffit, 1994). The result is that workers entering the job market today with a high school education or less can expect lower incomes than their fathers (Blank, 1994). In the 1960s and the 1970s, men between the ages of twenty-five and thirty-four had higher incomes than their fathers. By 1987 this trend reversed, leaving men twenty-five to thirty-four with lower median income than their fathers' generation. In 2002 this was still true (Bureau of the Census, 2004c, Historical Income Tables, table P-5).

The evidence, then, does support the argument that declining wages, high unemployment, and decreasing rates of employment characterize a larger percentage of all men today than in the past (Bound and Holzer, 1993; Bound and Freeman, 1992; Bound and Johnson, 1992). The ques-tion then becomes: what is the impact of these changes on family struc-ture? The evidence is mixed. Wilson and Neckerman (1986) compared the ratio of employed black men to employed black women in the same age cohort and found a significant decline since the 1970s. The decrease in employed black men occurred at the same time that marriage rates of blacks were declining quite dramatically. However, Mare and Winship (1991) found that only about 20 percent of the decrease in marriage rates for black men could be explained by their lower rates of employ-ment. Testa (1991), Ellwood and Crane (1990), and Ellwood and Rodda (1991) also concluded that changes in employment patterns of men, white and black, are rather modest compared to the steep declines in marriage rates. Thus, while male earnings and rates of employment and unem-ployment are related to marriage and perhaps divorce, this is just one factor contributing to the major increase in mother-only families (Lichter et al., 1992; Mare and Winship, 1991). In the next chapter, Cornel West, professor of African-American Studies at Princeton, offers a quite dif-ferent explanation for the decline in black marriage rates.

In summary, low wages and high rates of unemployment for many men, especially minorities, the independence provided women by their careers, a more liberal attitude toward premarital sex and single parenting, and the availability of welfare all have contributed to the major increases in divorce and out-of-wedlock births that have taken place over the last thirty years.

Why Are Mother-Only Families So Economically Vulnerable?

There is general agreement that mother-only families often suffer low income and high rates of poverty for at least five reasons: (1) historically the nation's major social welfare programs have not been designed to help single mothers become economically independent; (2) unemployment rates are very high among mother-only families living in poverty; (3) when women do work, their median incomes are low; (4) on average, there are fewer workers in mother-only families than in married-couple families; and (5) most single mothers receive little or often no support from absent fathers.

Poorly Designed Social Welfare Programs

Despite the fact that the dramatic growth in mother-only families is one of the most important demographic changes in the last century, public policy has been altered very slowly to deal with the reality of this massive change in the American family. Through most of its history, the Aid to Families with Dependent Children (AFDC) program was antifamily, denying assistance to almost all two-parent families. Poor women who married generally lost all assistance. Poor men often realized that their wives, girlfriends, and children would be better off if they abandoned the family. Even when AFDC was amended by the Family Support Act of 1988, the program continued to provide assistance almost exclusively to single mothers. Under AFDC most mothers could not enter the job market because child-care assistance was not provided, and they generally could not afford it given the incomes they could earn. Also, the jobs that AFDC mothers could obtain often did not provide health care, and employment resulted in the loss of Medicaid. The result was that when millions of mother-only families fell below the poverty level, welfare programs discouraged marriage and failed to help the vast majority of them escape poverty through supported work.

Additionally, as detailed below, between 1970 and the early 1990s, the inflation-adjusted value of AFDC benefits declined quite dramatically. Thus, the welfare program actually promoted single parenting,

Figure 3.14 **Percentage of Children Under Age 18 Living With at Least One Parent Employed Full Time All Year, by Family Structure, 1980–2001**

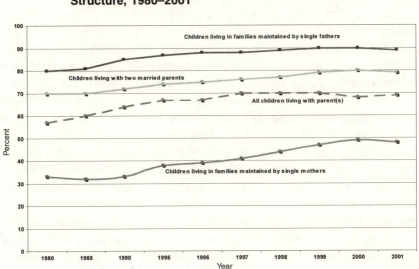

Source: Bureau of Labor Statistics (2004), *ChildStats, Current Population Reports*, table Econ2.

helped very few of those on welfare become employed, and provided increasingly inadequate assistance over time.

Women's Employment Income

The economic condition of mother-only families is also affected by a series of problems related to employment and wage earnings. Most obviously, unemployment rates for single mothers are high, especially for women heading poor families. In 2001, only 48 percent of all children living with a single mother had a mother who was employed full time year around (FTYR). Of those children living in a poor mother-only family, only 19 percent had a mother employed FTYR (Figure 3.14). By contrast, 79 percent of children living in a married-couple family had at least one parent who was employed FTYR. Children living with a single father were more secure than those living with a single mother. In 2001, 69 percent of children in a single-father household had a father who was employed FTYR. The percentage dropped to 29 percent for children living below the poverty level in these families.

Even when women are employed, they tend to earn less than male workers. In 2002 the median income for women working FTYR was $30,203, compared to $39,429 for men (Bureau of the Census, 2003b, figure 3). Among families with related children under the age of eighteen, the median income for married-couple families in 2002 was $65,399. For mother-only families the median was only $22,637, and $32,154 for families headed by single fathers (Bureau of the Census, 2004c, table ES 1.1). All the evidence makes it clear that children in married-couple families are much more likely to be economically secure than their peers in single-parent families, regardless of the sex of the family head.

Female workers earn significantly less than male workers for several reasons (Bergman, 1989; Fuchs, 1989). Many more women work only part time or part of the year. Women also tend to change jobs and move in and out of the work force more often. Among full-time workers the discrepancy between male and female wages is caused by many factors. First, the mean age of working women is considerably younger than that of male employees (which means that women tend to have less seniority). Second, women employees tend to be concentrated in jobs that are traditionally considered "women's work," and these jobs often pay a rather low wage regardless of the skill or training required. Third, some of the differences reflect "glass ceilings" and other forms of discrimination.

Lack of Adequate Child Support

One of the most obvious factors contributing to the poverty of mother-only families is the low level of child support by absent fathers. Until very recently, only about half of all women with minor children from an absent father have been awarded child support, and of these, only about half have received the agreed-upon amount (Bureau of the Census, 1994, tables 604–5). With the passage of the Family Support Act (FSA) of 1988, considerable new emphasis was placed on identifying absent parents and making them pay child support. The PRWORA of 1996 was built on the FSA provisions, and includes major new initiatives to identify absent parents and force them to pay their child support obligations. The provisions are explained in Chapter 7 and evaluated in Chapter 8. As will be detailed in those chapters, paternity establishment has been greatly improved as have child-support collections. There is every reason to believe that progress will continue in the years to come as the PRWORA provisions are fully implemented. In 2001 almost $19 billion was collected in child support, more than triple the amount collected in FY 1992. Paternity was established in 1.6 million cases, a 21 percent increase since FY 1997 (see Figure 8.15). Despite real progress, however, in 2001 only about 40 percent of all custodial parents received any support. Thus, child support has been significantly improving, but most mothers still do not receive the support they are owed, and this contributes significantly to the economic problems of these families.

Why Has Progress Slowed in Reducing Poverty?

As noted previously, despite both an economy that has been quite robust until the early 2000s and growing welfare spending over the last twenty years, progress in reducing American poverty has been disappointing. The lack of progress was one of the major reasons members of Congress cited for the major overhaul of welfare passed by Congress in 1996. As detailed in Chapter 5, critics of the welfare system blamed the lack of progress on evidence of an increasing willingness on the part of Americans to rely on welfare (Hoynes and MaCurdy, 1994), high rates of welfare fraud, drug and alcohol abuse by welfare recipients, and many other problems. Although much of what the critics cited may be true, considerable evidence suggests that three major trends played a significant role in slowing and even reversing progress against poverty.

First, as documented above, over the last thirty years, very significant changes have taken place in American families. One very important change is that an increasing percentage of all children live in mother-only households. In 1959 only 9 percent of all children lived with a single mother (Bureau of the Census, 2004d, Historical Poverty Tables, table 10). By 1984 over 20 percent of all children lived in a mother-only family and the rate since then has remained over 20 percent. In 2002, 23.2 percent of all children lived in a mother-only household. Thus, one reason that progress against poverty slowed is that a family type highly vulnerable to poverty has grown extremely rapidly over the last four decades.

A second problem that has made it difficult to reduce poverty is that wages for many workers have stagnated over the last twenty-five years. This is especially true for adults without college training or degrees. Figure 3.15 shows the changes that have taken place in income levels for the lowest 20 percent of all workers, the middle 20 percent, and the top 20 percent. Notice that between 1975 and 2002 the earning power of those workers at the bottom of the wage scale increased in only the most

Figure 3.15   **Average Income of Low-, Middle-, and Upper-Income Households by Quintile, 1975–2002**

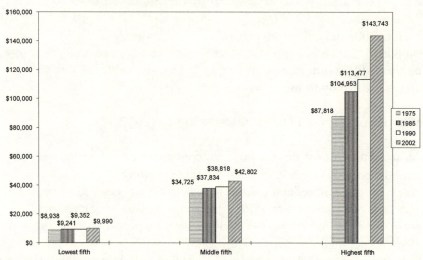

Source: Bureau of the Census (2003b), table A-4.
Note: All figures are adjusted for inflation and reported in 2002 dollars.

modest fashion. In fact, between 1990 and 2002 the yearly income of the workers in the lowest group of earners increased by only $638. The middle group of earners fared a little better, but still made only modest progress. The picture is completely different for the highest fifth of all income earners. This group's income on average increased from $85,131 in 1975 to almost $144,000 in 2002. College educated adults, especially those with advanced degrees, are doing exceptionally well in the market, while less well-educated adults, especially those with a high school degree or less, are doing very poorly.

Figure 3.16 shows how yearly income is divided among the population. These data reveal that income has become increasingly maldistributed; that is, an increasing proportion of the money is going to a smaller and smaller proportion of all earners. Figure 3.15 divides all households into five groups, ranging from the lowest 20 percent of all households with income to the highest 20 percent. The data show that only the top 20 percent of all households have been gaining income, and their share of the total pie increased from 43.2 percent in 1975 to 49.7 percent in 2002. The share of all income going to the bottom 20 percent shrank from an extremely modest 4.4 percent in 1975 to a paltry 3.5

Figure 3.16   **Share of Aggregate Household Income by Quintile, 1975–2002**

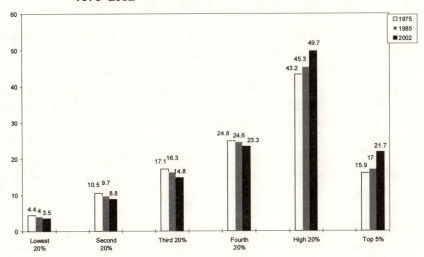

Source: Bureau of the Census (2003b), table A-3.

percent in 2002. The second, third, and fourth quintiles also saw their share of total income decline. By contrast, Figure 3.16 selects out the top 5 percent of all households. Notice that their share of all income increased very substantially between 1975 and 2002, increasing from 15.9 percent to 21.7 percent in 2002. In 2002 the top 5 percent of all households received far more of the cumulative income than the bottom 40 percent of all households, more than the middle 20 percent, and almost as much as the fourth quintile of earners.

Why has income stagnated for most of the workforce, while a small percentage of workers has gotten richer and richer? The basic answer is education. On average, the only workers enjoying real income gains over the last twenty-five years have been the college educated. As American society has changed from a manufacturing economy to a global economy based on information transfer, only the best educated of Americans have been prepared for the most competitive and lucrative jobs (Bound and Johnson, 1992; Juhn, Murphy, and Pierce, 1993; Murphy and Welch, 1993).

Both high school dropouts and high school graduates have suffered a steady decline in inflation-adjusted wages since the late 1970s (Freeman and Katz, 1995). However, workers with post–high school training and college degrees have made significant wage gains over the same period (Blank, 1997, 32–33). This is a trend that will certainly continue. Americans in search of economic gain and security will increasingly find education mandatory.

The last reason for the decline in progress against poverty in the 1980s and much of the 1990s was the decreasing effectiveness of welfare programs in helping recipients escape poverty. Welfare rolls increased quite dramatically during this period and spending simply failed to keep pace. The percentage of all American families on cash welfare was 1.7 percent in 1960 (see Figure 8.1). The percentage steadily increased to 5.2 percent in 1972, declined modestly during the 1980s, but moved up again in the 1990s. By 1994, 5.5 percent of all families with children were receiving cash welfare. The welfare reform debate in the early to mid-1990s was driven, in part, by these increases and played an important role in the passage of the PRWORA. The 1996 act and state reforms that preceded and tested many of the provisions of the act led to substantial declines in the welfare rolls (Figure 8.1).

As caseloads rose and remained high during both the 1980s and most of the 1990s, spending for the primary cash welfare program, AFDC, increased in inflation-adjusted dollars, but not enough to cover the rapidly increasing caseload. Thus, spending per AFDC family declined quite drastically. In 1970, for example, the average AFDC family received $734 a month (1996 dollars). By 1996 the average AFDC family received only $374 (see Table 7.5). As the real dollar value of AFDC declined, the number of welfare families pushed over the poverty line by cash assistance decreased throughout much of the 1980s and early 1990s (Danziger and Weinberg, 1994, 50).

The impact of social welfare spending on poverty rates began to improve in the late 1980s. While per capita AFDC benefits were being eroded, other programs for the poor were improving. The most important improvements were in the Earned Income Tax Credit (EITC). A study by the Congressional Research Service Office (2000) examined the impact of all cash and near-cash transfer programs on poverty among persons living in families with children under the age of eighteen between 1979 and 1994. The analysis included all means-tested cash transfers such as AFDC and Supplemental Security Income (SSI), plus Social Security, unemployment compensation, workers' compensation, food and housing benefits, and the EITC. This study found that these programs lowered the number of poor in these families by 36.6 percent in 1979. As per capita spending per family declined, the antipoverty effectiveness of the programs was greatly eroded. The poverty count was reduced by only 19.1 percent in 1983, slowly recovering to 23.9 percent in 1989, and 26.5 percent in 1993. Thus, in the early 1990s, both overall expenditures and poverty rates increased.

These three major trends that slowed progress against poverty provide some insights into the challenges involved in making additional progress in reducing poverty. The percentage of all households with children headed by single mothers remains high. As we have seen, the members of these households are extremely vulnerable to poverty. The PRWORA of 1996 focuses considerable attention on reducing out-of-wedlock births, especially among teenagers, on forcing both parents to accept financial responsibility for their children, and even on attempts to promote marriage. But even if the act is successful in reducing out-of-wedlock births and improving child support, it seems doubtful that divorce and separation will decline in any major fashion over the next decade. Thus, the proportion of all households with children headed by a single woman will remain very high, and perhaps even grow. This means that further poverty reduction depends in part on welfare and social policy ameliorating the major barriers to economic independence for single-parent families.

The declining wages of less educated adults is also a challenge. The forces that have altered the job market are not likely to reverse. In the future, a quality education will become increasingly important to economic security. The national challenge is to better educate all the population and to improve opportunities for adults to obtain additional education over their lifetime.

In later chapters we will examine the PRWORA of 1996 in some depth. One goal will be to determine if the new reform legislation is really responsive to the problems that have stymied progress in reducing poverty over the last twenty years.

Conclusions

This chapter has examined trends in American poverty and the demographics of the American poor. Poverty has proven to be an extremely stubborn problem. After decades of antipoverty initiatives and expenditures in the trillions, the rate of poverty in 2003 was higher than at any point during the 1970s. The problems that have stymied progress against poverty are considerable, but three broad societal and policy changes played major roles: the growth of mother-only families, the decline of wages for less well-educated workers, and the decline of per capita cash welfare assistance in the 1980s and much of the 1990s. The growth of mother-only families is the result of increasing rates of divorce, separation, and out-of-wedlock births. Changing social mores, the availability of welfare, the independence women have gained through education and employment, and problems with the employment and earnings of many men have all contributed to the breakdown of the traditional family.

America's poor tend to be its most vulnerable citizens—children, the aged, members of mother-only households, and the poorly educated stuck in jobs that pay wages that increasingly fail to keep pace with inflation. Children constitute about 35 percent of all the poor and a majority of them live in homes headed by single mothers. The rate of poverty for mother-only families has always been high, and has not markedly changed over the last two decades. What has changed is the number of mother-only families. As this type of household has increased, poverty among poor women and children has become an increasingly complex problem. Minority children are particularly likely to live with mothers who are divorced, separated, or never married, and this contributes significantly to their high rate of poverty.

4

Why Are People Poor in America?

Why are people poor in a country as rich as America? While many people, including some scholars, think the answer is simple, a thoughtful analysis suggests the antecedents of poverty are complex. As shown in Chapter 3, the poverty population is much more diverse than many people imagine. The poor are stereotyped as chiefly minorities, single women and their illegitimate children, and street people. In fact, the poverty population is an elaborate mix of people who vary by age, race, sex, geographic location, and family structure. Among the poor can be found the elderly, often living alone, married-couple families with children in which one or sometimes even both parents are employed, young healthy males who may be in the labor force, single or married adults without children, and farmworkers following crop rotations across the nation. The poor can be found in every state, in central cities, in suburbs and rural areas in every region of the nation. Does it seem reasonable that the same cause or reasons are responsible for the poverty of these diverse groups of people? Is an eighty-five-year-old widow poor for the same reasons as an eighteen-year-old single mother or a homeless alcoholic?

Not likely. The most common mistake in thinking about the causes of poverty is to generalize based on one group among the poor. If we think that poverty is only a problem related to minorities, teenagers having children out of wedlock, street people, or those who abuse alcohol or drugs, we are not likely to ever understand the complexities of the broader problem well enough to fashion creative solutions. Our understanding, or even biases, about the causes of poverty have a significant impact on the solutions we are willing to support (Schneider and Ingram, 1993; Barber, 1984; Wilson, 1973). Many people who might be willing to penalize adults who refuse to work or teenage mothers who will not attend parenting classes would likely have a different attitude about a parent who worked full time but could not escape poverty. It is important, therefore, to achieve as sophisticated an understanding as possible of the various causes of poverty.

When the assortment of people who are poor is examined, it becomes obvious that poverty is not a single problem, but rather a series of problems that affect diverse groups within our population. Also, being poor does not automatically mean that a person is a welfare recipient. Only some of the poor receive welfare (see Table 7.2). For various reasons many poor people never apply for support, and others would find qualifying for aid to be difficult because most aid is reserved for select groups of poor people. Stereotypes of the poor often result from the fact that only some of the poor receive the cash benefits that society thinks of as welfare. Those people who qualify for cash assistance—mostly female-headed families—tend to be thought of as the poor. But they are a subset of the poor.

Even being aware of the diversity and complexity of poverty and the use of welfare by the poor will not solve all the analytical problems. Fashioning public policies to solve poverty would be easier if there was agreement about the causes of poverty. But even when we examine the poverty of a particular person or a specific group of people, individual values impact opinions of why these people are poor. Think about this example. The poverty rate for married-couple families with children is low—about 7 percent. Several seemingly obvious causes make a small percentage of these families poor. Some of these families, for example, go through periods of unemployment, and some work full time but receive low wages, a not uncommon problem. Some family heads suffer illness, or become disabled, perhaps because of a job-related injury.

While the basic reasons these families suffer poverty may seem clear, there are many ways to diagnose their problems. If unemployment is a problem, how did the parents become unemployed? Did they fail to take employment seriously? Did they have the misfortune of being downsized? Do the parents misuse alcohol or drugs? Have the parents remained unemployed because they refuse to accept jobs they consider undesirable? Are they willing to relocate to an area with more jobs? Are both parents seeking employment? Is one parent forced to stay home because child care is too expensive or unavailable? Are the parents at fault for having children despite the parents' low income potential? Have the parents been wronged by employers who fail to offer acceptable benefits (for example, health care or day care) or display too little concern about the on-job safety of their employees?

Depending on individual values and perhaps the behavior of the individuals involved, there are notable grounds for differences in perspectives about why these families are poor, whether they should be offered any relief, and, if so, what help they should be given. The same is true, of course, for other subgroups of the poor. Thus, agreeing on the causes and cures for poverty is difficult.

The Dynamics of Poverty

Before examining specific theories of poverty, it is helpful to know some additional facts about America's poor population that have relevance to this discussion. An important question is what type of poverty are we dealing with? Does America have a large number of people who are poor for long periods, even a lifetime, or is poverty more likely to be a short-term problem? A permanent poverty class would be more complicated to deal with, and the causes of its poverty would probably be more intricate than that of people suffering from episodic spells of poverty. There are studies that answer this question. Research shows that most Americans who are identified as poor are impoverished for a short time. Gottschalk, McLanahan, and Sandefur (1994, 89) found that most poverty spells are short and that only a small percentage—7.1 percent—last seven or more years. They also found that poverty spells vary by race. Poverty spells are longer for blacks than for nonblacks. About 63 percent of nonblack poverty spells last less than one year. For blacks the matching figure is 48.4 percent. Blacks also suffer a higher rate of longer spells. While only 4.3 percent of nonblacks remain poor seven or more years, the rate for blacks is almost 15 percent (p. 90). If a person does become poor, how long will he/she be poor before moving above the poverty line for a full year? Gottschalk, McLanahan, and Sandefur's (p. 89) data show that for most of the poor, regardless of race, the answer is fewer than two years.

The U.S. Census Bureau conducted a study of new poverty spells, which is summarized in Figure 4.1. This study found that over half of all new poverty spells lasted less than four months. Within one year, 80 percent of poverty spells had ended. Only 2.7 percent lasted twenty-one to twenty-four months, and fewer than 6 percent lasted more than thirty-six months.

Figure 4.1   **Duration and Percent of Poverty Spells, 1996–99**

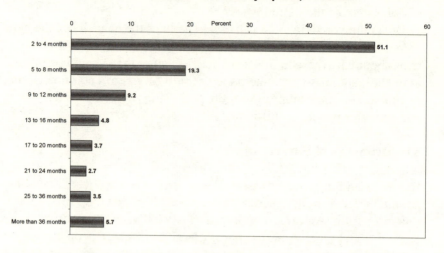

Source: Bureau of the Census (1996), Survey of Income and Program Participation; from John Iceland, *Dynamics of Economic Well-Being: Poverty 1996–1999*, P70–91, July 2003. See also www.census.gov/hhes/www/sipp96/sipp96.html.
Notes: Excludes spells underway during the first interview month. 2.0 percent of people were in poverty for all 48 months; they are not included in the above distribution.

Ruggles (1990) came to similar conclusions by examining monthly family income. This research also showed a great deal of income mobility among low-income groups. Over 80 percent of families with income below the poverty line in any one month suffered a poverty spell that lasted fewer than eight months. Examining these families over a two-year period, Ruggles found that only 11 percent were poor all twenty-four months.

For most people, therefore, new poverty spells are short. However, for some people poverty is a more long-term problem. By shifting focus and examining poverty spells in progress, rather than new spells, Gottschalk, McLanahan, and Sandefur (1994, 91) find a more troubled population. About 20 percent of people in poverty at any time have been poor for seven or more years.

Studies of income vulnerability also find that poverty is more than a fleeting problem for millions of people. Gottschalk, McLanahan, and Sandefur (1994, 91) tracked individuals who escaped poverty to discover how far they moved above the poverty threshold. They found that most of those who escape poverty remain economically marginal, considerably below middle-income levels. Some 91 percent of individuals who were poor in one year had incomes less than twice the poverty line in the next year. Living on the margins means that if they face any economic misfortune, many of the former poor are in jeopardy of falling back into poverty.

The evidence reviewed here reveals that poverty is a transitory problem for most people with incomes below the poverty line. Most of these people leave poverty, but remain economically vulnerable. However, a significant proportion of the poor live below the poverty line for long periods. If this information is correct, we should find three major patterns of welfare use. First, many people will be poor for too short a period to receive welfare. Second, most of those who do receive welfare will remain on the rolls for a short period. They may, however, cycle through the welfare system several times. Third, some 20 percent of the poor will be long-term users, remaining on the rolls for seven or more years. To see if these are the patterns of welfare use, we can examine welfare spells.

Welfare Dynamics

Table 7.2 shows the first pattern above is correct. Only 21.5 percent of those identified as poor in 2002 received cash aid, less than one-third received food stamps, and only a little over half were enrolled in Medicaid. Most of the poor never receive welfare, or benefit only from programs such as the school lunch program for poor and low-income families.

The second pattern is also confirmed by the data. Most welfare spells are short. Gottschalk, McLanahan, and Sandefur (1994, 94) in studying cash relief spells found that for nonblacks 44 percent of cases are closed in one year, while an additional 22.8 percent end in the second year. Spells last longer on average for black recipients, but 33.7 percent ended during the first year, with another 16.2 percent ending in the second year. By the end of two years, two-thirds of the spells for nonblacks and half the spells for blacks had ended.

Many recipients who leave welfare return. Recidivism, or multiple spells, significantly lengthens welfare use by many people. Looking at multiple spells over a ten-year period, Gottschalk, McLanahan, and Sandefur (1994, 95) found that 27.7 percent of black recipients received cash support for only two or fewer years. For nonblacks, 41.3 percent received aid for two or fewer years over a ten-year period. When multiple spells are added, 34.4 percent of blacks and 18 percent of nonblacks used cash assistance for seven to ten years. The average of all stays for recipients, counting multiple spells, is about four years (Moffit, 1992; Bane and Ellwood, 1994, 95–96). About 35 percent of all recipients leave the rolls only to return after losing a job or suffering another financial setback (Brandon, 1995). Rather than transitional users, they are episodic users (Bane and Ellwood, 1994, 41; Pavetti, 1993).

The third pattern is also confirmed. About half of all recipients remain on cash aid for more than four years, while about 25 percent remain on the rolls for ten years or more. Almost 6 percent of the cash assistance spells of nonblacks were still in progress at the end of seven years, while 25.4 percent of the spells for blacks were still in progress. One result is that while most of the poor who receive support are on the rolls for a short period, most of those people receiving aid on any given day have been on the rolls for a long time. This sounds contradictory, but it is not. Most people who receive assistance leave the system rather quickly, but a small percentage of recipients become long-term users. In a year's time, short-term users greatly outnumber long-term users. Thus, the typical user is short-term. Still, long-term users dominate the rolls on any given day. An often repeated example can make this clearer. Imagine a hospital room with four beds. Patients who remain in the hospital for the whole year occupy three of the beds. The fourth bed accommodates patients who stay in the hospital on average for one week. At the end of the year the hospital room will have served fifty-five patients, 94.5 percent of whom were short-term users. However, on any given day during the year, 75 percent of the patients in the room would be long-term. This is the way the welfare system works. Most people cycle through, some recycling. A small percentage of users are long-term, making up most recipients on any given day.

Bane and Ellwood (1994, 35–37) provide some important insights into the differences between long- and short-term users. The long-term users tend to be young, never-married mothers, especially those who drop out of school and have little job experience. While only about 14 percent of divorced women remain on the rolls for ten or more years, about 40 percent of all never-married mothers do so (Green Book, 1994, 444). Banes and Ellwood also find that when cash assistance recipients remain on the rolls for more than two years, they are in danger of becoming long-term users. On the other hand, when recipients manage to leave the rolls and stay off for at least three years, they usually do not return to cash aid (Hoynes and MaCurdy, 1994).

With this understanding of the poverty population and their use of welfare, we can examine and evaluate some specific theories of the causes of poverty.

Theories of Poverty

Theories of poverty generally fall into one of two categories: cultural/behavioral or structural/economic. Cultural/behavioral theories make the case that the only real cause of poverty is the behavior, values, and culture of the poor. Structural/economic theories usually contain some behavioral component, but argue the precipitating cause of poverty is a lack of equal opportunities for all Americans. Structural/economic theories usually focus on unequal economic opportunities (high unemployment or subemployment), educational systems that disadvantage the poor, or discrimination in its various forms. Conservatives favor cultural/behavioral arguments, while moderates and liberals usually stress structural/economic explanations that contain a behavioral component.

Cultural/Behavioral Theories

In *The Dream and the Nightmare* (1993), Myron Magnet offers a conservative interpretation of American poverty. Magnet argues the basic cause of poverty is the culture and behavior of the poor. People become poor, Magnet argues, not because they lack social, political, and economic opportunities, but because they lack the inner resources to seize the ample opportunities that surround them. Magnet believes the poverty of the poor is mainly a destitution of the soul, a failure to develop the habits of education, reasoning, judgment, sacrifice, and hard work required to succeed in the world. To Magnet the poor are not hardworking, decent people who have fallen victim to economic problems. Rather, he says, they are people who engage in leaving school, illegitimacy, drug and alcohol abuse, welfare misuse, and often crime.

The primary job of any civilization, Magnet says, is soulcraft: the transmission of values that combine to develop mature, educated, honest, hardworking, caring, and responsible people. The poor represent society's failures, those who have not inherited the central values of mainstream culture. Magnet believes the values of today's poor reflect the revolutionized culture of the 1960s, which taught that it was legitimate to blame the system for personal failures and expect government handouts rather than seek success through education, hard work, and sacrifice. This same 1960s culture also promoted the sexual revolution, endorsing premarital sex, promiscuity, and illegitimacy, while degrading marriage, sacrifice, education, and industriousness.

Magnet's concluding point is that an individual's values and behavior determines his/her opportunities, economic or otherwise. Economic opportunity can abound, but if a person lacks the inner resources to take advantage of opportunities, he/she will fail. Giving welfare to those who fail only makes matters worse. Welfare reinforces the belief that people are not responsible for their behavior, that they cannot overcome their problems through hard work, and that welfare is something they deserve.

Moderate and liberal critics believe the image of the poor drawn by Magnet and others who accept his view is nothing but a narrowly drawn stereotype. This vision of the poor, they argue, is based on a subset of the poor, which ignores the complexity of the poverty population, and as noted above, empirical evidence about poverty spells and welfare use. Out of a population of 35 million poor people, Magnet, they argue, bases his theory of poverty on the behavior and welfare use of a few million of the poor, a group often labeled as the undeserving poor or, more recently, the underclass. Those poor people with obviously dysfunctional habits or lifestyles have long interested society. But what part of the poor do they represent?

A considerable body of research has tried to define and identify the underclass. Scholars who have attempted to identify and count the members of this class have used a number of definitions and methodologies. Some studies have tried to define the underclass as those poor who are isolated in inner-city impoverished neighborhoods, essentially separated from the workforce (Bane and Jargowsky, 1988; Gottschalk and Danziger, 1986; Hughes, 1989; Nathan, 1986; Ricketts and Sawhill, 1988). These studies identify a small underclass population ranging from under 1 million to about 6 million.

Another group of scholars has tried to identify those long-term poor people, often including those who live in neighborhoods with high concentrations of poverty, who engage in dysfunctional behavior such as chronic unemployment, drug use, out-of-wedlock births, crime, leaving school, and antisocial attitudes and behavior (Adams, Duncan, and Rodgers, 1988; Reischauer, 1989; Kasarda, 1992; O'Hare and Curry-White, 1992). These studies identify a population that ranges from fewer than 1 million to slightly more than 8 million, depending on definitions, methodologies, and number of cities studied.

While these various studies arrive at estimates that differ, they agree that most of the poor are not the highly dysfunctional people described by Magnet. The proportion of the poor population that does display serious social problems, however, is large, visible, and expensive users of social services. It is not too surprising that this group is often thought of as the poor.

Many conservative scholars, on the other hand, are not concerned about stereotyping the poor because they think Magnet's basic arguments are correct. They believe the welfare system is so perverse in design that it has the capacity to spread a contagion of pathologies among the poor. Charles Murray in his influential book *Losing Ground* (1984) argued the real culprit of the poor is welfare. Welfare, Murray argues, robs the poor of initiative, breaks up families by encouraging men either not to marry the mothers of their children or to abandon them, provides an incentive to women to have children out of wedlock, so they can get on welfare or increase their benefits, and discourages work by providing a combination of cash and noncash benefits that amounts to better compensation than could be earned through employment.

Murray's arguments have attracted strong criticism, in part, because he proposes a radical solution. Murray argues the best way to lessen poverty is simply to abolish all welfare programs (Murray, 1994). Labeled the cold turkey approach, Murray's arguments are almost the perfect foil for those sympathetic toward the poor. But even critics of Murray often agree that welfare does produce some antifamily impacts. As noted in Chapter 3, Danziger et al. (1982), Ellwood and Bane (1985), and Bassi (1987) all found a significant link between welfare receipt and increased rates of divorce. Garfinkel and McLanahan concluded that although welfare receipt often delays remarriage, it has a modest impact on divorce and out-of-wedlock births (Garfinkel and McLanahan, 1986; 1994, 211).

Also as noted in Chapter 3, there is little relationship between state cash relief and state out-of-wedlock birthrates (Acs, 1996; Ellwood and Bane, 1985; Duncan and Hoffman, 1988; Plotnick, 1989). The out-of-wedlock birthrate, in other words, is not higher in states that pay high cash aid benefits than the rate in states that pay low benefits. In fact, Mississippi, one of the lowest-paying states in the nation, has one of the highest out-of-wedlock birthrates. Murray's response is that the generosity of state benefits is less important than the fact that an out-of-wed-lock birth makes women eligible for welfare or may increase her ben-efits, even modestly. Murray argues that if states gave no money to single mothers, especially teenagers, parents would put more pressure on teen-agers to avoid pregnancy, and women would be more careful about hav-ing children with men who did not have the prospect or interest in being parental partners.

Other scholars take a different approach than Murray, but argue that welfare programs play an important role in making and keeping people poor. In a pair of influential books, Lawrence Mead (1986, 1992) ar-gued the welfare system had become too permissive, placing too few obligations on recipients. By not requiring the healthy poor to work, Mead contended, the welfare system undermined both the confidence of the poor and public sympathy for them. One of Mead's theses was that passive poverty, that is an idle poverty population, reflected a welfare-nurtured defeatism among recipients rather than a real lack of economic opportunity. Mead focused, first, on proving the healthy poor could work and, second, on documenting ample economic opportunity for those with motivation. Mead argued the poor would be substantially better off eco-nomically and psychologically if they were moved into the workforce and that society would be much more positive about helping low-income working families than in aiding passive welfare families. Thus, Mead did not contend that all welfare is wrong or harmful, but rather that welfare, especially long-term, is the wrong solution to the problems of the able-bodied poor.

James L. Payne (1998) agrees with the fundamental position of con-servatives that welfare is harmful to the poor. Payne makes the familiar argument that welfare destroys the integrity of the poor while promoting and prolonging poverty by asking too little in return. Payne advocates what he calls "expectant giving," basing most assistance to the poor on the understanding that they must give something in return. "What the poor need," argues Payne, "is to be asked to give, not be given to" (p. xii). "Expectant giving" requires the poor to engage in productive efforts to help themselves. The best assistance programs, Payne argues, are those that require the greatest contribution from the poor.

Payne takes the conservative argument one step further. He contends that government can never pass or administer effective welfare reform. The reason, he argues, is that governments will always yield to a hand-out mentality, based on the belief that the poor, regardless of why they are poor, deserve help. "Expectant giving" requires judgments about why people are poor, what they need, what they should give in return, and whether they have lived up to the terms of their agreement or contract. Effectively helping the poor, Payne argues, requires that they be treated selectively or unequally, a role government is unsuited to play. With heavy caseloads, endless rigid rules, and a bias toward uniformity, government programs, he says, will always drift to handouts. The best alternative, Payne suggests, is to turn welfare over to private, voluntary efforts that can be more flexible and creative. Only then, says Payne, can we avoid the extremes of indulgence and cruelty that aggravate America's poverty problems.

The cultural/behavioral approach, in summary, places responsibility for America's poverty problem on the personal inadequacies of the poor, welfare in general, or the design flaws of welfare programs.

These conservative arguments played an important role in shaping the 1996 welfare reform. PRWORA gives states the authority to treat welfare applicants and recipients selectively (rather than uniformly), depending upon their personal situation and the state of the local economy. PRWORA presumes that the poor have an obligation to take responsibility for themselves and their families. It requires mutual obligation contracts between recipients and the state. In return for assistance, recipients agree to engage in responsible behavior. If the state decides that recipients have not lived up to their side of the agreement, their support can be terminated. PRWORA also incorporates work obligations and gives states the authority to regulate and even terminate support for teen mothers. Considerable emphasis is placed on forcing absent parents to support their children. Thus, the influence of conservatives can be clearly seen in the design and implementation of PRWORA.

Structural/Economic Theories

Moderates and liberals explain poverty in terms of limited and unfair economic opportunities, inadequate and unfair educational systems, lack of political power, biased government policies, and sometimes racial and/or sexual discrimination.

An interesting example of a structural/economic theory is offered by William J. Wilson in *The Truly Disadvantaged* (1987). Wilson examines the impact of civil rights laws on changes in economic oppor-

tunities for inner-city minorities. Wilson's theory focuses on the growth
of poverty and social problems in urban black ghettoes. In the early to
mid-twentieth century, blacks, Wilson notes, migrated from the South
to the major cities of the Midwest and North in search of economic
opportunities. Because of housing discrimination, almost all black
people, regardless of education or skills, became concentrated in central city ghettos. By the 1970s, Wilson maintains, civil rights laws and
changes in the nation's economy were producing important changes
that would have major impacts on black ghettos. Wilson explains these
dynamics with four hypotheses.

First, Wilson hypothesizes that changes in the inner-city employment
market harmed low-income, low-skilled blacks, especially black men.
These changes involved the general decline of manufacturing jobs, which
paid good wages for low-skill work, and the migration of hundreds of
thousands of these same types of manufacturing jobs from central cities
to the suburbs. Replacing these manufacturing jobs in the inner city
were clerical and white-collar jobs. These jobs, Wilson argues, required
more post-secondary or specialized skills than many ghetto residents
possessed. Wilson labels these changes slow economic growth, skills
mismatch, and spatial mismatch. Slow economic growth reduced the
number of manufacturing jobs, the jobs that increased in urban areas
were those that many poor blacks were unqualified to fill, while those
jobs they could perform were increasingly found in the suburbs.

Second, Wilson hypothesizes the resulting joblessness among inner-
city men encouraged many of them to turn to idleness and hustling,
including criminal activities such as the drug trade. The combination of
unemployment and crime among so many men left ghetto women with
fewer qualified or desirable partners, significantly reducing the marriage rate while increasing the incidence of out-of-wedlock births and
the use of welfare.

Third, ironically, Wilson argues, the civil rights laws passed in the
1960s played an important role in making these problems worse. Civil
rights and affirmative action laws extending equal employment opportunities and fair housing increased the income of the most educated and
skilled inner-city residents and allowed them to move to the suburbs.
Wilson calls this selective out-migration.

Fourth, Wilson theorizes that selective out-migration harmed the ghetto
community in important ways. Those who migrated had been the communities' best role models and civic leaders. Gone were those commu-

nity leaders who had championed the importance of education, quality schools, and high academic standards while resisting crime, illegitimacy, and idleness. In turn, those left behind had less education, skill, and motivation. This produced what Wilson labels a contagion effect—the degeneration of aspirations, morals, schools, and the general health of the community—leading to ever-increasing rates of poverty and other social problems.

Wilson's theory is interesting and important because it provides a tightly reasoned explanation of the growth of the black underclass in American ghettos. Wilson highlights a loss of low-skilled, decent-paying jobs as the precipitating event in increasing poverty in ghettos, but there is also a behavioral component. Wilson openly says that many poor people engage in behaviors that make and keep them poor. He believes, however, that economic problems set off the chain of events that increased poverty and other social problems.

Wilson's theory has attracted opposition on two points. First, some scholars condemn Wilson, a black scholar, because he places no emphasis on racial discrimination as a cause of ghetto poverty. Wilson, in fact, believes that racism plays a declining role in black life and black poverty (1980). Other scholars have argued that racism is the primary reason for the increasing marginalization of black males (Massey, 1990; Darity and Myers, 1983). Second, other scholars fault Wilson for not crediting welfare with making any real contribution to ghetto poverty. Scholars such as Mead, Murray, and Payne, of course, believe that welfare played a pivotal role. Mead (Wilson and Mead, 1987) criticizes Wilson's theory by pointing out that low-skilled immigrants have a history of preserving high employment levels, often doing so despite language barriers. Mead believes that immigrants sustain high employment levels because they were not raised in welfare families. Blacks, on the other hand, Mead says, often grew up in or around welfare families and are, therefore, more willing to turn to welfare rather than accept low-paying jobs that they consider unpleasant, degrading, or unrewarding or gain the education or job skills required for better employment.

Mickey Kaus in *The End of Equality* (1995) takes a different position. Kaus argues that welfare might not be the cause of poverty, but that welfare sustains it. Kaus raises the question of why inner-city blacks have often failed to follow low-skill jobs as they moved to the suburbs. Wilson's answer is that for many ghetto residents the jobs, once increased transportation and housing costs were factored in, do not pay enough to make relocation realistic. Kaus finds that answer suspect. He notes that blacks left the South in large numbers and traveled long distances in search of employment opportunities, but they often failed to follow jobs as they moved to the suburbs. Why, asks Kaus, did they travel a thousand miles to seek improved economic opportunities before the 1960s, but later failed to follow jobs that were twenty-five miles away? His answer is welfare. Blacks migrated from the South, he says, because they had no choice. The welfare system did not exist and was not an alternative. However, when urban jobs migrated to the suburbs, black citizens often had a choice. Rather than follow the jobs, they could qualify for welfare and become idle; and, that, Kaus says, is exactly what many of them did.

There is empirical evidence to support some of Wilson's hypotheses. Considerable research supports Wilson's skills-mismatch and spatial-mismatch hypotheses. Kasarda (1990, 1989, 1988) and Johnson and Oliver (1991) have documented the loss of decent-paying manufacturing jobs to the suburbs, especially in the major cities of the Northeast and North-Central regions. Holzer (1991) found that when jobs left the central cities for the suburbs, inner-city blacks lost more jobs and employment opportunities than did whites or suburban blacks. Research also documents a general decline in the wages of low-income workers (Holzer and Stoll, 2001; Hoynes, 2000). Since the mid-1970s wage increases have mainly taken place only in jobs that require higher levels of skill and education.

The empirical literature provides no support for Wilson's hypothesis that lack of economic opportunity explains the declining black marriage rate (Wilson and Neckerman, 1986). The marriage rate for blacks has been declining at least since the 1950s, and seems to be little influenced by shifting black male employment levels or the skill-level, education, or income of black males (Ellwood and Crane, 1990; Lerman, 1989; Hoffman, Duncan, and Mincy, 1991). As we will note below, Cornel West has a different explanation for the decline in black marriage rates.

Wilson's out-migration hypothesis is supported by empirical research (Gramlich and Laren, 1991). There is clear evidence that black citizens with the economic ability have fled the inner city for better neighborhoods, as have many other people. Wilson's contagion hypothesis has not been rigorously tested, but there is some evidence in support. Jencks and Mayer (1990) found that peers significantly affect academic achievement. Students perform better when they attend schools with peers who take education seriously and perform at higher levels. Hoffman, Duncan, and Mincy (1991) found the higher the proportion of single welfare mothers in a neighborhood, the higher the rate of teenage pregnancy. Anderson (1990) and Fagan (1992) found that young inner-city men turn to hustling when good jobs are unavailable.

In summary, much of Wilson's theory is supported by empirical and ethnographic research, although the role that welfare and racism do, or do not play, is seriously contested, and there is little support for the marriage hypothesis.

Culture as Structure

Another prominent black scholar offers a structural theory of black poverty, which includes some of the fundamentals of Wilson's theory. Wilson believes that black poverty stems from economic problems, and he believes that economic reform would go a long way toward reducing the poverty and social problems of low-income neighborhoods and individuals. But Cornel West in his book *Race Matters* (1993) argues that while there is an economic antecedent, the problems of the black population are more complex than Wilson imagines. West agrees with Wilson that many black people, especially those who live in central city ghettos, engage in self-destructive behavior. But West argues that this dysfunctional behavior has complicated antecedents, reflecting problems not just of the economy, but also of America's culture, and, thus, cannot be reversed simply by economic reform.

West attributes the poverty and social problems of poor blacks to four causes:

- First, the economic decline that has taken place within the inner cities of America and the change in compensation for low-skill jobs. His analysis of economic problems that have harmed the black population is similar to Wilson's.
- Second, a history of racism with continuing discrimination that West believes has done great emotional harm to millions of black people.
- Third, a prevailing American culture that stresses materialism and material gain to the exclusion of other, more important values, especially intellectual, moral, and spiritual growth. Materialism, West argues, is such a dominant value in American society that it is the core of American culture. As such, says West, it should be admitted

that this perverse culture is a form of structure, much like the economy and the political system (p. 12). When mainstream culture is so shallow that it reflects primarily market moralities, he argues, it misdirects and teaches low value, thus keeping people from becoming fully developed, successful humans with meaningful values and culture.

• Fourth, a lack of quality black leadership. West is critical of black leadership, arguing that most black leaders are unprepared to transcend narrow racial issues, be examples of moral and spiritual growth, and lead with real vision and courage (p. 23).

West believes the combination of flawed cultural values, racism (past and present), economic problems, and poor leadership has produced battered identities in much of black America. These battered identities express themselves in two ways. First, West contends, many black people suffer from nihilism, a disease of the soul that reveals itself by producing lives of "horrifying meaninglessness, hopelessness, and (most important) lovelessness" (p. 14). "Life without meaning, hope, and love," West concludes, "breeds a cold-hearted, mean-spirited outlook that destroys both the individual and others" (pp. 14–15). Second, is racial reasoning. Racial reasoning, West says, is not moral reasoning. "The humanity of black people," says West, "does not rest on deifying or demonizing others" (p. 28). Racial reasoning leads to closing-ranks thinking that takes the form of inchoate xenophobia (poorly thought out fears and dislikes about foreigners), systematic sexism (which West says contributes significantly to the declining black marriage rate), and homophobia.

West believes that racial reasoning must be replaced with moral reasoning, which would produce mature black identities, coalition strategies that cross racial lines, and black cultural democracy. Mature blacks could be honest about themselves and other black people, would be willing to work with other groups to achieve collective goals, and would promote a society in which black people treated everyone with respect, regardless of race, ethnicity, sex, or sexual orientation.

West's recommended solutions go beyond reducing black poverty, and they can be summarized in four parts. First, West believes that black people need a love ethic that would confront the self-destructive actions of many black people. Second, black people, he says, must also understand that the best source of help, hope, and power is themselves. Black people, argues West, must take charge of their lives and become involved in the civil soul of their communities. They must play a role in the debate, design, and passage of enlightened public policies that teach and celebrate quality values and stable, prosperous families. Third, government programs to aid low-income and poor people must be increased. Last, there needs to be a new generation of black leadership with genuine vision, courage, and commitment to ethical and religious ideas.

West's theory is provocative, controversial, and challenging. He argues that just improving economic opportunities will not solve the fundamental problems of American society. He believes that millions of black Americans suffer from battered identities, destructive reasoning, perverse cultural values, and inadequate leadership. Solving the problems of many people, he argues, requires a change in the basic values of American culture, more insight on the part of whites about racism, along with enlightened public policies and better leadership.

Tobin's Structural Theory of Poverty

The economist James Tobin (1994) offered another structural theory, one much more purely economic in nature. Tobin's theory rests first on his empirical research on the relationship between the yearly rate of poverty in America and the health of the economy. Tobin found that in those years in which there have been real (inflation adjusted) increases in wages and decreases in unemployment, poverty has declined (p. 148). The performance of the economy, in other words, is important. Tobin's findings are consistent with those of a considerable body of research (Bartik, 1996; Blank, 1997; Fitzgerald, 1995; Harris, 1993; Hoynes, 1996; Moffit, 1992). However, as Tobin documented, between 1973 and the early 1990s the economy often performed less well, and poverty rates declined less during good economic times than in the past (p. 149).

Tobin argued there are five reasons for the decreased impact of economic performance on poverty rates:

1. An expanding proportion of the population is excluded from the more viable sectors of the market economy because they do not have the increasingly sophisticated skills required by employers (p. 161).
2. Jobs, especially good-paying low-skill jobs, are increasingly found outside the central cities (p. 160).
3. Wage rates have been held down because corporations can ex-

port jobs to low-wage markets in other nations and because corporations must spend more on fringe benefits. Corporations,
Tobin notes, think about labor costs in terms of the total expense, rather than just in wages. As the cost of fringe benefits
(especially health care) has increased, employers have tried to
hold down wages to cover some of the increasing expense of
fringes. However, fringes, says Tobin, go mostly to better-paid
workers. The lowest-paid workers often do not benefit from
fringes, but their wages still suffer.

4. The welfare population has changed over time, becoming increasingly comprised of female heads of households and poorly
   educated unattached males, with both groups less willing or able
   to take advantage of economic opportunities (p. 155).

5. The Federal Reserve has allowed the economy to grow too slowly
   (p. 164).

Tobin argued that the Federal Reserve's policies were too conservative, constituting a drag on the growth of the economy. Tobin argued that
fundamental changes have taken place in the economy that allow faster
growth without setting off inflation. The major changes Tobin documented
are the increasing globalization and deregulation of the economy. Globalization increases available labor and product markets. The increase in
labor pools and products lessens the chances of product or labor shortages that set off inflation. Since consumers have access to more markets
for goods, there is less chance of consumption producing shortages and
thus inflation. Global markets also hold down prices by restraining labor
costs and labor demands because employers have options in other nations. Deregulation lowers business costs while allowing companies to
be more creative, reducing costs and improving productivity.

Tobin argued that these changes allow the economy to grow faster
than in the past, without setting off inflation. He recommended the Federal Reserve consent to the economy growing at a rate of about 3 to 3.5
percent a year, one percentage point higher than in the past. If the
economy were allowed to grow faster, Tobin maintained, more jobs would
be created, employers would pay their employees better because labor
markets would be tighter and profits higher. Companies, Tobin argued,
would be more willing to invest in their employees by giving them more
training and more opportunities.

The economic history of the United States in the 1990s and early twentieth-first century bear out Tobin's arguments. The economy has grown faster than the Federal Reserve intended without setting off inflation. Also, in the second half of the Clinton administration a healthy economy resulted in a lower poverty rate, dropping the black poverty rate below 30 percent for the first time in American history. As the economy has struggled during the Bush administration, poverty rates have risen.

Tobin's theory is about as pure as structural theories ever are, but even his theory recognizes that some poor people do not take advantage of opportunities as they become available and that other poor people need considerable help to get into and stay in the job market.

Comparative studies of poverty rates in advanced capitalist democracies (for example France, Germany, Italy, Belgium, United Kingdom, United States, Switzerland, Canada, etc.) also support structural theories. These studies find the poverty rate is lowest in those nations in which a large percentage of the working population is employed in industry, where the unemployment rate is low, and where emphasis is placed on paying decent wages to workers (Moller et al., 2003. Also, the more generous the welfare state, the lower the poverty rate.

PRWORA was clearly a conservative victory, but some of the arguments made by moderates and liberals are incorporated in the law. First, PRWORA recognizes that not all poor adults can work. States can exempt up to 20 percent of their adult recipients from work requirement and time limits. Second, states cannot start the clock until support services are available to those adults required to move into the job market. Third, the food stamp and Medicaid programs remain as entitlements and there are no time limits on assistance. Fourth, states are given the latitude to adopt policies that make work pay better. Last, Congress recognized that many jobs pay poverty wages by significantly expanding the Earned Income Tax Credit (EITC).

What Do These Theories Tell Us About Poverty and Welfare Reform?

There are many insights gained by this review of theories of poverty. First, poverty is not a single problem; it is a series of rather complex problems. There are both cultural/behavioral and structural/economic causes of poverty, which vary by the subgroups of people found among the poor. Culture and structure are also connected. Opportunities influence culture, which influences behavior, which influences opportunity, which influences culture, ad infinitum.

Even when the same set of factors causes poverty, the problem of poverty varies because of the differential reactions of those who become poor. Some single mothers, for example, might seize the chance to gain job training, and transitional health and child care to allow them to enter the workforce, while others may be unwilling to accept responsibility for themselves. Therefore, both variations in causes and reactions to poverty make the problem complex.

Second, the economy is important. The economy must be kept healthy and growing to provide quality opportunities for low-income and poor people. Government policies, such as the EITC, can smooth out some of the deficiencies of the economy. Third, many families cannot take advantage of economic opportunities without a better education or advanced job training. Fourth, similarly, many of today's poor people, especially parents, cannot work without child care and health care aid. Fifth, some people will need extra help, encouragement, even sanctions, to make the transition to employment. These people will need not only education and skill training, but also help with interpersonal skills, self-esteem, hope, and confidence before they believe in themselves enough and interact with others well enough to benefit from assistance and become self-sufficient. Some people will need help more than once. When they fail, they will need a second or even third push to get on their feet. Some people will need support in overcoming alcohol and drug dependency and domestic violence problems before they can be successful in the job market.

Sixth, discrimination based on sex, race, or ethnicity cannot be tolerated. Assistance programs and the employment market must be free of bias. Last, poverty, especially among the elderly, would be lessened if the government sponsored more programs to help people save during their employment years.

5

The Evolution of Welfare

Ending Welfare as We Know It

Of the major Western industrial nations, the United States has always been the most conservative about social welfare policy (Patterson, 1986; Skocpol et al., 1993; Rosenblatt, 1982). America's welfare programs are the most recent in origin and the most restrictive in eligibility, coverage, and cost among the major Western powers (OECD, 1976; Smeeding, 1992a, 1992b; Wilensky, 1975, 11). The reason is that American philosophy about the role of government in providing support to low income citizens differs from the philosophy that prevails in the major industrial nations of Western Europe (see Figure 1.1). The American public philosophy stresses freedom and opportunity over equality (Bobo and Smith, 1994; Feagin, 1975; Shapiro et al., 1987). Americans believe that everyone should be given an opportunity to succeed, that opportunity may not be truly equal but that it is bountiful, and that economic failure generally reflects personal failings. Although public surveys show that Americans are generally sympathetic toward the poor, they are not comfortable with policies that financially support healthy unemployed adults unless the support is transitional. The public believes that anyone can suffer a financial setback, but that with a little help there are ample opportunities for people to recover if they work hard. The public fears that welfare that is too generous, or poorly designed, may undermine core American values by rewarding, supporting, and encouraging indolence and even immoral behavior (Mead, 1986, 1992; Bobo and Smith, 1994). Thus, the public supports long-term aid only for those who cannot care for themselves, and temporary aid to help the able-bodied become settled in the workforce. The American philosophy can be thought

77

of as a belief in "rugged individualism" and personal responsibility, and faith in the power of the economic market. Emphasis is placed on keeping the economy healthy, vigorous, and competitive to create opportunity, while insisting that all who can support themselves through the market do so. This philosophy has shaped the establishment and evolution of the American welfare system. At any point in which welfare seemed to evolve into a system that conflicted with this philosophy, public officials have struggled to reform the system.

The Historical Context

The first federal assistant program was a modest program to aid widowed mothers passed in 1911 (Allard, 2004; Skocpol et al., 1993). Decades after the other major Western industrial nations had developed and begun to refine their welfare programs, the United States laid the foundation for a national welfare system with the passage of the Social Security Act of 1935. This act was passed in response to the Great Depression (Katz, 1986; Piven and Cloward, 1971). The economic collapse brought about by the depression was so massive that by 1933 one-fourth of the nation's adult males were unemployed, millions of families were losing their homes, and thousands stood in bread lines each day. Millions of those who suffered from the economic crisis had formerly been viable members of America's middle class (Rodgers, 1979, 43–72).

When Franklin D. Roosevelt became president in 1933, he was reticent about using public funds directly to assist those individuals devastated by the economic crisis. Reluctantly, under the Federal Emergency Relief Administration, President Roosevelt sent billions of dollars to the states to help them aid their citizens (Leuchtenburg, 1963). The states handed out most of this money in the form of cash relief and public service jobs, many of which were considered "make-work." Roosevelt became alarmed when the relief rolls continued to grow. In 1935 some 20 million Americans were receiving support. In his State of the Union address in 1935, Roosevelt warned Congress that relief undermined the character of the public and the strength of the nation:

> Dependence upon relief induces a spiritual and moral disintegration fundamentally destructive to the national fiber. To dole out relief in this way is to administer a narcotic, a subtle destroyer of the human spirit. . . . I am not willing that the vitality of our people be further sapped by the giving

of cash, of market baskets, of a few hours of weekly work cutting grass, raking leaves, or picking up papers in the public parks. We must preserve not only the bodies of the unemployed from destitution but also their self-respect, their self-reliance and courage and determination (Roosevelt, 1938; Israel, 1966).

As an alternative to most cash relief, Roosevelt convinced Congress to pass the Works Progress Administration (WPA), a program designed to employ over 3 million people in jobs such as housing, highway and public sector construction, slum clearance, and rural electrification. The able-bodied were hired in these jobs, while those unable to work continued to receive relief. The WPA provided jobs to millions of needy citizens, but most of the able-bodied unemployed still could not find work. It has been estimated the WPA provided jobs to only one in four applicants and that some 8 million able-bodied males could not find any work (Piven and Cloward, 1971, 98). Those millions who could not find work, along with the aged, the handicapped, and orphans, turned to state and local governments for assistance. Many states, however, could not handle the burden. Some cut the size of grants so more of the needy could receive some help; others abolished all relief. New Jersey offered the indigent licenses to beg (Piven and Cloward, 1971, 109).

The Social Security Act of 1935

The continuing hardship spawned increasing criticism of the Roosevelt administration. Under pressure, Roosevelt launched what historians refer to as the "second New Deal." This New Deal had three primary thrusts: first, the government used Keynesian economics to stimulate and, it was hoped, moderate economic cycles; second, aid to business was increased in hope of promoting an economic recovery; third, to assist many of those who continued to be impoverished by the depression, Roosevelt proposed and Congress passed the Social Security Act of 1935, setting up relief programs for those who were outside the labor force.

The Social Security Act consisted of five major titles:

- Title I provided grants to the states for aid to the aged.
- Title II established the Social Security system.
- Title III provided grants to the states for the administration of unemployment compensation.

- Title IV established the Aid to Dependent Children (ADC) program.
- Title V provided grants to the states for aid to the blind and disabled.

The Social Security Act created a new federal governmental role, which, at the time, was radical. In the past, the federal government had subsidized state and local relief programs, but this was the first time that major assistant programs would be run by the federal government (Social Security) or in partnership with the states (ADC).

As fundamental a departure as the Social Security Act was, its benefits were originally modest. Grants under Social Security were extended only to those who worked in certain occupations and industries, and payments were delayed until 1942. Domestic workers and farm laborers were excluded, effectively denying aid to most employed minorities (Patterson, 1986). It was not until 1950 that half the retired population received any benefits under the program. ADC was sold as a program for widows and their dependent children, and until 1950 only orphans and poor children received assistance. In 1950 the program was changed to Aid to Families with Dependent Children (AFDC), allowing benefits to one parent (normally the mother) in a family with eligible children.

With the passage of the Social Security Act of 1935, the United States became the last of the major industrial nations to set up a national welfare system—one that by European standards was modest. Three features of the act reflected American reservations about welfare, especially for the able-bodied, and have had long-term consequences for U.S. social welfare programs. First, unlike European programs, benefits under the various Social Security titles were designed for only select groups within the poverty population. Even as social welfare programs expanded in the 1960s and 1970s, they continued to be designed for only some of the poor.

Second, various Social Security titles allowed the states to decide who would receive aid and how much they would receive. This meant that needy citizens would be treated differently, depending on the state in which they lived (Rosenblatt, 1982; Patterson, 1986. As AFDC expanded to become the nation's primary cash aid program for the non-aged poor, this feature remained. Variations in state coverage and benefits to the poor are huge under AFDC/TANF, with some states providing much more generous assistance than others (Howard, 1999; Peterson and Rom, 1990; Skocpol, 1996). Titles I and V also allowed a great deal of local autonomy and variation in funding relief to the aged and the blind.

Last, the Social Security Act did not include health insurance. By 1935 most other Western industrial nations already had health insurance programs. Roosevelt considered including health insurance in the Social Security Act, but eliminated it because opposition from the American Medical Association and southern members of Congress was so intense.

State control over the benefit levels under Titles I, II, IV, and V of the Social Security Act substantially limited growth in these programs through the 1950s. By 1960 only 787,000 families (1.7 percent of all families) were receiving benefits under AFDC, and only 144,000 blind and disabled citizens were receiving assistance under Title V. Thus, by 1960, twenty-five years after the passage of the Social Security Act, U.S. welfare programs were still modest, and, as events would prove, poverty was severe.

The Civil Rights Movement

Just as the Great Depression had served as the catalyst for establishing the nation's first major social welfare programs, the civil rights movement and the ghetto riots of the 1960s served as the stimulus for the next substantial expansion of the welfare state. The civil rights movement, which matured in the late 1950s and the early 1960s, focused attention on the economic conditions of millions of U.S. citizens. Civil rights workers often charged that many U.S. citizens of all races were ill-housed, ill-clothed, medically neglected, malnourished, and even suffering from hunger. Most of the nation's public leaders simply dismissed the latter charge, but slowly the evidence of acute poverty, malnutrition, and poverty-related diseases began to be documented (Rodgers, 1996, 72–73).

In 1967 the Senate Subcommittee on Employment, Manpower, and Poverty held hearings on U.S. poverty. The testimony of many civil rights leaders contained graphic allegations of acute poverty and hunger in the South. These charges were largely dismissed, but the testimony convinced two liberal members of the subcommittee—Robert Kennedy (D-NY) and Joseph Clark (D-PA)—to tour the Mississippi Delta. The visit turned into a major media event that documented severe hunger and malnutrition among Mississippi's poor.

The subcommittee's initial investigation also encouraged the Field Foundation to send a team of doctors to Mississippi to investigate the health of children in Head Start programs. The team issued a report documenting extensive poverty, poverty-related diseases, and malnutrition among the children and their families (Kotz, 1971, 8–9; Kotz, 1979). This report was followed in the mid-1960s by another well-documented finding of severe poverty. The Field Foundation and the Citizen's Crusade Against Poverty formed the Citizen's Board of Inquiry into Hunger and Malnutrition in the United States. After hundreds of on-site investigations and hearings, the Citizen's Board reported its findings in late 1967 and 1968. The findings confirmed the worst suspicions of welfare reform advocates. Investigators had discovered, within the larger population of the United States, a population that might best be described as an underdeveloped nation. They reported "concrete evidence of chronic hunger and malnutrition in every part of the United States where we have held hearings or conducted field trips" (Citizen's Board of Inquiry, 1968, iv).

These widely publicized findings contributed powerfully to pressures on Congress for improvements in, and expansion of, welfare programs. As leaders of the civil rights movement lobbied for relief for the poor, their arguments were bolstered by the outbreak of hundreds of riots in U.S. cities between 1965 and 1969 (Downes, 1968). The nation was divided as to the causes of the riots (Hahn and Feagin, 1970), but a national commission (the Kerner Commission) identified the source as pervasive racism and poverty among black Americans. President Lyndon Johnson convinced Congress that both new civil rights laws and expanded social welfare programs were needed. Thus, with the cities on fire and media attention focused on the struggles of the black population and the poverty of millions of U.S. citizens, Congress passed major civil rights acts in 1964, 1965, and 1968. Congress also expanded existing welfare programs and created new ones. The changes included:

1. In 1961 the AFDC program was amended to allow states to provide support to families where both parents were unemployed (fewer than half the states adopted this option).
2. The food stamp program was formally established in 1964 (initially only twenty-two states opted to participate).
3. The Medicare and Medicaid programs were enacted in 1965.
4. Congress adopted national standards for the food stamp program in 1971, which were extended to all states in 1974.
5. The Supplemental Security Income Act (SSI) was passed in 1972, effective in 1974.

The 1960s and early 1970s, then, saw the second significant installment in developing American social welfare programs. Still, American welfare programs retained much of the early design imposed by the Social Security Act of 1935. Programs continued to be designed for only some of the poor (Moynihan, 1992). Those who qualified were mainly single mothers and their children, the aged, and the handicapped. AFDC benefits varied greatly by state and Medicaid benefits were tied to welfare. If a welfare mother left the rolls for a job, her family lost Medicaid coverage and often other critical support. If the mother married, she usually lost all support. Thus, the nation's major cash welfare program was antifamily and unsupportive of poor mothers who wanted to work.

In keeping with America's conservative attitudes about welfare, President Lyndon Johnson campaigned for an expanded system, but one that reflected the Roosevelt philosophy. Johnson distrusted cash welfare and wanted to help the poor become independent through work. Johnson's proposals focused on job training, education, legal aid, and community action (Lemann, 1991, 164–69; Moynihan, 1970; Patterson, 1986, 138–41). The theme of his War on Poverty was "a hand up, not a hand-out." In signing the War on Poverty legislation in 1964, President Johnson announced that "the days of the dole in this country are numbered" (Lemann, 1991, 149).

But, as we will see below, for over three decades welfare moved in exactly the direction that Roosevelt, Johnson, and other presidents and leaders feared most. AFDC grew much faster than anyone predicted, supporting millions of families headed by single mothers who were unattached to the workforce. Not only did millions of single mothers—many of whom had children out of wedlock—become welfare recipients, but a small percentage became long-term users. A system that supported poor mothers outside the job market became increasingly unpopular over time, especially since nonpoor mothers were joining the workforce in record numbers (Bernstein and Garfinkel, 1977, 155).

There are several reasons welfare moved in this unintended direction. First was the unexpected explosion in the growth of single-parent families, largely the result of unprecedented rates of out-of-wedlock births and increasingly high rates of divorce (Moynihan, 1992). Second, as noted above, since the expectation was the programs would serve only a small number of mother-only families, little emphasis was placed on job training or support services to help single mothers leave welfare and become settled in the workforce. Mothers who did leave welfare were left without health care for themselves and their children. Third, welfare became a method of aiding many minorities who had been victims of racism. Welfare became an extension of civil rights, a method of compensating and aiding people who had been mistreated. Fourth, when the welfare rolls grew to unexpected levels, public officials realized that, at least in the short run, moving welfare recipients into the job market would be expensive. Welfare recipients would often need education, job training, child care, health care, and many others expensive services to make the transition. Until the cost of Medicaid became expensive in the mid-1980s and 1990s, it seemed cheaper to just leave most welfare recipients at home and on the dole. But as Medicaid and other welfare programs grew in enrollments and costs, presidents and the members of Congress began to rethink the nation's antipoverty programs. After false starts and some experimentation, Congress passed major reform in 1996.

As far back as the Kennedy administration (1961–63), there was recognition the welfare system was moving in unintended directions and required reform. President Kennedy proposed that Congress pass legislation encouraging and enabling employment of welfare recipients. Congress passed bills designed both to encourage employment and, during the Nixon administration (1969–74), to make employment compulsory for a larger group of welfare mothers. Believing the welfare system was oversized and wasteful, Nixon campaigned for a version of the negative income tax to take the place of many welfare programs. Under Nixon's version of a negative income tax, a household or individual's income would have been compared to a predetermined income standard. If a family's income was below the standard, the family had a "negative income," and the government would have transferred income to the family. Families below the standard with earnings would have received more aid than those without earnings. Nixon's plan was twice passed by the House but could not pass in the Senate.

Although President Nixon's proposal finally failed, for a time it promoted a consensus about the most plausible approach to reducing the number of welfare programs while efficiently helping the poor. President Ford (1974–77) made a modest effort to recoup Nixon's momentum on the issue by offering another reform package based on the negative income tax. Ford abandoned the effort when the economy turned increasingly sour. President Carter (1977–81) hoped that welfare reform would be a major accomplishment of his administration. He proposed a system based on a negative income tax for those able to work and a guaranteed income for those who were unemployable. President Carter's plan also foundered in Congress.

The defeat of Carter's plan cast a pall over reform for most of a decade. The concepts on which that plan was based had been debated during three administrations, and it seemed clear that Congress was unlikely to embrace reform based on substantial use of the negative income tax or a guaranteed income. The consensus on which debate centered during three administrations had clearly dissolved (Ellwood 1989, 269).

A New Consensus—Supported Work

President Reagan (1981–89) argued for a new direction. He believed the welfare system was too expensive, too indulgent, and too centralized at the federal level. Reagan argued for compulsory work requirements for the able-bodied poor, substantial consolidation of programs, budgets for major welfare programs rather than open entitlements, and the transfer of more funding, authority and autonomy to the states. Reagan's philosophy would prove important in shaping both the debate and the reform of welfare in the 1990s. Reagan also impacted the welfare debate by convincing Congress to cut federal taxes while substantially increasing spending for defense. Reagan's belief was the tax cuts would stimulate the economy, producing more, not less, revenues. Time proved Reagan wrong. The result of Reagan's tax and spending policies was the largest deficits in the nation's history. The huge new national debt made it unlikely that Congress would entertain welfare reforms that raised federal outlays, even temporarily (Tobin, 1994). Reform also stalled because in the early and mid-1980s there was no generalized crisis of the magnitude that had spawned programs in the 1930s, 1940s, 1960s, or early 1970s to lend urgency to welfare reform. Poverty increased dramatically during the Reagan years, but Reagan argued that welfare programs were to blame, not his economic policies.

Still, by the end of Reagan's presidency, a new approach to welfare reform was developing in Congress and at the state level focusing on many of the policies that he had supported. Increasingly popular were the concepts of supported work for the able-bodied poor, including single mothers, budgeted rather than open-ended entitlements, and increased autonomy by states. Supported work required programs designed to move able-bodied adults into the employment market, backed by intermediate support like child and health care to help recipients become fixed in the workforce. Supported work involved a mutual-obligation contract between the recipient and the state. In return for support, the recipient would agree to engage in a good faith effort to leave the welfare rolls through employment. This approach is substantially different from programs that simply require welfare recipients to work in return for benefits. Supported work assumes the recipient will receive help in making the transition to self-sufficiency. This new approach accepted Reagan's argument that welfare recipients should leave the rolls for employment, but it obligated the government to help with the transition. In 1988 Congress embraced this philosophy by passing the Family Support Act.

The Family Support Act of 1988

Throughout much of the 1960s, 1970s, and 1980s, Congress had increasingly mandated that able-bodied welfare recipients engage in work. But because there were no support services for those who left welfare, only a small percentage of welfare recipients worked. Most members of Congress seemed convinced that the welfare system had to help recipients and ex-recipients become successfully employed, but given the nation's huge deficits, funding was scarce. In 1988 Congress ended years of debate on welfare reform by passing the Family Support Act (FSA). The FSA was poorly funded, with a phase-in over five years. It was not destined to impact a large percentage of AFDC recipients. The importance of the FSA was its foundation in reforming welfare by helping the poor become self-sufficient through employment and its assumption that both parents should be responsible for the welfare of their children.

In principle, the goal of the FSA was to lessen considerably the time that families remain dependent on AFDC by providing recipients with services such as education, job search skills, and career skills required by the labor force. To make employment a viable option, the bill provided some funding for child and health care for enrolled mothers, and extended these support services to the family heads for a limited period while they settled into the job market. The bill also strongly emphasized improving child support from absent parents. The major terms of the bill were in five titles.

Title I. Child Support and Paternity

Starting in November 1990, all states were required to provide wage withholding of child-support orders in all cases in which the custodial parent received public assistance or in which the custodial parent had asked for help in collecting support. By 1994 states were required to set up wage withholding of child support for almost all support orders, even when the custodial parent was not on welfare. More uniform guidelines for all child-support awards were required by the bill, and these guidelines were to be reviewed regularly.

States faced penalties if they failed to determine paternity in a certain proportion of all cases of out-of-wedlock children receiving benefits. To help states locate missing parents, the bill provided access to both Internal Revenue Service (IRS) and unemployment compensation data. Procedures were established to collect child support from noncustodial parents residing in another state.

Title II. Job Opportunities and Basic Skills Training Program (JOBS)

All states were required to establish a JOBS program. All single parents with children over the age of three (or at state option, over one) could be required to participate, unless they were ill, incapacitated, or had some other valid reason for nonparticipation. States were given a great deal of discretion in designing the training programs, but they had to be approved by the Department of Health and Human Services at least every two years. All states were required to have the JOBS program in place by October 1990 and statewide by October 1992.

The FSA required the state agency in charge of AFDC to assess the needs and skills of all AFDC heads. From this consultation an employability plan for each recipient was to be developed, specifying the activities the head would undertake and the supportive services the participant would receive. State programs could include education, job training, job readiness training, and job placement. Post–secondary education and other approved employment activities could also be offered. Parents under age twenty without a high school diploma were required to engage in an educational program leading to graduation. Some states were also allowed to set up programs to provide education, job training, and placement to noncustodial parents.

In an effort to lessen long-term welfare dependency, the bill required the states to spend at least 55 percent of all JOBS funds on (1) families that had received aid for more than thirty-six months during the preceding five years, (2) families in which the head was under age twenty-four and had not completed high school, and (3) families that would lose benefits within two years because of the age of their children.

Title III. Supportive Services

The states were required to provide child care to participants engaged in education, employment, or job training. To help recipients stay in the workforce and leave welfare, the states could assist in child care for up to one year after families left welfare. The cost of the care to the parent was to be assessed on a sliding scale based on the income of the parent. Families leaving the AFDC ranks because of employment were eligible for Medicaid coverage for up to one year.

Title IV. AFDC Amendments

The FSA required all the states to establish an AFDC-UP (unemployed parent) program to cover two-parent families with an unemployed head. Until the FSA, only about one-half of the states allowed two-parent families to receive AFDC benefits. States new to the AFDC-UP program were allowed at their option to limit benefits to a minimum of six months a year. However, Medicaid benefits would have to be continuing.

The money that an AFDC family could earn without losing benefits was raised to $90 a month from $75. The child-care cost the family could deduct from earned income was raised from $160 a month to $175 (or $200 if the child was under age two). Expenditures for child care would not be counted as income in calculating AFDC benefits. States were given the option of requiring single parents who were minors to reside with a parent or guardian.

Title V. Demonstration Projects

The bill funded a wide range of innovative demonstration projects at the state level to discover how well various experimental programs alleviated problems or promoted certain desirable outcomes. States could experiment with requiring able-bodied welfare recipients to work, they could select adults to leave welfare for work after a specified period, and they could engage in wide-ranging test projects to promote self-sufficiency. Other experiments were allowed, but modestly funded. For example, $6 million over a three-year period was allocated to encourage innovative education programs for poor children. Three million dollars was authorized to fund programs to train poor family heads to be child-care providers. Eight million dollars was provided to establish programs to improve noncustodial parents' access to their children. Other programs provided counseling for high-risk teenagers and incentives to businesses to create jobs for AFDC recipients.

The Impact of the Act

The FSA represented agreement in Congress that welfare needed to change, and it incorporated some clear principles about how welfare should be reformed. But because the bill was so modestly funded, the importance of FSA is chiefly in the philosophy it establishes about some of the ways Congress could agree that welfare needed to be reformed and the insights provided by the various experiments that were carried out by the states. In passing FSA, most conservatives, moderates, and liberals agreed, at least in principle, that able-bodied welfare recipients should be moved into the job market and given the support services they needed to become established in the workforce. There was also broad support for holding both parents responsible for the sustenance of their children. Both establishment of paternity and support from the noncustodial parent increased because of the act (*Green Book*, 1994, 500–1). Still, because of funding shortages for training and support services, states were slow in establishing JOBS programs required by FSA. By 1994 only about 13 percent of all AFDC heads were receiving JOBS training.

The innovative welfare reform experiments sanctioned by FSA yielded information that would be important in future welfare reform. The FSA allowed the states to petition the Department of Health and Human Services for waivers to provide them with the flexibility to be creative in the design of their welfare programs and specific experiments. The waivers allow states to treat welfare recipients within the state differently as long as they were participating in an approved experiment. The state had to agree to pay for any additional costs associated with the implementation and evaluation of such experiments. By late 1996, forty-three states had gained approval to carry out and test some ninety innovative programs. A few states, such as Wisconsin, Michigan, Oregon, and Vermont, led the way. The plans these states and others put into effect would later serve as models of how states could reform their welfare systems and would substantially influence the reform plan passed in 1996.

The Clinton Administration Plan

President Clinton (1993–2001) had considerable experience with the welfare system as governor of Arkansas and included welfare reform in his presidential platform (Blank and Ellwood, 2002). Clinton believed the FSA was on the right track and the experiments had yielded valuable insights into viable reform options. But, he believed, reform required better funding and a more comprehensive approach. Once elected president, Clinton put together teams of experts to design a new reform plan based on the FSA that would, he pledged, "end welfare as we know it." The resulting plan proposed by President Clinton was based on the continued use of entitlement programs to ensure that all categorically eligible poor were given support. The plan rested on six principals:

1. *Make work pay.* Clinton believed that to reform welfare, it had to be more profitable for families to work than to receive welfare. To achieve this end, Clinton favored raising the minimum wage, improving the Earned Income Tax Credit (EITC), and expanding child care and Medicaid coverage for those leaving or avoiding welfare by entering the work force.
2. *Improve child-support enforcement.* Clinton believed the FSA was moving in the right direction on this policy, but the process by which absent parents were identified and required to support their children needed improvement. Clinton proposed wage withholding of all child-support orders and penalties for mothers who failed to cooperate in identifying the father(s) of their children, and a few changes designed to make it easier to identify and track absent parents.
3. *Pregnancy prevention.* Funds would be granted to help states establish antipregnancy programs for teenagers based on counseling, moral suasion, and incentives. To improve supervision of teen mothers, Clinton proposed that to be eligible for cash assistance, unwed mothers younger than eighteen be required to live with a parent or guardian.

4. *Job assistance for welfare heads.* Building on the FSA, Clinton proposed increased funding for job training, education, and support programs for AFDC family heads. An additional $10 billion would be earmarked to job training and child care to move AFDC family heads into the workforce and help them to stay employed.

5. *Set time limits on cash benefits.* In a substantial departure for a Democratic president, Clinton proposed that recipients who were born after 1972 and were healthy and able to work be required to accept a combination of education, training, or job placement help to enable them to leave the welfare rolls, often within two years. This provision was known as "two years and out," but actually meant a transition to a job, subsidized if necessary.

6. *Public service and subsidized jobs.* If welfare heads could not find employment in the private sector, Clinton proposed that as a last resort they be placed in either a public sector job or that their employment in the private sector be subsidized. Once employed, parents would be given child care and Medicaid assistance to help them become settled in the work world.

President Clinton summarized his proposal in a speech to the National Governors Association in early 1995: "Anyone who can work should do so. Welfare reform should include time limits. Anyone who brings a child into the world ought to be prepared to take financial responsibility for that child's future. Teen pregnancy and out-of-wedlock childbearing are important problems that must be addressed through comprehensive welfare reform."

Clinton's proposals represented a substantial alteration in the welfare system, especially his emphasis on time limits. While Clinton had made welfare reform an important part of his campaign for the presidency, during the first two years of his administration he concentrated on health-care reform, believing that it was a necessary first step. The Republican members of Congress, interested in reducing the size and cost of the federal government, especially welfare, kept the issue on the agenda and by 1995 had raised welfare reform to a central political issue.

The Republican Party Plan

In 1995 the Republican Party had a majority in both houses of Congress. One goal of the Republican majority was a thorough overhaul of the nation's welfare system. The Republicans were never united on how to reform welfare, but they did agree the system needed major renovation. Some of the Republicans were mostly interested in reducing costs, others wanted to move welfare recipients into jobs even if it was initially expensive, others wanted to turn welfare over to the states, and a few just wanted to get rid of welfare because they believed it did harm to recipients (Bryner, 1998, 152). Republicans in the House tended to be more conservative than their colleagues in the Senate. While some Democrats vigorously defended AFDC, the majority was interested in a fundamental overhaul and often joined their Republican colleagues in supporting various reform proposals.

Given the divisions within the Republican Party, opposition from many Democrats, and significant differences between the two chambers, the debate was vigorous, emotional, and even hostile. Throughout 1995 the House and Senate debated various reform proposals and struggled to agree on a welfare reform bill. In November 1995, Congress sent President Clinton a reform plan as part of a larger budget reconciliation bill (H.R. 2491). President Clinton vetoed this bill on December 6, 1995. Congress made some minor changes in this plan and sent it back to the White House in late December 1995 (H.R. 4). President Clinton vetoed this bill on January 9, 1996.

After Congress amended its proposal to meet some of the president's objections, on August 22, 1996, President Clinton signed into law the third version of welfare reform passed by Congress. President Clinton made it clear that he did not agree with all the provisions of the bill he signed but wanted welfare reform to pass and pledged to work to amend those provisions of the bill he found objectionable. The reform bill finally passed was a true bipartisan compromise. All major public policies result from many compromises, but the new reform bill represented an unusual degree of compromise between the Republican and Democratic members of Congress and with a president who was flexible and moderate. The liberal wing of the Democratic Party lobbied and voted against the bill and was very disappointed by its passage and eventual support by President Clinton.

The major policy differences between the Republican majority in Congress and President Clinton varied during the most intense months of the debate, but some of the most important differences included the following:

1. *Capping welfare spending.* Clinton's reform proposals would have continued to treat major welfare programs as entitlements,

meaning that all persons who qualified for assistance under a program would be served. This "open-ended" spending on welfare was a major concern of the Republican majority, especially those interested in realizing cost savings from reform. The Republicans proposed eliminating entitlements by placing a yearly cap on spending for most welfare programs.

2. *Turn welfare programs over to the states.* The Clinton plan envisioned less administration of welfare by the federal government, and more state autonomy, but not to the extent supported by the Republicans. The Republican plan proposed major devolution of welfare programs to the states. It proposed giving the states block grants and then allowing them to use these funds to design their own welfare systems. Most of the nation's governors, represented by the National Governors Association, vigorously promoted this approach.

3. *Time limits*, *sanctions*, *and caps.* Clinton supported time limits, but the Republican proposals were more stringent. The Republican majority bills would have required states to cut off cash benefits to any family that over its lifetime had received aid for a total of five years. States could exempt up to 15 percent of their caseloads from time limits. Penalties for noncompliance would have also been tougher under the Republican plans. Assistance would have been denied to any adult who refused to cooperate in proving paternity or who failed to assist a state child-support enforcement agency. If a recipient had received a year of education or training, benefits could be terminated. Any adult recipient who received welfare for two years (or a shorter period at state option) would be required to engage in work.

In several versions of its plan, the Republicans proposed that both the food stamp and Medicaid programs be capped and turned over to the states in the form of block grants. Agricultural and nutrition lobbies convinced Congress to preserve the food stamp program, while President Clinton forced the Republicans to back away from their plans to give states control over Medicaid. Thus, the reform plan sent to the President in August 1996 allowed recipients who were rendered ineligible for cash assistance by deadlines to retain the right to apply for noncash support such as food stamps and Medicaid.

4. *Employment deadlines.* To force states to make substantial progress in moving welfare recipients into the job market, the Republican plan imposed yearly benchmarks. As the Republican plan evolved, states would have been required to enroll half of all caseload family heads in work or training programs by 2001 or suffer a 5 percent reduction in funding. The goal was to require 1.5 million welfare family heads to find employment by the year 2001.

5. *Deny or reduce cash assistance to some families.* Although the Senate and House often disagreed on the details, the Republicans' proposals significantly increased the opportunities for denying assistance to certain recipients. States would have been allowed to make teen mothers under age eighteen ineligible for cash assistance, except in cases of rape or incest. At state discretion, the ban could have been extended to all unwed mothers under twenty-five. Children born to families on welfare could have been denied assistance. The savings realized could have been used to fund orphanages, adoption services, and homes for unwed mothers. States would have been given the option of issuing vouchers to teen mothers and to women who had additional children while on welfare, which could have been used to purchase baby supplies.

6. *Eliminate most aid to legal immigrants.* The Republican proposals varied over time, but all placed major restrictions on assistance to legal aliens. Until they became citizens, most legal immigrants would no longer have been eligible for cash assistance, SSI, social services block grant funds, Medicaid, and food stamps. The only exceptions would have been refugees, permanent residents over age seventy-five who had lived in the United States for at least five years, legal immigrants who had honorably served in the U.S. military, and, in some cases, legal immigrants who had lived in the United States for at least five years. The financial responsibility of immigrant sponsors would have been extended, usually until the immigrant became a U.S. citizen or paid Social Security taxes for ten years.

7. *Change food stamp rules.* As noted, in several versions the Republican plans sought to cap food stamp expenditures but still allow everyone qualified by need to receive assistance. If demand were high, each recipient would have received less. All

able-bodied food stamp recipients would have been required to obtain employment within ninety days or enroll in job training or a government-sponsored work program.

8. *Tighten eligibility for SSI.* Adults suffering from alcoholism or drug addiction would no longer have been eligible for SSI. The definition of a disabled child would have been changed. Under the law in place, a child was defined as disabled if mental, physical, and social functioning was substantially less than that of children of the same age. Under the proposed law, a child would be disabled if he or she had a medically verified physical or mental impairment expected to cause death or last more than twelve months.

9. *Enforce child-support orders.* The Republican proposals would have established new state and federal registries to help enforce child-support orders. States would have been required to establish a central-case registry to monitor all child-support orders. They would have also been required to establish a worker registry to which employers would send the name, Social Security number, and address of all new hires. The states would have been required to put Social Security numbers on most licenses and to suspend licenses of parents who fell behind in child-support payments. Federal registries would have been established to track absent parents nationwide.

Clinton's Response

President Clinton seriously disagreed with many of the Republican proposals. He particularly objected to the proposed funding caps or annual budgets for major welfare programs. Clinton was afraid that when the economy was weak, causing more citizens to apply for aid, the programs would run out of funds, leaving eligible applicants without assistance. Clinton was also concerned that if welfare was turned over to the states and financed by block grants, many states would rely only on federal money and cut back on state welfare expenditures. Clinton wanted the law to require the states to continue to spend at current levels or very close to current levels.

Clinton also disagreed with the Republican rejection of guaranteed jobs for recipients forced off the rolls by time limits who could not find employment in the private sector. While the Republicans felt confident that the economy would provide ample jobs for serious job seekers, Clinton wanted to guarantee that willing applicants who could not find employment in the private sector could be placed either in a subsidized private sector job or in public sector employment. Additionally, Clinton argued, jobs would be of little value to welfare parents if quality, affordable child care was not available and if the recipients lacked the education or training required to make them qualified for employment. Thus, Clinton pressed Congress to expand funding for child care, education, and training programs. Clinton also objected to Republican plans to cut funding for nutrition programs and the EITC, which were critical to his efforts to make work pay. Last, Clinton felt that the restrictions on assistance to legal aliens were punitive and an attempt to use welfare reform to rewrite the nation's immigration laws. If the new law contained time limits, Clinton argued, there was no reason to treat legal immigrants any different than other recipients.

Compromises

After twice vetoing the welfare reform plans passed by Congress, Clinton was successful in convincing the Republican majority to increase funding for child care, education, job training, and nutrition programs. He was also successful in convincing Congress to set required spending levels for the states. Congress also agreed to continue to fund the food stamp and Medicaid programs as entitlements. The Republican majority, however, convinced Clinton to accept many of its key proposals. In the final bill signed by Clinton, spending for cash welfare and several other programs is capped. Welfare administration is turned over to the states, and states are given considerable discretion in the design of their programs. Stringent time limits are imposed, assistance to legal immigrants is significantly restricted, and states are allowed to impose serious penalties for noncompliance.

The new reform bill, therefore, represents a major set of compromises produced by divided government. Both the president and the Republican Congress won concessions on the design of the new bill, but it is a conservative victory. President Clinton took an unusually moderate posture on welfare reform for a Democratic president, and in the end he signed into law an act that gave the Republicans much of what they wanted. Although the new reform's foundation can be traced back to the

Family Support Act of 1988, it represents a radical change in the design and administration of welfare in America. Below we will describe the bill in some detail and then in Chapter 7 examine how the states have implemented the bill, and in Chapter 8 examine the early evidence on the impact of the new legislation.

Personal Responsibility and Work Opportunity Reconciliation Act

The Personal Responsibility and Work Opportunity Reconciliation Act (PRWORA) was signed into law by President Clinton on August 22, 1996. The major goals of this legislation include:

- Turn responsibility for welfare administration over to the states; allow states more flexibility in designing their programs, and help states deliver services more efficiently;
- Cap annual federal expenditures for a number of major welfare programs;
- Place the emphasis of welfare programs on helping recipients become independent through employment;
- Sharply limit the duration of federally funded cash welfare benefits for most recipients;
- Increase sanctions for noncompliance;
- Lower the out-of-wedlock birth rate;
- Increase the identification and financial responsibility of absent parents;
- Restrict the ability of legal immigrants to receive welfare assistance.

Major provisions include the following:

1. *Turn welfare programs over to the states.* A number of major welfare programs are consolidated into two block grants to the states. States receive yearly lump sum payments under each of the block grants and are given considerable discretion in designing their own welfare programs. The Temporary Assistance to Needy Families (TANF) block grant replaced four cash welfare and related programs: AFDC, AFDC Administration, the JOBS program, and the Emergency Assistance Program.

The TANF block grant provides cash and other assistance to advance a number of welfare goals, including funds to help needy families support their children while making the transition to work.

The second block grant consolidates four child care programs into the existing Child Care and Development block grant, which provides funds to states to improve the quality of child care and to subsidize child care for families on welfare, families becoming established in the workforce, and families who might become dependent without child-care assistance.

2. *Cap welfare spending.* Federal funding for the TANF block grant is capped at $16.4 billion annually from fiscal 1996 through fiscal 2001. (This funding level was continued through 2004.) The block grant approach means that TANF is not an entitlement program. If the states spend all the funds, except under limited circumstances noted below, no additional federal funds are made available even for qualified recipients. States, of course, have the discretion of spending their own funds once federal funds are exhausted.

3. *Grant distribution.* Grant dollars are distributed to each state based on its federal funding for AFDC and related programs in either fiscal 1995, fiscal 1994, or the average of fiscal 1992–94, whichever was higher. Additional funds to states include:

(a) Beginning in fiscal 1997, $2 billion in contingency funds were designated for matching grants to states with high unemployment or rapidly growing food stamp rolls.

(b) A $1.7 billion loan fund was made available to states beginning in fiscal 1997. States must repay the loans with interest within three years.

(c) Over four years, $800 million is available for states with growing populations and low welfare benefits per recipient.

(d) Beginning in fiscal 1998, states that reduce out-of-wedlock births by 1 percent in any year compared with the base year of 1995, while also reducing abortions, receive an additional 5 percent of their block grant. States that reduced such births by 2 percent receive an additional 10 percent.

(e) Beginning in fiscal 1999, $1 billion will be allocated over five years to those states most successful in moving welfare recipients into the workplace.

(f) Four hundred million dollars is made available to states to teach abstinence as a means of birth control.

4. *Maintenance of effort.* States must continue to spend the equivalent of at least 75 percent of the funds they allocated to welfare programs in 1994. States that do not meet mandatory work requirements for welfare recipients must maintain 80 percent of previous funding. To qualify for contingency funds described below, states must maintain spending at 100 percent.

5. *Encouragement of innovation.* States are encouraged to be innovative in designing their welfare policies. Programs may vary across a state, but all qualified families must receive fair and equitable treatment. States are not required to provide cash assistance; instead they may substitute vouchers or services. States may also opt to privatize welfare programs by turning them over to charities, religious organizations, or other private entities. To encourage innovation and flexibility, states are allowed to transfer up to 30 percent of their TANF block grant into the Child Care and Development block grant, or a maximum 10 percent into the existing Title XX Social Services block grant. Funds transferred into the Social Services block grant may be used only for programs and services to children and families with incomes below 200 percent of the poverty level.

6. *Employment guidelines and goals.* Adult welfare recipients are required to begin work within two years, or sooner at state discretion. Work activities are defined to include actual work in the private or public sector, plus, to a limited degree, education, vocational training, and job search. After the year 2000, not more than 30 percent of the required number of work participants can qualify by participating in vocational training or by being teen heads of households attending secondary school.

States may take parents of children under the age of one out of the participation rate, but only for a total of twelve months. Parents with children under six are exempt unless child care is available, but they still count in the state's participation rate. States must have at least 25 percent of single adult recipients engaged in work in fiscal 1997, rising to 50 percent in 2002.

To count toward the employment goal, single parents must be involved in work activity at least twenty hours a week in 1997, rising to thirty hours in 2000. States may allow parents with a child under the age of six to work twenty hours a week. Two-parent families must work thirty-five hours a week. The requirements for single parents and two-parent families are summarized below:

Fiscal year	One-parent families (percent)	Minimum hours	Two-parent families (percent)	Minimum hours
1997	25	20	50	35
1998	30	20	50	35
1999	35	25	75	35
2000	40	30	90	35
2001	45	30	90	35
2002	50	30	90	35
2003	50	30	90	35

States that fail to meet the work requirements will have their block grant reduced by 5 percent, which will grow by 2 percent per year, rising to a maximum reduction of 21 percent. The secretary of Heath and Human Services may approve "reasonable cause" for failure to meet the goals.

7. *Time limited assistance.* Block grant funds can be awarded to adults for a lifetime limit of five years. States can write their regulations to deny federal funds to assist adults who do not work after receiving TANF for two years. States may exempt up to 20 percent of their caseload from these requirements. States may also opt to set a shorter time limit for all families, or they may opt to continue to provide assistance after the time limit using only state dollars or funds transferred from the TANF block grant into the Social Services block grant.

8. *Sanctions and restrictions on assistance.*
   (a) Adults who do not cooperate with work or training requirements or in establishing paternity will have their benefits reduced proportionately, or at state option, will be rejected for assistance.
   (b) Individuals convicted of felony drug crimes are not eligible for welfare benefits and food stamps. States may pass a state law to amend this provision if they wish.
   (c) States may deny assistance to children born to welfare recipients or assistance to unwed parents under age eighteen. If a state provides assistance to unwed parents un-

der the age of eighteen, they must live with an adult and attend school or be enrolled in other specified work or training programs.

(d) Welfare recipients who move to a new state may, at state option, be limited to those benefits that they would have received in their former state for twelve months.

9. *Federal waivers.* States that have received federal waivers in order to establish experimental welfare programs can continue to carry out those programs until the waivers expire, even if the experimental programs are inconsistent with this bill.

10. *Food stamps.* Eligibility for food stamps is tightened and states are given more flexibility in designing and implementing the program, but it remains an entitlement program. Benefits are adjusted yearly for inflation, although individual allotments are reduced from 103 percent of the Agriculture Department's Thrifty Food Plan to 100 percent. Additionally, benefits are reduced by changes in various deductions that recipients are allowed to count against income, and state and local energy assistance is counted as income. The base fair market value above which the value of a car is counted as an asset is frozen at $4,650, and the housing deduction was capped at $300 in 2001.

Welfare recipients who fail to comply with work requirements can be denied food stamps. Able-bodied adults without dependents (ABAWDs) between the ages of eighteen and fifty must work an average of twenty or more hours per week or participate in a work program. Those not employed or enrolled can receive food stamps for only three months out of every three years, unless they are laid off or live in a community with high unemployment (10 percent or more). If these conditions exist, the state can apply for a waiver that would allow recipients another quarter of eligibility. In 1997 this provision was amended to allow states to exempt 15 percent of all ABAWDs who have used up their three "free" months of food stamp eligibility. Additionally, funds were provided to enable states to create workfare or subsidized job slots for ABAWDs.

States are given the option of aligning the food stamp program with their revamped welfare programs by establishing a single set of eligibility requirements for assistance. States are also given the option of converting food stamp benefits to wage subsidies for employers who hire recipients. These recipients will receive wages rather than stamps.

11. *Child nutrition programs.* Child nutrition programs, including the Child and Adult Care Food Program, are reduced by about $3 billion over six years. The act eliminates the option of serving an additional meal or snack to children who are in childcare centers for more than eight hours per day. Congress repealed this provision in 1997.

12. *Medicaid.* The act does not establish a block grant for Medicaid. Generally, states must provide Medicaid to families that would have been qualified for AFDC under the eligibility standards in existence on July 16, 1996. Thus, qualified families who lose cash assistance because of employment will continue to qualify for Medicaid unless their income exceeds the old AFDC income limit set by their state. States must continue to provide Medicaid coverage for one year to those individuals who lose their welfare eligibility because of increased earnings (six months of full Medicaid; six months of subsidized Medicaid if family income is less than 185 percent of the poverty level). States may, however, deny Medicaid to adults who lose cash aid by not meeting work requirements and restrictions on many legal aliens are tightened.

13. *Restrictions on assistance to legal immigrants.* Illegal aliens and legal nonaliens are generally ineligible for welfare assistance, except short-term emergency aid. The provisions covering legal aliens in the 1996 law were amended in 1997. After amendment, the reform law provides that legal immigrants residing in the United States on the date that the bill was signed (August 22, 1996) will continue to be eligible for SSI and Medicaid. States were given the option of making this group of legal aliens eligible for food stamps but at state cost. In 1998 the law was further amended to restore food stamps to this group of legal immigrants, estimated to number about 250,000, including about 75,000 children. The 1997 amendments also allowed the states to decide if they want legal aliens residing in the United States on August 22, 1996, to be eligible for TANF and services provided by Social Services block grant funds. Legal aliens residing in the United States on that date achieve regular assistance

eligibility when they become citizens or when family members work a total of forty quarters.

Legal immigrants who enter the United States after the new law's enactment are much more restricted. During the first five years, they are barred from receiving most nonemergency means-tested federal help, including child-care, food stamps, SSI, nonemergency Medicaid, and TANF. After the first five years, the income of sponsors will be counted in assessing the eligibility of legal immigrants for assistance until the immigrant (or immigrant family) has worked in the United States for forty quarters or has become a citizen. Refugees, American military veterans, and those granted asylum are exempt from these restrictions.

14. *Supplemental Security Income.* The law tightens eligibility for SSI for both adults and children. Previously children could receive SSI benefits if their mental, physical, or social functioning was substantially less than children of the same age or if they engaged in age-inappropriate behavior. Under this law a child is disabled only if he/she has a medically proven physical or mental disability that results in marked and severe functional limitations. This disability must be expected to cause death or to last more than twelve months. In 1997 the law was amended to provide continuing Medicaid coverage for any disabled child losing SSI benefits because of changes in the law.

15. *Child-support enforcement.* Over fifty statutory changes were made in existing laws. The reforms pursue five major goals: (a) automating many child support enforcement procedures; (b) establishing uniform tracking procedures; (c) strengthening interstate child-support enforcement; (d) requiring states to adopt stronger measures to establish paternity; (e) creating improved enforcement tools to increase actual child-support collections.

States are required to create a central-case registry to track all child-support orders created or modified after October 1, 1997. Information must be updated regularly and shared with the federal-case registry. States were required to establish a new-hire registry by October 1, 1997, to collect the name, address, and Social Security number of new hires. States must review information on new hires and order employers to withhold child-support payment from delinquent employees. A similar federal registry will track nonpaying parents nationwide. States are given the authority to suspend all licenses held by parents who owe past due child support. All funds collected from parents of children receiving assistance will go to the state.

In 1998 President Clinton supplemented these provisions by signing into law the Deadbeat Parents Punishment Act. This law created two new categories of felonies against parents who seek to evade child support: (1) Any parent traveling across state or country lines to evade child support commits a felony if the amount owed is $5,000 or more and has been outstanding for twelve months or longer; (2) If the child support obligation is more than $10,000 or has gone unpaid for over two years, willful failure to pay this support to a child living in another state constitutes a felony.

16. *Child Care.* The Child Care and Development block grant provides child care for low-income families, funding to improve the quality and availability of child care, child-care services for welfare recipients who accept jobs or enter job training, and child-care assistance to families in jeopardy of becoming welfare recipients.

Federal funding was set at $16 billion through fiscal 2002, starting at $1.1 billion in 1996, growing to $2.7 billion in fiscal 2002. This represented an increase of about $4 billion in funding for child care. At least 70 percent of the funds must be used to assist welfare recipients, those attempting to leave welfare, and those in danger of needing welfare assistance. Child-care services are also funded at the state level by Social Services block grant funds. This block grant was cut by 15 percent, but states were given the flexibility to use these funds to provide noncash vouchers for children whose parents exceed the five-year time limit on benefits.

17. *Earned-income tax credit.* This tightens eligibility for this program for low-income workers, requires that applicants use a valid taxpayer identification number to make it easier to track recipients and their income, and expands the types of income counted in determining eligibility and excludes some income losses that were previously taken into consideration.

Additional 1997 Amendments

In 1997 Congress added another amendment to create a $3 billion Welfare to Work Jobs Challenge fund. In 1998 and 1999, $1.1 billion was allocated annually to the states by formula to help them move long-term welfare recipients into lasting, unsubsidized jobs. These funds were used for job creation, job placement, and job retention, including wage subsidies to private employers and other post–employment support services. In each of the two years, $400 million was made available on a competitive basis to fund innovative job programs in high poverty areas recommended by the states.

Additionally, employers are given an additional incentive to hire long-term welfare recipients by providing a credit equal to 35 percent of the first $10,000 in wages in the first year of employment, and 50 percent of the first $10,000 in the second year. The credit is for two years per worker to encourage not only hiring but also retention.

Other Federal Welfare Initiatives

Mobilizing the Business Community

In May 1997 the Welfare to Work Partnership was launched to encourage businesses to hire people from the welfare rolls. Some 800 companies have accepted President Clinton's initial challenge to help move those on assistance into jobs in the public sector. In August 1997 the partnership established a toll-free hotline (1–888–usajob1), a Web page (www.welfaretowork.org), a "Blueprint for Business" manual to help companies across the nation hire people off welfare, and a city-to-city challenge to help promote innovative and effective welfare-to-work initiatives in twelve cities with high levels of poverty.

Helping Welfare Recipients Get Off and Stay Off Welfare

The Welfare to Work Coalition to Sustain Success, a coalition of civic groups committed to helping former welfare recipients stay in the workforce and succeed, was established in 1997. The goal was to tailor services to meet welfare recipients' needs. The coalition focuses on providing mentoring and other support services. Charter members include the Boys and Girls Clubs of America, the Baptist Joint Committee, the United Way, the YMCA, and fourteen other civic groups.

Federal Government Hiring Initiative

In March 1997, President Clinton directed each head of a federal agency or department to develop a plan to hire and retain welfare recipients in jobs in the government. The goal is to hire 10,000 welfare recipients over four years without displacing current employees.

Transportation

In May 1997, President Clinton announced Department of Transportation grants to twenty-four states to develop welfare-to-work transportation strategies. The president also urged Congress to adopt a six-year, $600 million grant program that would support flexible, innovative transportation systems in rural, urban, and suburban areas to get people to jobs.

Conclusions

The 1996 welfare reform act was a major alteration in the welfare system that evolved over the sixty-year period since the Social Security Act of 1935. Based on a fundamentally altered philosophy, it places federal spending for several major welfare programs on a yearly budget and turns welfare administration over to the states. States are given a great deal of discretion in designing and administrating their welfare programs, as long as they focus on moving actual or potential welfare recipients into the job market. The deadlines for moving caseloads into employment are short, especially since most welfare families lose eligibility for federal cash assistance after a lifetime limit of five years.

State governors and conservative politicians won a major victory in convincing Congress and the president to turn welfare administration over to the states. Now, however, the states are faced with a major obligation. They are basically required to work toward the goal of converting the welfare system into a supported jobs program. In the next chapter we will examine state implementation of the law.

6

State Welfare Plans Under PRWORA

The Personal Responsibility and Work Opportunity Reconciliation Act (PRWORA) of 1996 has resulted in the most innovative period in the history of American welfare. All fifty states, the District of Columbia, and several territories have designed new welfare systems, with the ultimate goal of finding ways to help the poor become independent through self-employment. Although the 1996 act places many requirements and restrictions on the states, it allows considerable flexibility in designing new welfare systems. Most states have used this discretion to test experimental programs, and many have used it to redesign their welfare systems. States are experimenting with a wide range of policies designed to move welfare recipients, and would-be recipients, into the job market, and assist them with support services while they become settled in the workforce. The plans being implemented across the nation vary, even within states, where different approaches are often being tested in one or more counties.

There are considerable differences in the quality of state programs. Public officials in some states have been interested in comprehensive welfare reform for many years. Wisconsin, Michigan, Indiana, Kansas, and Oregon, for example, were leaders in gaining permission to test innovative policies in the early 1990s. The Clinton administration approved demonstration projects (experimental plans) in forty-three states before the 1996 act was passed. This allowed states to test alternative programs, or even to engage in major welfare reform, years before the new law was passed. A few states designed and tested programs that became models for reform.

Even many of the states conducting demonstration projects were in the early stages of experimentation and reform when PRWORA became law in 1996. The combination of short deadlines required by the act, slow startups by many states, and a healthy economy in the late 1990s allowed most states to focus chiefly on quickly moving recipients off the rolls directly into jobs. Most states modeled their program around "Work First," a policy that de-emphasizes education and job training in favor of job search and rapid job placement. Recipients are essentially required to take any job, based on the assumption the best job training is a job. The primary challenge to states under this approach is in setting up the infrastructure to provide recipients with incentives and support services—mostly income disregards, health care, and subsidized child care. Although all the states have toughened work requirements and most have some incentives for workers, support services for family heads that leave welfare for work are modest in many states. Child care and other support services are often inadequate, unavailable, or available only by waiting lists. At the other extreme, some states have done an excellent job of using PRWORA to design innovative policies that effectively help healthy adults leave welfare for sustainable employment or combine work with welfare.

The sophistication of state welfare programs can be gauged in part by the percentage of Temporary Assistance to Needy Children (TANF) recipients who meet work activity requirements. In 2001 only twelve states had welfare systems in place that were sophisticated enough to engage at least 50 percent of their TANF caseload in work activities (see Table 6.1). In fourteen states and the District of Columbia fewer than 30 percent of the TANF caseload was involved in work activities in 2001. The two most populous states, California and Texas, belonged to the laggard group. In New York, the third most populous state, only 33 percent of the TANF caseload was engaged in work activity.

Characteristics and Impact of State Programs

To provide insights into how states are carrying out PRWORA, two approaches are taken below. First, we start with a case study of Wisconsin, which is recognized as one of the states that has led the way in welfare reform. The Wisconsin plan is not typical; it is, in fact, arguably the most sophisticated reform plan adopted by any state. A study of the Wisconsin plan is valuable because it provides insights into the options states have at their disposal under PRWORA. Wisconsin chose among those options to organize and implement a comprehensive set of programs designed to substitute supported work for welfare for almost all the state's healthy able-bodied poor and low-income population. Second, the major provisions of PRWORA are reviewed to show how the fifty states and the District of Columbia have chosen among the various options to design their welfare plans.

Wisconsin: A Case Study

Wisconsin has designed and implemented one of the most comprehensive welfare plans in the nation (Mead, 2004). An early leader in reform, Wisconsin experimented with alternatives to traditional AFDC during the 1980s and early 1990s, and then became the first state to pass a fully articulated reform plan under PRWORA (Corbett, 1995). The Wisconsin plan is informed by its past experimentation, and is overtly designed to require, even force, most able-bodied adults to accept or find employment rather than receive cash welfare (Wiseman, 1996). As a result of the new program, welfare rolls in Wisconsin declined 82 percent between 1994 and 2001. After a shaky start, the plan has been hailed as one of the best in the nation (Mead, 2004). Wisconsin's innovations and successes have been influential in shaping both the welfare debate and the plans of many other states.

No Entitlement to Welfare ("For those who can work, only work should pay.")

The Wisconsin plan is formally named Wisconsin Works, but is known as W-2, a reference to the tax form reporting wages received by workers. W-2 was implemented statewide in late 1997. The basic assumption of W-2 is there is no entitlement to welfare. Basing reform on a clear declaration that people are not entitled to aid, but must earn it was a major change from the assumptions that Aid to Families with Dependant Children (AFDC) had been based on. AFDC was an entitlement program for certain types of families with children, even if the family head was detached from the job market. The Wisconsin plan plainly states that no one is entitled to aid, but those who are willing to work will be assisted in gaining and keeping employment that matches their abilities. For almost all able-bodied adults, employment is a precondition for assistance. Rather than employment following enrollment, recipients generally must first be employed before they can obtain services. Additionally, unlike Wisconsin's AFDC program, which was restricted to single parents, W-2 is available to all poor or near-poor adults with limited assets and incomes below 125 percent of their poverty level.

W-2 was designed to make work the core obligation of healthy adults, but not for purposes of reducing costs. W-2 is available to custodial parents with gross incomes below 115 percent of the poverty line. Parents may be single, married, or cohabiting. The asset limit is $2,500, excluding a vehicle valued up to $10,000 and one home. It was understood from the beginning that W-2 would be more expensive. Costs, however, would shift from cash aid to support services with the goal of nurturing a more self-reliant and productive population.

Focus on Employment

As a nonentitlement, W-2 is grounded in a mutual obligation philosophy. Applicants for aid do not meet with a caseworker as in the past, but with a Financial and Employment Planner (FEP), who helps them develop an Employment Plan (EP). Part of the EP is a mutual obligation contract in which applicants pledge, among other things, to be courteous and cooperative, refrain from certain behaviors (e.g., drug and alcohol abuse), accept responsibility for themselves and their children, and take training, education, and employment seriously. This contracting and planning stage is designed to (1) discourage applicants who have alternatives to welfare or who do not wish to cooperate, (2) establish ground rules for those who want assistance, and (3) creatively help those determined to require services through evaluation, counseling, training and/or education. If necessary, applicants are enrolled in several weeks of supervised job search. During job search sessions, applicants are given remedial instruction in topics including time management (particularly on how to get to work on time), accepting criticism from supervisors, getting on with coworkers, and transportation options. Job search sessions normally last half a day, with applicants spending the rest of the day in actual job interviews.

Employment Ladder

As part of the EP, applicants must lay out their goals and develop a plan of action. This exercise is designed to elevate the morale of applicants by convincing them that they can start out in low-paying jobs and through diligence work their way up. The second stage is to place applicants within a four-stage employment ladder, starting them at the highest stage possible. As an incentive, the income of participants increases as they move up the job ladder. The four levels are:

Level 4: Unsubsidized Employment

This is the highest rung of the ladder, and the one that recipients are encouraged to achieve. If qualified and the job can be found, applicants are placed here. Those placed in unsubsidized employment receive no cash aid, but they are often eligible for the Earned Income Tax Credit (EITC), food stamps, medical assistance, child care and job access loans.

Level 3: Trial Jobs (Subsidized Employment)

If an unsubsidized job cannot be found, but the applicant is willing to work, he/she may be placed in a subsidized job. Employers prepared to hire willing applicants who need three to six months of on-the-job training are given subsidies of $300 per month. The expectation is that after the subsidized training period, the employer will hire the trainee for a regular position. If not, the trainee is placed into another subsidized job. While in a training position, the trainee receives no cash assistance, but is paid at least the minimum wage, and may be eligible for the EITC, food stamps, medical assistance, child care, and job access loans.

Level 2: Community Service Jobs

Applicants who are not ready for regular employment may be placed in community service jobs (CSJs), which are designed to allow clients to learn work habits and job skills. CSJ participants receive a monthly grant of $673 for up to thirty hours per week of work activities and up to ten hours a week in education or training. Participants may be eligible for food stamps, medical assistance, child care, and job access loans, but not for the EITC. Clients who miss any work or training without good cause may be penalized at the rate of the minimum wage.

Level 1: W-2 Transition

The lowest rung of the employment ladder is reserved for adults who are unable to perform independent, self-sustaining work. Transition participants receive a monthly grant of $628 for up to twenty-eight hours per week of

work or developmental activities and up to twelve hours per week in education or training. Transition participants may also be eligible for food stamps,
medical assistance, child care, and job access loans, but not the EITC.

Adults who are placed in any of the three lower rungs of the employment ladder (below unsubsidized employment, where there are no time
limits) are restricted to twenty-four months in any one category, and a
lifetime limit of sixty months in the various level 1 to 3 work options.
Exceptions can be made when local labor markets limit opportunities.
The grants for CSJs and W-2 transition jobs do not vary with family
size, but are adjusted for cost increases at the discretion of the legisla-
ture. Uniform grants, or caps, are designed to mimic private sector jobs
where wages do not reflect family size. W-2 is built on the premise that
welfare should be as much like work as possible. Benefits do not vary
by family size, nor are they subsidized. Recipients are treated as much
as possible like other low-income working families.

W-2 participants who fail to live up to the terms of their EP have their
benefits reduced or eliminated. Counties that do the best job of placing
applicants in jobs receive financial rewards. If a county does a poor job
of managing programs, responsibility can be turned over to private contractors. To make the point that W-2 is a jobs program, administration of
the employment programs was shifted from Wisconsin's Department of
Health and Social Services to the Department of Workforce Development (DWD). The DWD is responsible for subcontracting employment
and training programs with both private and public entities. W-2 specifi-
cally charges DWD to open competition for the management of the work
programs to the private sector in hope of improving administration.

Support Services

Wisconsin officials have given a great deal of thought to the support
services that applicants require to be able to enter and stay in the job
market, while balancing employment with training, education, and parenthood. The services include:

One-Stop Job Centers

Located throughout the state, Job Centers offer one-stop shopping for
job seekers and employers. Those searching for a job can receive counseling, career planning, education, training, and job placement. W-2

agencies are either found within individual Job Centers or linked electronically within a Job Center network. Individuals arriving at a Job Center site are evaluated by a resource specialist to determine the support they need and then referred to those services within the site. The array of services include information about employment opportunities, career options, and the local labor market, with testing, training, job skills evaluations, job search, and job placement.

Job Access Loans

Small grants are available to help families meet immediate financial needs that may be preventing them from working. The grants cover such costs as car repairs, required clothing or equipment, and moving expenses. Repayment must begin almost immediately and can be done through cash or a combination of cash and volunteer community service. Generally the loans must be repaid within twelve months, but some exceptions are made.

Transportation Assistance

Various transportation options are available to ensure that clients can get their children to day care and themselves to work sites. Public transit services have been expanded to a broader range of communities, and service hours have been extended. Financial support has been offered to employers to finance van and shuttle services and to establish volunteer driver programs. W-2 agencies are also encouraged to develop buyer plans with local car dealers, vehicle repair services with local high schools and technical schools, and free bike programs.

Child Care

Wisconsin has substantially expanded funding for child-care assistance. All families with a gross income equal to or less than 185 percent of the poverty line and assets below the W-2 standard are eligible. There are no time limits on eligibility. Family heads must cooperate in identifying absent parents. Parents must be employed or, if twenty or younger, enrolled in high school or a high school equivalency program. Also, parents must be engaging in one of the employment tiers, enrolled in job training, or in unsubsidized employment.

Parents eligible for child-care assistance receive vouchers that can be used to place their children in licensed day-care centers, licensed family day-care homes, or even with neighbors or relatives as long as basic health and safety standards are met. Parents pay a co-payment based on their income and family size, the number of children in subsidized care, and the type of provider. As the income of parents increases, the subsidy may phase out.

Child Support

Both parents are expected to contribute to the support of their children. Child-support payments are aggressively pursued, and all collections are paid directly to the custodial parent and do not result in a reduction in benefit payments. Wisconsin is the only state that passes all collected child support to the family head. This policy is consistent with the philosophy of treating working welfare recipients like other low-income adults.

Health Care

Health care services have improved a great deal since the late 1990s. Currently, Wisconsin combines Medicaid, the state's Child Health Insurance Program (SCHIP), and state funds to provide free health care to all recipients below 150 percent of the poverty line. Above this limit, recipient co-payments are limited to 3 percent of family income. Wisconsin limits the overall costs of health care by requiring employed family heads to enroll in their employer provided program as soon as they are eligible.

Local Networks

W-2 encourages communities to establish volunteer boards to coordinate local community resources helpful to low-income families. Outreach programs publicize the assistance the families can find in their community. W-2 also encourages communities to set up committees that focus on creating local employment and training opportunities for needy adults. These committees also work on innovative ways to address child-care and transportation barriers on behalf of W-2 participants.

Education and Training

The Wisconsin plan is based on the philosophy that a job is the best training for self-sufficiency. Still, the plan assumes that parents will often need continuing education and training to perform better on the job and to prepare them for advancement up the employment ladder before they reach the sixty-month time limit for public assistance benefits. The opportunities that may be made available include employment workshops, job search skills, and life skills training.

As noted above, the type of education and training that W-2 parents need is determined when the FEP develops their EP. The EP details the participant's employment, education, and training goals. Additionally, W-2 parents may voluntarily pursue post–secondary education after fulfilling the requirements of their EP. Financial aid provided through the Higher Education Act of 1965 is not counted as income in determining W-2 eligibility.

At each rung of the W-2 employment ladder there are education and training choices. At the top two rungs of the ladder, employers have the flexibility to direct the education and training participants require to succeed on the job. Participants also may seek education and training through services offered at Job Centers, and they may compete for scholarships, financial aid, and loans to continue education after work. The Employment Skills and Advancement Program (ESAP) provides grants of up to $500 for education and training. Applicants must be working forty or more hours a week and must match the state funds. Participants in W-2 community service jobs may be required to spend up to ten hours a week in education or training, and the requirement for W-2 Transition participants may be as much as twelve hours a week. W-2 participants and workers earning less than 165 percent of their poverty line who have been in unsubsidized employment for at least nine months are eligible for up to one year of child care while they pursue additional education and training. In order to receive child-care assistance, the client's FEP must approve the education and training.

Summary

It is easy to understand why the Wisconsin plan is a national model for welfare reform. The emphasis on work rather than welfare, backed up by education and training programs, child care, medical assistance, transportation assistance, community support networks, job access loans, the job ladder, and many other innovative policies make the Wisconsin plan comprehensive and sophisticated. Clearly, the plan has been well-thought out, and it has produced high work rates for recipients and large reductions in welfare rolls. In 2001 over 70 percent of all TANF family heads were engaged in work activities, one of the highest rates in the nation. There were about 40,000 recipients on TANF in 2001, down from 288,000 in 1985 and 226,000 in 1994. Many former recipients have on their own found jobs, but W-2 has also moved thousands of poor family heads into employment. Wisconsin's first study of families leaving welfare between January and March of 1998 found that 83 percent had been employed since leaving welfare; however, 38 percent were not employed when interviewed. Of those employed, the average wage was $7.42, and a majority was working forty or more hours a week (www.dwd.state.wi.us/desw2/leavers1.pdf).

In the first few years after the launch of W-2 there were serious problems with coordination between private sector contractors and state employees, and some support services, especially child care in the Milwaukee area, were inadequate. Also, staff support was often inadequate, especially in Milwaukee. In recent years these problems have mostly been resolved.

Although the Wisconsin plan is sophisticated and comprehensive, its most distinguishing characteristic is its declaration that welfare is not an entitlement. PRWORA was meant to end the practice of giving aid to poor adults who are physically able to join the labor force, but refuse to do so. However, for a state to make this policy a reality, it must have the administrative ability to screen recipients or potential recipients to determine their suitably for work, provide counseling and job search assistance, establish required support services, move adults into the market, and supervise them until they become established and independent. This requires strong case management, and a very professional bureaucracy. Most states simply lack the administrative skills and infrastructure to execute this type of sophisticated plan (Mead, 2004, 243–60).

The Wisconsin plan is less focused on economics than it is on hearts and souls. It is designed to change the value systems and behavior of healthy adults who expect society to support them. It seeks to teach and defend core American values such as personal responsibility, commitment to hard work, education, parenthood, and obedience of the law. In this sense the plan is conservative. But, it is also a liberal plan because it provides quality support services not only to the poor, but to other low-income families. Under PRWORA many states focus on removing or diverting the poor from cash aid, but then fail to provide even modestly adequate case management and support services to improve the chance that they will work, or that if they do, that employment will lead to a better life.

State Plans

As noted, the Wisconsin plan is not typical. By tradition, Wisconsin is a state that believes in using government to solve problems (Elizar, 1984). Wisconsin officials wanted to end the entitlement approach to welfare and believed that a well-designed plan could help most of the poor gain independence through employment. Wisconsin was confident that it had the professional bureaucracy, experience, imagination, and will to design and execute a viable plan. Most of the states do not have Wisconsin's faith in the problem-solving abilities of government, nor do they have the professional bureaucracy and administrative infrastructure required to carry out a sophisticated plan.

This is not to say that the governors and political leaders of the states did not want change. There was general agreement that the AFDC approach to poverty was bankrupt, and almost all saw PRWORA as an opportunity to design a better plan. They liked the idea of imposing time limits, stiffer work requirements, sanctions for noncompliance, improved support services for workers, and better enforcement of child-support orders. Lowering the out-of-wedlock birth rate, especially among teens, also struck a responsive cord. But so far most of the states lack the determination, experience, and professionalized bureaucracy required to execute reform on the Wisconsin level. Most states have done the basics, but still lack the evaluative, supervisory, and bureaucratic skills required to put most of their healthy TANF family heads into work activities, and provide quality support services for those who have been diverted from or moved off welfare.

Still, Wisconsin is not the only innovative state or the only one that got off to an early start. Oregon, Kansas, Indiana, Illinois, Massachusetts, and Indiana, among others, had given considerable attention to reform well before the passage of PRWORA. These states designed programs that effectively put most of their able-bodied TANF recipients into work activities while providing quality support services to

Table 6.1

TANF Work Participation Rates, FY 2001

State	All family rates	State	All family rates
United States	34.40	Minnesota	36.20
		Nevada	35.10
Kansas	80.70	Hawaii	35.00
Massachusetts	76.50	Kentucky	34.00
Indiana	76.00	Michigan	33.80
Wisconsin	75.00	Missouri	33.10
Oregon	72.00	Arizona	32.90
Wyoming	71.80	North Dakota	32.00
Illinois	65.80	Tennessee	32.00
South Carolina	58.70	Florida	29.90
Ohio	53.20	California	25.90
Washington	50.40	Utah	25.90
New Hampshire	50.20	Rhode Island	25.30
Idaho	46.90	Delaware	24.60
New Mexico	46.40	North Carolina	24.40
Maine	45.90	Arkansas	21.90
Montana	44.40	West Virginia	21.60
Virginia	44.30	Mississippi	20.90
Alaska	43.40	Dist. of Col.	20.30
South Dakota	43.00	Oklahoma	18.60
Texas	41.50	Nebraska	18.10
New York	41.40	Vermont	12.90
Iowa	41.20	Pennsylvania	10.80
Connecticut	40.60	Georgia	8.70
New Jersey	39.00	Virgin Islands	6.70
Alabama	38.90	Maryland	6.60
Colorado	38.20	Puerto Rico	6.60
Louisiana	37.40	Guam	0.00

Source: Department of Health and Human Services (2004a), table 3.1.

families who left welfare for work (Mead, 2004, 6). Table 6.1 ranks the states by the percentage of their TANF caseload involved in work activities in 2001. This table shows which states have made the most progress in setting up the infrastructure required to move TANF family heads into work activities. The data provide a rough measure of how effective states have been in implementing PRWORA. Notice that the average for all the states was 34.4 percent. In the top ranks, seven states placed more that 65 percent of eligible adults into work activities. On the low end, fifteen states and the District of Columbia placed less than 30 percent of their eligible adults in work activities.

These states have shown little ability to design and implement the administrative structure and support services required to carry out effective reform.

A few of the states that have made median-level progress under PRWORA were early leaders in welfare reform. They have invested considerable energy in reform, but for various reasons have fallen short of being able to put most of their TANF recipients into work activities. They have also often struggled to establish quality support services for ex-welfare recipients and other low-income adults trying to become settled in the workforce. These states include Michigan, Colorado, and Minnesota. Many of the provisions of PRWORA were borrowed from the states that were early leaders in testing new ways to help the poor, including some of the states that have struggled with execution.

Changes in State Welfare Expenditures

One indicator of the changes in state plans is that under PRWORA the states are spending more on welfare, but spending those dollars very differently than in the past (Volden, 2003; Allard and Danziger, 2000; Ellwood and Boyd, 2000; Rom, Peterson, and Scheve, 1998). Rather than simply dispensing cash, the states are spending more TANF dollars on services, child care, work-related activities, and system administration. Figure 6.1 shows the changes that have taken place in the expenditure of federal and state TANF dollars since 1997. The obvious trends are increased overall spending, with a shift away from cash toward work activities and services to support employment. In 2001, slightly more than one-third of TANF funds were spent on cash, compared to 1997 when cash aid represented more than two-thirds of expenditures. In 2001, 26 percent of expenditures were for "other expenditures," which included spending for transportation, pregnancy prevention, refundable tax credits, and family formation. In 1997 this type of expenditure represented 8 percent of spending. In 2001 the states also spent $5.2 billion on child care and $2.7 billion on work-support activities. These are huge increases over spending for these activities in 1997. The increase and shift in expenditures is clear evidence that welfare policy is moving in the direction prescribed by PRWORA. Some states, of course, are making the transition much faster than others.

Figure 6.1   **Combined Federal and State Expenditures by Type** (in millions)

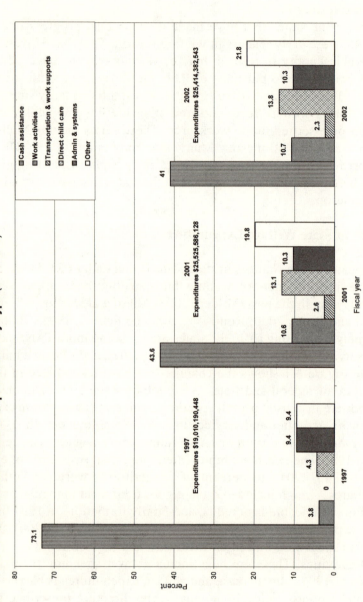

Source: Department of Health and Human Services, Administration for Children and Families. *Temporary Assistance for Needy Families*, 6th Annual Report to Congress, 2004, pp. 11–14.

State Program Options

The decisions states have made in exercising their options under PRWORA create a varied and complex matrix. We review state options by examining a dozen major provisions of PRWORA and discussing the decisions states have made in implementing each of these policies. Since the District of Columbia is treated as a state, the number of entities reviewed is fifty-one if all data are available. These data are summarized from the Department of Health and Human Development's annual report to Congress (Department of Health and Human Services, 2004a).

Individual Responsibility Plans

All the states require TANF applicants and recipients to sign an Individual Responsibility Plan (IRP), although the plans carry many different titles. PRWORA mandates that each state assess TANF applicants and recipients in terms of their education and job skills, work experience, and qualifications for employment. The IRPs are the way states meet this requirement. IRPs typically require applicants to pledge cooperation with all aspects of state welfare policy, including avoidance of alcohol and drug abuse, immunization of dependent children, identification of absent parents, and any required job training and education programs. Failure to sign an IRP most often disqualifies an applicant from assistance. Noncompliance with the provisions of the plan results in either disqualification or reduction in benefits. Continued noncooperation generally results in loss of all benefits.

- Thirty-two states deny all benefits to applicants who refuse to sign an IRP or fail to comply with a plan they have signed.
- Fourteen states and the District of Columbia limit the maximum sanction to a reduction in family benefits.
- Four states do not specify sanctions for noncompliance.

Time Limits on Assistance

Under PRWORA families are limited to a lifetime limit of five years (or less at state option) of cash assistance. States may exempt up to 20 percent of their caseload from time limits, and they may use Social Services block grant funds to provide cash and noncash assistance and vouchers to families that have exhausted the time limit. States may also use their own funds to assist families that have used up their five-year limit in federal funds.

- Thirty-seven states and the District of Columbia have set the time limit at sixty months. About a third of these states have intermittent time limits, requiring recipients to leave welfare for some fixed period after some specified number of months on welfare. Most of these states require time off welfare after twenty-four months of enrollment. Two states, Arizona and Texas, continue assistance to children after the intermittent limit.
- Eight states and the District of Columbia have no time limit for children.
- Eight states have set the limit at less than sixty months.
- Eight states use a variety of other options, with Arizona, Oregon, Vermont, Michigan, and Massachusetts having no time limit. Texas varies the limit to twelve, twenty-four, or thirty-six months for adults only, depending on the education and employability of the head. In Texas an adult who receives benefits for the specified limit may not receive additional assistance for five years.

Exemptions From the Time Limit

States have the option of exempting up to 20 percent of their caseload from the sixty-month limit. Exemptions are generally based on high unemployment rates in a particular area of the state, and the mental and physical ability of the family head or a caretaker. Victims of family abuse, minors, and those actively seeking employment also frequently qualify for exemption.

Extensions of the Time Limit

PRWORA does not provide for extensions, but some states allow nonexempt families that have exhausted the time limit to receive state-financed assistance for an additional period, normally three to sixty months. Extensions are most often given to allow individuals to finish a training program, or to family heads making an honest effort to find work.

Time Frame for Work

Most state plans are based on "Work First" policies, which require recipients to quickly move into available jobs. PRWORA requires those receiving TANF to engage in work (as defined by the state) when ready or within twenty-four months. States determine when recipients are ready and they may use timelines shorter than twenty-four months.

- Thirty-four states and the District of Columbia require TANF recipients and applicants to engage in immediate work.
- Nine states set the number of months at twenty-four; Vermont at thirty months.
- Six states set the time limit at two or three months.

Exemption From Work Requirements Based on Age of Children

States are given the option of exempting single parents with children under the age of one from work requirements, and they may disregard them in calculating work participation rates for a cumulative lifetime total of twelve months.

- Twenty-two states and the District of Columbia exempt single parents with a child younger than one year old.
- Seventeen states exempt single parents with a child younger than age twelve, thirteen, or sixteen months.
- Four states exempt some parents with children older than one year.
- Five states provide no automatic exemptions.

Making Work Pay

Under AFDC states were required to follow federal guidelines that specified how earnings were treated in determining eligibility for cash assistance (Acs et al., 1998). PRWORA drops this rule and allows states to make their own decisions about earning disregards for eligibility and benefit determination.

- All of the states disregard either a fixed dollar amount of earning in determining eligibility, a certain percentage, or a combination of dollars plus a percentage. Fifteen states, for example, exempt the first $90 earned monthly. Ten states exempt 18 to 50 percent. The other states use an assortment of formulas.

- Only New Jersey and Wisconsin allow no income disregard in calculating benefits. All the other states allow a fixed dollars exemption, a percentage of earnings, or a combination of the two. Many of the states limit the number of months that the exemption can be applied. The states struggle with conflicting goals in this area. If exemptions are generous, TANF heads have greater earning power. But, if the exemptions make staying on TANF too attractive, the family is more likely to exhaust its lifetime limit.
- Almost all the states have raised the asset level for recipients from the old AFDC limit of $1,000. Many of these states now allow recipients to have $2,000 or more in assets. Ohio has no asset limit.
- Almost all the states have increased the vehicle asset limit to help recipients own reliable transportation. Twenty-eight states simply disregard the value of one automobile. Several others exempt the vehicle if it is used for work. Other states have increased the asset range up to $8,000 to $12,000. In twelve states the limit is still $5,000 or less.

Individual Development Accounts

In one of its most innovative provisions, PRWORA allows Individual Development Accounts (IDAs) to be established by or on behalf of a TANF applicant or recipient. IDAs are restricted saving accounts that allow recipients to accumulate funds that can be used for specific purposes, such as post–secondary education, purchase of a first home, tools required for employment, or start-up funds for a business. IDA accounts are not considered as assets and are not counted in determining TANF eligibility or benefits (Sherraden, 1991).

- Thirty-three states allow IDAs. A few states place no dollar limit, but most allow $5,000 or less.
- Nineteen states have some type of matching formula for recipient contributions to IDAs.

Almost all the states with IDAs allow the recipient to use the funds for post–secondary education.

Sanctions for Failure to Comply With Work Requirements

PRWORA allows states to either reduce or end cash assistance to individuals or families that refuse to comply with work requirements. Sanctioning authority is much stronger under TANF than under AFDC.

- Fifteen states cut off all funds for the first failure to meet work requirements. All the other states use partial reductions to encourage compliance. Maine and Pennsylvania have policies that allow full or partial reductions depending on the number of months the family head has been on assistance.
- Suspensions or reductions in cash assistance generally last until compliance or for three or fewer months. No state suspends the family for more than three months for the first infraction.

Sanctions for Noncooperation With Child-Support Requirements

PRWORA requires recipients to cooperate in establishing paternity and child-support orders. Any applicant or recipient who refuses to cooperate can have his/her benefits reduced by 25 percent or be refused cash assistance.

- Twenty-seven states end all cash assistance to recipients who are not cooperative in identifying the father of their children.
- All the other states reduce benefits by at least 25 percent.
- Most states restore cash assistance if the parent decides to comply.

Family Caps

PRWORA does not contain a specific provision on family caps. However, states have the discretion to deny added benefits to any TANF recipient who has an additional child (Acs, 1996).

- Twenty-three states have passed laws that allow either no additional cash assistance or reduced amounts for a child born to a TANF head.
- Most of these states make exceptions for children born within ten months of the beginning of TANF enrollment.

- Most of these states make exceptions for children born as the result of rape or incest.
- Most of these states also make exceptions for first-time minor parents.

Cash Diversion Programs

PRWORA gives the states the flexibility to offer potential TANF recipients a lump sum payment. In return for the payment, the applicant agrees not to reapply for assistance for a specified period. The payment is usually equal to one to four months of benefits.

- Twenty-nine states and the District of Columbia offer diversion payments.
- Thirteen of the states with diversion programs refer the family head to job search or job placement programs.

This review of some of the major options provided the states by PRWORA provides insight into the rich mix of decisions that have been made. State welfare programs vary more now than at any time since the passage of the Social Security Act of 1935. The mix of strategies being employed by the states creates a complex set of policies but, in the long run, should provide considerable insight into the best ways to help able-bodied adults make the transition to employment.

How Do States Make Decisions About Options?

There is a considerable body of research that examines state welfare policy choices (Meyers, Gornick, and Peck, 2001; Mettler, 2000; Schram, 1999; Mead, 1997) and research that asks why states vary in the decisions they have made (Berry, Fording, and Hanson, 1998; Howard, 1999; Rom, Peterson, and Scheve, 1998; Brace and Jewett, 1995; Brown, 1995; Peterson and Rom, 1990; Barrilleaux and Miller, 1988; Plotnick and Winters, 1985). Since the 1996 law represents the replacement of a welfare system that many had come to see as too permissive, it allows the states to adopt policies that are tough, stringent, and even harsh. However, if states chose the strict approach, they have to go beyond adapting the basic changes required by the law and design a more innovative and even less incremental set of policies. The willingness of states to be policy innovators has long interested social scientists. Studies have found

that states show a long-standing pattern of either being policy innovators or policy laggards (Walker, 1969; Gray, 1973; Berry and Berry,
1990; Lieberman and Shaw, 2000). This research raises a question: could
the states that have adopted tougher options be the most innovative states?
Interestingly, the evidence reviewed below suggests that the answer to
this question is no (Soss et al., 2001).

Research has also shown that states tend to be either conservative or
liberal (Erikson, Wright, and McIver, 1993; Berry et al., 1998), and that
conservative states have more restrictive eligibility rules and less generous benefits (Rom, 1999). Another body of research examines the impact on policy decisions of competition between the states. The focus of
this research is whether states set welfare benefit rates at levels that will
protect the state from being a "welfare magnet" (Allard, 2004; Peterson
and Rom, 1990). States, in other words, might not want to set benefits at
higher rates than neighboring states because this might prompt potential
recipients to relocate to their jurisdiction. A considerable body of research has found that neighboring state policies do have an impact on
policy design and generosity of benefits (Peterson and Rom, 1990; Rom,
Peterson, and Scheve, 1998; Saavedra, 2000; Volden, 2003). Berry,
Fording, and Hanson (2003) dissent, arguing that neighboring effects
are statistically significant but of modest consequences. Bailey and Rom
(2004) expand this research by examining the impact of neighboring
effects on benefit levels, access to, and costs of state AFDC, Medicaid,
and Supplemental Security Income Supplements (SSI-S). They find the
neighboring state policies impact state decisions about AFDC benefits
and access, Medicaid costs, and SSI-S benefits, access and costs.

V.O. Key (1949) argued that the degree of competition among parties
in a state had an impact on policy decisions about benefit levels. Key's
thesis was that states with competitive party systems would compete for
the support of low-income voters by supporting more generous public
policies. Brace and Jewett (1995) found support for this hypothesis.
Barrilleaux, Holbrook, and Langer (2002) found that even within a party,
competition played a role. They found that Democratic state legislators
who won election in close races supported more generous welfare policies than Democrats elected in less competitive races. Other studies have
added support by finding that in states in which the low-income population was most active, welfare policies are more generous (Piven and
Cloward, 1988; Hill, Leighley, and Hinton-Andersson, 1995; Hill and
Leighley, 1992).

Another body of research has examined the relationship between the racial makeup of states and their welfare programs (Schram, Soss, and Fording, 2003; Sears, Sidanius, and Bobo, 2000; Lieberman, 1998). This research has found that states with the largest black populations tend to provide the least generous welfare benefits (Fording, 2001; Fording, 2003; Wright, 1976; Howard, 1999). Racial attitudes have also been shown to be good predictors of white attitudes toward welfare. White adults are much less likely to support welfare programs if they believe that the primary users and beneficiaries are minorities (Kinder and Sanders, 1996; Gilens, 1999). Fording (2003) and Brown (1999) find multiple links between race and the evolution and design of welfare policies. Racial attitudes, then, may be good predictors of state welfare plans.

Soss et al. (2001) recently conducted a study that tests the findings of many of the studies discussed above. They focused on why states would choose to adopt the most stringent TANF options. They concentrated on four stringent or tough options: (1) work requirements shorter than the maximum twenty-four months allowed by the law, (2) lifetime TANF eligibility less than sixty months, (3) family caps, and (4) strong, rather than, weak or moderate, sanctions. During the debate at the national and state levels, these four options commanded a great deal of attention (Bryner, 1998).

Soss et al. found that the best predictors of state adoption of tough welfare policies were the general conservatism of the state and the percentage of a state's AFDC/TANF roll that was minority. States with a higher rate of minorities on the aid rolls were much more likely to adopt the four stringent welfare options. Strict time limits and family caps were found to be almost entirely the products of state conservatism and race issues. Strong sanctions were also related to the competitiveness of the party system within the state. States with limited party competition were the most likely to adopt strong sanctions.

Conclusions

PRWORA has certainly "ended welfare as we know it." PRWORA fundamentally changed the philosophy of welfare policy in America, placing the focus on moving most able-bodied poor into the job market. Changes in the patterns of welfare spending show the states moving in the direction of supporting employment rather than dispensing cash. Although many states have been slow to make major alterations in their welfare policies, by 2004 even the lagging states had made important changes in their approach. A handful of states have been very inventive, and other states that have made less progress are testing innovative policies in at least a few counties.

The review above shows how comprehensively states can overhaul their welfare systems if they wish, and it shows the range of options that states can choose to design welfare systems that meet the unique needs of their state or even specific geographic regions. The various options allow the tailoring of reform to the economy and culture of a state. PRWORA also allows the states to alter their approach over time, based on experiences in the state or evidence produced by studies of experiments in other states. However, the particulars of a plan are of limited importance if the state cannot put together and execute a plan to engage most of its TANF recipients in work activities, or if the state fails to provide adequate support services to those who leave welfare for employment. Without quality infrastructure and administration, a plan may look progressive and even dynamic on paper, but the results will be disappointing.

The flexibility given states by PRWORA in designing their welfare systems means that the poor are treated differently depending on the state in which they live, or sometimes even the area of the state in which they reside. PRWORA allows differential treatment to give states the flexibility to tailor reform to the conditions of the state and to allow the states to experiment. On the positive side, reform can be more inventive and responsive to state and local conditions, although states seem restrained by the decisions made by neighboring states. On the negative side, the poor may be treated differently on the basis of race or sex. A minority living in a state with low minority use of welfare is likely to be treated better than minorities in states with high enrollments. Women in conservative states, or states with high minority enrollments, are more likely to face tougher work requirements, stricter time limits, family caps, and harsher sanctions. These are some of the costs of devolution.

In Chapter 7 we will review the early evidence on the impact of the new welfare programs on actual or potential welfare recipients.

7

After PRWORA

The American Welfare System

The welfare system that evolved from the Social Security Act of 1935 and various reforms over time is complex and expensive (Howard, 2003). The modest welfare programs established in 1935 have evolved and been transformed into much more sophisticated and expensive programs, and dozens of new programs have been established. The result is a modern welfare system composed of at least eighty-five programs that provide means-tested cash and in-kind assistance to low-income citizens. Table 7.1 lists eighty-five FY 2002 programs, along with the combined federal and state expenditures for each. The programs serve only individuals who meet low-income and minimum-asset guidelines and other eligibility requirements. Social Security and unemployment compensation are not included, because they are not welfare programs. A review of Table 7.1 shows that the programs vary greatly in size, cost, and recipient base. A few of the programs account for the vast majority of all welfare expenditures. Expenditures for medical aid programs account for 54 percent of total costs, while cash aid programs account for another 19 percent. Food assistance is only 7.5 percent of expenditures, while housing programs constitute another 6.8 percent. The combined costs of education, job training, energy, and other services account for less than 13 of total costs (Figure 7.1).

Figure 7.2 shows the growth of welfare spending and expenditure levels at the federal and state levels. In FY 2002, the total cost of the eighty-five income-tested programs was $522,156 billion—$373,152 in federal funds and $149,004 in state dollars. Federal expenditures accounted for 71 percent of the total, and were 18.6 percent of the federal

Table 7.1

Income-Tested Benefit Programs, 2002 (in millions of dollars)

Medical aid

1. Medicaid	258,216
2. Medical care for veterans without service-connected disability	8,185
3. State Children's Health Insurance Program (SCHIP)	5,407
4. General assistance (medical care component)—no federal dollars	4,956
5. Indian health services	2,758
6. Consolidated health centers	1,328
7. Maternal and child health services block grant	1,279
8. Title X family planning services	265
9. Medical assistance to refugees, asylees, other humanitarian cases	74

Cash aid

10. Supplemental Security Income (SSI)	38,522
11. Earned Income Tax Credit (EITC)—refundable portion only	27,830
12. Temporary Assistance for Needy Families (TANF)	13,035
13. Foster care	8,618
14. Child tax credit—refundable portion only	5,060
15. General assistance (non-medical care component)— no federal dollars	3,251
16. Pensions for needy veterans, their dependents, and supervisors	3,177
17. Adoption assistance	2,472
18. Dependency and indemnity compensation (DIC) and death compensation for parents of veterans	84
19. General assistance to Indians	66.5
20. Cash assistance to refugees, asylees, other humanitarian cases	41

Food aid

21. Food stamps	24,054
22. School lunch program (free and reduced price segments)	6,064
23. Special Supplemental Nutrition Program for Women, Infants, and Children (WIC)	4,350
24. Child and adult care food program, lower-income components	1,638
25. School breakfast program (free and reduced price segments)	1,638
26. Nutrition program for the elderly	801
27. The Emergency Food Assistance Program (TEFAP)	361
28. Summer food service program for children	307
29. Commodity Supplemental Food Program (CSFP)	105
30. Food distribution program on Indian reservations	74
31. Farmers' market nutrition programs	36
32. Special milk program (free segment)	1

Housing aid

33. Section 8 low-income housing assistance	18,499
34. Low-rent public housing	8,213

(continued)

Table 7.1 *(continued)*

35. Rural housing loans (section 502)	3,499
36. Home investment partnerships (HOME)	2,500
37. Housing for special populations (elderly and disabled)	895
38. Rural rental assistance payments (section 521)	705
39. Section 236 interest reduction payments	579
40. Housing opportunities for people with AIDS (HOPWA)	314
41. Rural rental housing loans (section 515)	114
42. Rural housing repair loans and grants (section 504)	62.4
43. Farm labor housing loans (section 514) and grants (section 516)	61.8
44. Section 101 rent supplements	53.7
45. Rural housing self-help technical assistance grants (section 523) and rural housing site loans (sections 523 and 524)	27.1
46. Indian housing improvement grants	19.6
47. Section 235 home ownership aid	10.8
48. Rural housing preservation grants (section 533)	8.6
49. Home ownership and opportunity for people everywhere (HOPE)	3.8

Education aid

50. Federal Pell grants	11,364
51. Head Start	8,172
52. Subsidized Federal Stafford loans and Stafford/Ford loans	7,523
53. Federal work-study program	1,000
54. Federal Trio programs	827
55. Supplemental educational opportunity grants	760
56. Chapter 1 migrant education program	395
57. Perkins loans	166
58. Leveraging educational assistance partnerships (LEAP)	134
59. Health professions student loans and scholarship	58
60. Fellowships for graduate and professional study	45
61. Migrant high school equivalency program (HEP)	23
62. College assistance migrant program (CAMP)	15
63. Close Up fellowships	1.5

Other services

64. Child care and development block grant	8,589
65. TANF services	6,147
66. Social services block grant (Title XX)	2,743
67. TANF child care	2,322
68. Homeless assistance	1,044
69. Community services block grant	739
70. Legal services	329
71. Social services for refugees, asylees, other humanitarian cases	159
72. Emergency food and shelter program	143

Jobs and training aid

73. TANF work activities	2,727
74. Jobs Corps	1,532

Table 7.1 *(continued)*

75. Youth activities	1,000
76. Adult activities	950
77. Senior community service employment program	494
78. Welfare-to-work grant program	413
79. Food stamp employment and training	410
80. Foster grandparents	155
81. Senior companions	69
82. Targeted assistance for refugees, asylees, other humanitarian cases	49.5
83. Native employment works (NEW)	7.6

Energy aid

84. Low-income home energy assistance program (LIHEAP)	1,800
85. Weatherization assistance	352

Source: Congressional Research Service (2004), tables K10–12.

Notes: These programs provide income-tested benefits. Within each category, the programs are listed in the order of their total cost in fiscal year 2002 to federal and state and local governments.

budget (Congressional Research Service, 2004, table K-1). Welfare expenditures have increased quite considerably over time, with particularly sharp increases since the late 1980s. In FY 2002 expenditures were thirty-two times as great as in 1968. The growth in welfare costs has greatly exceeded population growth. Controlling for inflation, expenditures for these programs increased by 523 percent between 1968 and 2002. During this same time period, the U.S. population grew by 43 percent. Per capita welfare spending grew in inflation-adjusted 2002 dollars from $416 in fiscal 1968 to $1,826 in FY 2002 (table K-3). The picture is clear: the rather modest set of programs established in 1935 has grown into a large, complex, and expensive welfare system.

Figures 7.3 and 7.4 break down federal and state-local spending by type of expenditure from FY 1968 to FY 2002. The clearest insight in these two graphs is that the most expensive and fastest growing programs at both the federal and state levels are those that provide medical services. In FY 2002, medical programs at the federal and state levels cost $282,468 billion, 54.1 percent of all outlays. Medical services were almost 80 percent of state-local expenditures, and almost 44 percent of federal costs. Cash benefits were the most expensive programs at the federal level until 1980, when medical expenses became predominant. In FY 2002 cash assistance accounted for only 22 percent of federal costs and 13.2 percent of state-local costs. Although individually they

Figure 7.1   **Spending for Income-Tested Welfare Programs by Type, 2002**

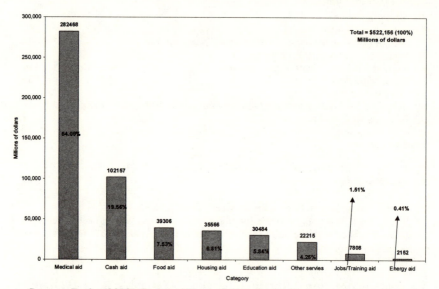

Sources: Burke (2003) *Cash and Noncash Benefits for Persons with Limited Income*; Congressional Research Service (2004), tables K10–13, pp. 412–37.

Figure 7.2   **Expenditures for Income-Tested Programs, 1968–2002**

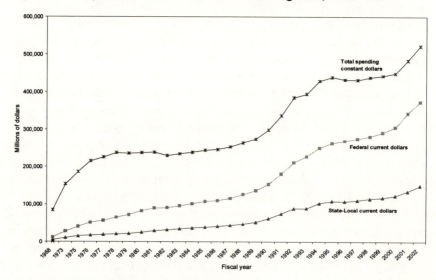

Sources: Burke (2003) *Cash and Noncash Benefits for Persons with Limited Income*; Congressional Research Service (2004), table K-1.

135

Figure 7.3 **Federal Spending for Income-Tested Programs by Form of Benefit, 1968–2002**

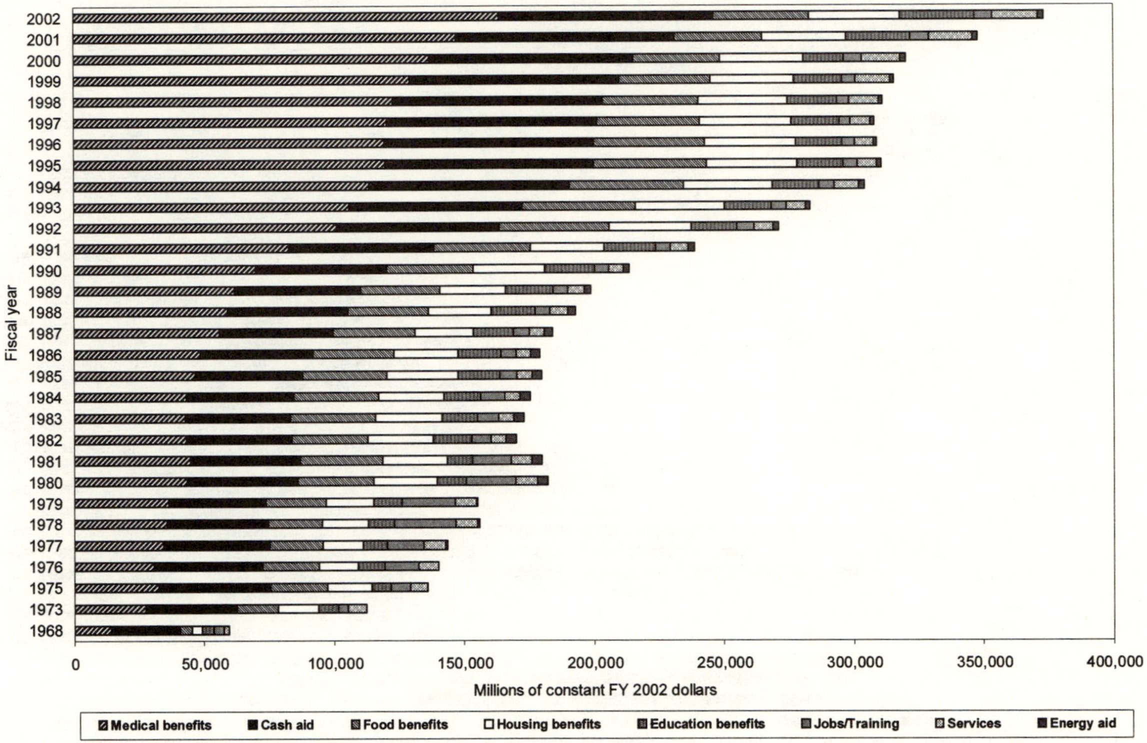

Sources: Burke (2003), *Cash and Noncash Benefits for Persons with Limited Incomes;* Congressional Research Service (2004), table K-2.

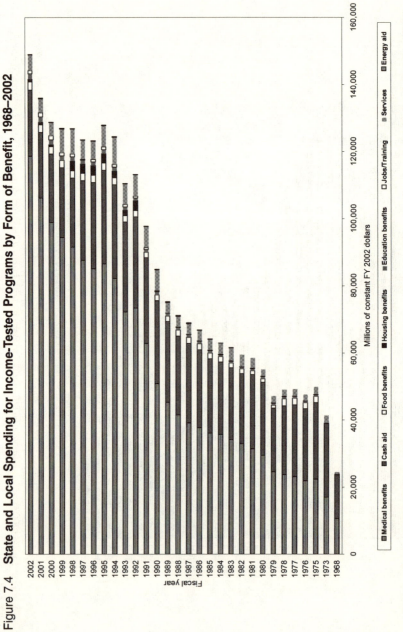

Figure 7.4 State and Local Spending for Income-Tested Programs by Form of Benefit, 1968–2002

Sources: Burke (2003), *Cash and Noncash Benefits for Persons with Limited Income;* Congressional Research Service (2004), table K-2.

Figure 7.5 **Share of Federal Budget Used for Income-Tested Aid Programs by Form of Aid, 1968–2002** (selected fiscal years)

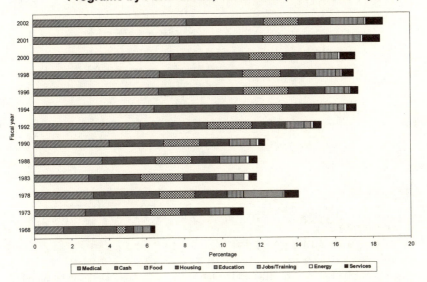

Sources: Burke (2003), *Cash and Noncash Benefits for Persons with Limited Income*; Congressional Research Service (2004), table K-5.

are rather modest contributors to total spending, food assistance, housing, education, and job training nonetheless are significant items on the federal budget. By contrast, at the state level, 93 percent of all spending is for medical services and cash assistance, with very little spending on other services. As Chapter 6 showed, states are shifting their cash expenditures toward services such as child care, but health care is by far the major category of spending.

As programs and costs have grown, the total share of the federal budget devoted to welfare spending has substantially increased. Figure 7.5 shows the share of the total federal budget expended on various types of income-tested programs between FY 1968 and FY 2002. In 1968 income-tested programs constituted 6.4 percent of all federal expenditures. By 2002 these costs had climbed to 18.6 percent of the total budget. Much of the overall increase in costs is attributable to the mounting costs of medical services. Cash assistance costs have increased over time, but expenditures for education and job training have grown very little. In 1968 medical programs accounted for only 1.54 percent of the total federal budget. By 2003 they were 8.14 percent of the federal budget. Cash

Figure 7.6   **Recipients of AFDC/TANF, 1960–2002**

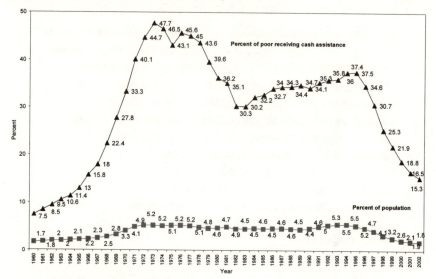

Source: Department of Health and Human Services (2004a). Data can be found at www.acf.hhs.gov/news/stats/69097rf.htm.

assistance increased in cost because the number of families receiving cash assistance spiked in the late 1980s and early 1990s, and because of the introduction and growth of both the Supplemental Security Income (SSI) program and the Earned Income Tax Credit (EITC). Food assistance also increased as a percentage of the federal budget while housing aid was fairly stagnant after the early 1970s.

The cost of income-tested programs, then, increased very substantially over the last thirty-five years. As a percentage of both federal and state-local budgets, means-tested programs expanded greatly. But, as we will see below, the poverty rate often increased during periods in which programs and welfare use were expanding and expenditures were escalating.

Welfare Rolls

Figure 7.6 shows the percentage of the nation's population receiving AFDC/TANF benefits from 1960 to 2002. As national attention was focused on civil rights issues and hunger in the 1960s, Aid to Families with Dependent Children (AFDC) rolls grew substantially. Growth continued in the early 1970s, exceeding 5 percent of the population between 1972 and 1977. The rolls declined somewhat after 1978, but averaged 4.6 percent until 1991. Five percent of the population received means-tested cash assistance in 1991, and the rate remained above 5 percent until 1996. With the debate, passage, and implementation of the Personal Responsibility and Work Opportunity Reconciliation Act (PRWORA) of 1996, welfare rolls began to decline. Between August 1996 and September 1998, the rolls dropped by 35 percent and continued to decline into the 2000s. In 2002 only 1.8 percent of the population was receiving Temporary Assistance for Needy Families (TANF), the program that took the place of AFDC when PRWORA was passed. In a very short time, the percentage of the population receiving assistance from the nation's major cash welfare program dropped back to the 1960–61 rates. In Chapter 8 we examine in more depth the causes and implications of this rapid decline.

Figure 7.6 also shows the percentage of all the poor receiving cash assistance by year. These data show that cash assistance has always been limited to only a subset of the poor. It was not until 1968 that slightly more than 20 percent of the poor received cash assistance. The percentage of the poor receiving cash welfare rose to 40.1 percent in 1971 and stayed above 40 percent until 1978. As the poverty rate increased in the 1980s and most of the 1990s, less than one in four of the poverty population received cash assistance. By 1998, the rate dropped to 25.3 percent of the poor, and by 2002 only 15.3 percent of the poor received cash assistance. The drop in cash welfare recipiency among the poor reflects the policy changes brought about by PRWORA.

Table 7.2 provides a more comprehensive examination of welfare assistance in 2002. The data show that a significant percentage of all American households received at least one form of means-tested assistance. In 2002, 25.1 percent of all American households received assistance that was income tested. This includes all households that received benefits from one or more of the programs listed in Table 7.1. Assistance might be substantial and costly, or involve more modest benefits like free or reduced-cost school meals or energy assistance. Medicaid benefits went to over 18 percent of all the population, while much smaller proportions of the population received cash, food stamps, and help with housing.

Among those in households with incomes below the poverty level, 23 million (or about two of three) received assistance from one or more programs. This means that about one-third of those counted among the

Table 7.2

Receipt of Means-Tested Benefits, 2002

Percent of population receiving
Any type of benefit	25.1
Medicaid	18.6
Cash aid	6.1
Food stamps	6.7
Public and subsidized housing	3.9

Average number of monthly recipients
Food stamps	20.2 million
TANF	5.1 million
SSI	6.9 million
EITC	16.8 tax filers
Medicaid	50.9 million

Percent of people below the poverty line
Two out of every three people counted as poor lived in a
   household that received means-tested assistance

Medicaid	52.7
Cash aid	21.5
Food stamps	32.9
Public or subsidized housing	17.5

   Source: Department of Health and Human Services, *Indicators of Welfare Dependency.* Annual Report to Congress, 2003, tables Ind 3a, 4, and 4a.

poor received no assistance. Only 21.5 percent of the poor received any type of cash assistance (TANF, General Assistance, SSI, EITC), and 32.9 percent received food stamps. A slight majority received Medicaid benefits, and only 17.2 percent received housing assistance. Thus, even among the poor, a significant percentage received no assistance, and among those who did receive assistance, a rather small percentage received cash or food aid.

Of those individuals who do receive assistance, many obtain benefits from more than one program. Table 7.3 shows the overlap in welfare receipt in 2002. Among TANF recipients about 81 percent received food stamps, almost 100 percent were enrolled in Medicaid, and a significant percentage received WIC (Women, Infants, and Children) assistance and help with housing. Over 60 percent of TANF families included children who participated in free or reduced-price school meal programs. Almost all SSI recipients are enrolled in Medicaid, and over 40 percent

Table 7.3

Overlap in Receipt of Assistance, 2002

Other assistant programs	TANF	SSI	Social Security	Unemployment compensation	Medicare
Food stamps	80.8	40.2	6.7	10.6	6.3
WIC	35.1	5.2	1.2	8.4	0.8
Medicad	99.6	96.4	18.2	23.5	17.8
Free or reduced-price school meals	62.3	17.7	4.3	16.1	3.0
Public or subsidized rental housing	37.6	22.9	5.6	3.0	5.6
VA compensation or pensions	1.0	3.6	4.6	1.4	4.8
Number of recipients in household receiving benefits (in thousands)[a]	1,393	5,207	31,358	3,209	28,452

Source: Congressional Research Service (2004), table 15-1.
Note: [a]Number of recipient households in February–May 2002.

receive food stamps. Alternatively, a rather small percentage of Social Security, Unemployment Compensation, and Medicare recipients receive traditional welfare benefits.

Antipoverty Effectiveness of Means-Tested Programs

Despite the nation's extensive array of welfare programs, they have never been designed, individually or cumulatively, to alleviate poverty. Even PRWORA does not include poverty reduction in its list of goals. Until the passage of PRWORA in 1996, welfare programs were designed as a temporary patch to allow recipients to recover from a financial setback. Many recipients stayed on the rolls for long periods, and many clearly were too old, incapacitated, or needy to correct their problems through employment, but the philosophical foundation continued to be that the poor only needed a short-term fix. To admit otherwise was to risk supporting a large class of unemployed poor, undermining personal motivation, or funding expensive support services to help family heads become established in the workforce. Thus, cash benefits, which varied by state, were generally very modest and support services that family heads required to move into the job market were generally not available.

Table 7.4

Antipoverty Effectiveness of Cash and Noncash Programs, 2002

	Persons in families with an unmarried head and children	Children under 18	65 and older
Number removed from poverty	5,301	5,138	14,004
Percent removed due to:			
Social insurance (including Social Security)	11.36	11.7	76.9
Means-tested cash	3.79	3.5	2.2
Means-tested noncash	10.79	9.7	3.0
EITC and federal payroll and income taxes	10.90	10.90	−0.1
Total percent removed from poverty	36.75	35.90	82.0

Source: Congressional Research Service (2004), pp. H35–H43.

With the passage of PRWORA in 1996, the philosophy changed, but the emphasis on modest, temporary cash assistance continues. Under PRWORA, the philosophy is that the able-bodied poor can best solve their problems through employment. Cash benefits continue to be modest, and restrictive, but support services to help family heads move into the job market have been greatly improved. The costs of support services are being paid for by greatly restricting access to cash assistance.

Given the national philosophy, it is not surprising that the majority of cash welfare recipients have always remained below the poverty level (Congressional Research Service, 1998, table H-23, 1341). Table 7.4 shows the effectiveness of cash and noncash transfers in reducing poverty in 2002. To demonstrate the differential impact of the programs, three groups of people are separately analyzed. Table 7.4 also includes three social insurance programs (Social Security, Unemployment Compensation, and Workman's Compensation) even though they are not means tested. Social insurance is included to contrast its impact with that of means-tested programs.

What the data show is that social insurance programs play a major role in helping the elderly escape poverty. In 2002, over 14 million persons sixty-five years of age and over escaped poverty because they received social insurance payments (mostly Social Security) and other means-tested assistance. Almost 77 percent of the elderly who escaped poverty did so because of social insurance. Another 5.2 were pushed over the poverty line by means-tested cash and noncash assistance. The combination of social insurance and means-tested programs allowed 82 percent of the at risk elderly to escape poverty.

By contrast, a much smaller number of people in families with an unmarried head and children were moved over the poverty line by the combination of benefits. In 2002 about 5.3 million people living in households with an unmarried head and children escaped poverty because of the combined benefits they received from social insurance, welfare programs, and the EITC program. The least effective program in helping people in this type of family was cash assistance. TANF, SSI, and General Assistance were responsible for removing only 3.8 percent of the total. By contrast, social insurance (11.36 percent), the cash value of means-tested noncash programs (10.79 percent) and the EITC (10.90 percent) each played a more significant role in preventing poverty. The combined programs lowered the poverty rate among people in this family type by 37 percent. The effectiveness of these programs in helping this group of people avoid poverty is far below the impact on persons sixty-five and over, but it is a considerable improvement over prior years. The reasons will be detailed below, but basically the reasons are that benefits under the EITC were improved by Congress in the late 1990s, and because noncash programs have been significantly expanded under PRWORA. Table 7.4 also shows the number of children under the age of eighteen who were sheltered from poverty in 2002 by a combination of programs. As with the other two groups, cash assistance played a rather minor role, but social insurance, noncash benefits, and the EITC combined to lower the poverty rate among vulnerable children by 36 percent.

Why do the very expensive income-tested programs play such a modest role in reducing poverty among the nonaged? There are several reasons. First, a majority of all program costs at the federal and state level are for medical assistance. At the state level almost 80 percent of all expenditures are for medical assistance. The services provided by these programs are very important, but they do not provide recipients with disposable income. Second, when we examine the TANF program below, we will see that none of the states sets cash benefits at a level that would move families over the poverty line. In fact, in most of the states TANF benefits are quite modest. Even adding the value of food stamps, the fungible value of health-care benefits and housing does not add up to a package of benefits generous enough to push recipient families over the poverty line. This does not mean that the programs are not helpful. TANF families receive much needed cash, food stamps clearly improve nutrition, and medical benefits certainly improve the health of recipients. If the family head is employed, the EITC significantly improves take-home pay.

Major Welfare Programs

Temporary Assistance for Needy Families

From 1935 to 1996 AFDC was the core cash-welfare program for poor families with children. In passing PRWORA of 1996, Congress replaced AFDC with TANF. TANF is a very different program. It is basically a supported-work program. A family can qualify for TANF only if it contains a minor child or a pregnant person. The states must move most TANF heads into the workforce within a relatively short time frame. States are required to help able-bodied recipients move into employment by providing transitional support services such as child care and medical coverage. To assist the states, TANF gives them much stronger sanctioning power than existed under AFDC. States have considerable discretion in screening recipients, and they decide how needy people have to be to receive aid and how much they will receive. States are given flexibility in designing their cash-welfare programs, and they are encouraged to experiment with various ways of helping poor families. As a result, there is significant variation among the states in how recipients are served and how much cash assistance they receive.

TANF is a budgeted program, as opposed to an open-ended entitlement, and most recipients are allowed to receive benefits for sixty or fewer months. The program is budgeted at $16.5 billion through 2004, with each state receiving an allocation that reflects its past expenditures for several welfare programs. There are supplemental grants for states with below average spending and high population growth. There are bonuses for reducing unwed births without increasing abortions, bonuses for superior performance in meeting goals, and a contingency fund. States are required to maintain their prior spending levels on the programs replaced by TANF (including child care) at a minimum of 75 percent, rising to 80 percent if they fail to meet work requirements.

Almost all the states have set TANF cash benefits at rates very similar to those paid under AFDC. About half the states have frozen rates at July 1996 levels. The other states have increased benefits, but only very modestly. Most states have increased asset limits for TANF eligibility and earning disregards to encourage employment and make work pay better. Benefit levels in a state often reflect experiments. Oregon, for example, gives recipients a bonus for cooperation, and West Virginia for marriage. Wisconsin and Idaho give flat rates to all families regardless of size. Twenty-three states have capped family benefits, allowing either no cash increase or a reduced rate boost if a new child is born into a TANF family. In twenty-nine states and the District of Columbia there are diversion or avoidance grants to help families meet emergencies without becoming TANF recipients. These grants are generally lump sum payments that remove the family's eligibility for TANF assistance for a specified period.

Maximum cash benefits under TANF are far from generous. With freezes and the failure of most states to make any meaningful adjustments for inflation over the last thirty-five years, benefits have declined significantly in all of the states. As an example, Table 7.5 shows maximum benefits for a family with one adult and two children from July 1970 to January 2003. Notice that in all the states, benefit levels have declined in inflation-adjusted dollars. In almost all of the states the decline has been quite large. In twenty-three states and the District of Columbia and several other major urban areas the decline has exceeded 50 percent. In several of these states the decrease has been well over 60 percent. In the average state, the maximum TANF grant is about $400 for a mother and two children.

Although cash benefits under TANF are low, TANF is designed to interact with other welfare programs to improve the family's situation, and, if possible, help the head move into employment. TANF families automatically qualify for Medicaid, over 80 percent receive food stamps, and they may receive child care, housing, and other assistance. If the family head becomes employed, she/he additionally qualifies for cash benefits under the EITC. The EITC is designed to make work a better option than welfare alone. Through income disregards and supplements to the EITC, states can improve on the package of benefits for employed heads, significantly improving their total yearly income while helping them become established in the job market.

Table 7.6 shows the combination of benefits a single-parent family with two children would receive in each state by working full time at the

Table 7.5

Maximum AFDC/TANF Benefit for a Family of Three (parent with two children), **July 1970–January 2003**

State	July 1970	July 1975	July 1980	January 1985	January 1990	January 1995	January 2000	January 2003	Percent real change, July 1970–January 2003[a]
Alabama	$65	$108	$118	$118	$118	$164	$164	$215	−29
Alaska	328	350	457	719	846	923	923	923	−39.6
Arizona	138	163	202	233	293	347	347	347	−46
Arkansas	89	125	161	192	204	204	204	204	−50.8
California	186	293	473	587	694	607	626	679	21.7
Colorado	193	217	290	346	356	356	356	356	−60.4
Connecticut	283	346	475	569	649	680	636	636	−51.8
Delaware	160	221	266	287	333	338	338	338	−54.7
District of Columbia	195	243	286	327	409	420	379	379	−58.3
Florida	114	144	195	240	294	303	303	303	−43
Georgia	107	123	164	223	273	280	280	280	−43.8
Hawaii	226	428	468	468	602	712	570	570	−46.2
Idaho	211	300	323	304	317	317	293	309	−68.6
Illinois	232	261	288	341	367	377	377	396	−63.4
Indiana	120	200	255	256	288	288	288	288	−48.5
Iowa	201	294	360	360	410	426	426	426	−54.5
Kansas	222	321	345	391	409	429	429	429	−58.5
Kentucky	147	185	188	197	228	288	262	262	−61.7
Louisiana	88	128	152	190	190	190	190	240	−41.5
Maine	135	176	280	370	453	418	461	485	−22.9
Maryland	162	200	270	329	396	373	417	473	−37.3
Massachusetts	258	259	379	432	539	579	565	618	−50.5
Michigan–Washtenaw Cty.	NA	NA	NA	447	546	489	489	489	NA
Michigan–Wayne Cty.	219	333	425	417	516	459	459	459	−55

Minnesota	256	330	417	528	532	532	532	532	-55.4
Mississippi	56	48	96	96	120	170	170	170	-34.8
Missouri	104	120	248	274	289	292	292	292	-39.7
Montana	202	201	259	354	359	416	469	507	-46.1
Nebraska	171	210	310	350	364	364	364	364	-54.3
Nevada	121	195	262	285	330	348	348	348	-38.3
New Hampshire	262	308	346	389	506	550	575	625	-48.8
New Jersey	302	310	360	404	424	424	424	424	-69.9
New Mexico	149	169	220	258	264	381	439	389	-43.9
New York–New York City	279	332	394	474	577	577	577	577	-55.6
New York–Suffolk Cty.	NA	NA	NA	579	703	703	703	703	NA
North Carolina	145	183	192	246	272	272	272	272	-59.7
North Dakota	213	283	334	371	386	431	457	477	-51.9
Ohio	131	204	263	290	334	341	373	373	38.9
Oklahoma	152	217	282	282	325	324	292	292	-58.8
Oregon	184	337	282	386	432	460	460	460	-46.3
Pennsylvania	265	296	332	364	421	421	421	421	-65.9
Rhode Island	229	278	340	409	543	554	554	554	-48.1
South Carolina	85	96	129	187	206	200	204	205	-48.2
South Dakota	264	289	321	329	377	430	430	483	-60.7
Tennessee	112	115	122	153	184	185	185	185	-64.6
Texas	148	116	116	167	184	188	201	201	-70.9
Utah	175	252	360	376	387	426	451	474	-41.9
Vermont	267	322	492	583	662	650	708	709	-43
Virginia	225	268	310	354	354	354	354	389	-62.9
Washington	258	315	458	476	501	546	546	546	-54.6
West Virginia	114	206	206	249	249	253	328	453	-14.7
Wisconsin	184	342	444	533	517	517	628	628	-26.7
Wyoming	213	235	315	360	360	360	340	340	-65.7

Source: Congressional Research Service (2004), tables 7-13.

Note: [a] The inflation factor used to convert July 1970 dollars to January 2003 dollars was 4.659 (representing the change in the Consumer Price Index for all Urban Consumers).

Table 7.6

Earnings and Selected Major Benefits for Single Parents With Two Children, Working Full Time at Minimum Wage, in the Thirteenth Month of Work, Annualized, January 1, 2003

State	Net[b] earnings	EIC (Federal)	TANF	Food stamps	Combined total	As a percent of the 2003 poverty guidelines[a]				
						Net[b] earnings	EIC (Federal)	TANF	Food stamps	Combined total
Alabama	9,885	4,204	0	2,304	16,393	64.8	27.5	0.0	15.1	107.4
Alaska	13,724	3,966	3,564	1,500	22,754	72.0	20.8	18.7	7.9	119.4
Arizona	9,885	4,204	0	2,304	16,393	64.8	27.5	0.0	15.1	107.4
Arkansas	9,885	4,204	0	2,304	16,393	64.8	27.5	0.0	15.1	107.4
California–Region 1	12,956	4,141	2,472	756	20,325	84.9	27.1	16.2	5.0	133.2
California–Region 2	12,956	4,141	2,088	876	20,061	84.9	27.1	13.7	5.7	131.4
Colorado[c]	9,885	4,204	0	2,304	16,393	64.8	27.5	0.0	15.1	107.4
Connecticut	13,244	4,075	7,632	0	24,951	86.8	26.7	50.0	0.0	163.5
Delaware	11,804	4,204	0	1,800	17,808	77.4	27.5	0.0	11.8	116.7
District of Columbia[c]	11,804	4,204	924	1,524	18,456	77.4	27.5	6.1	10.0	121.0
Florida	9,885	4,204	0	2,304	16,393	64.8	27.5	0.0	15.1	107.4
Georgia	9,885	4,204	0	2,304	16,393	64.8	27.5	0.0	15.1	107.4
Hawaii	11,996	4,204	1716	3,732	21,648	68.4	24.0	9.8	21.3	123.5
Idaho	9,885	4,204	0	230	14,319	64.8	27.5	0.0	15.1	107.4
Illinois[c]	9,885	4,204	1,176	1,944	17,209	64.8	27.5	7.7	12.7	112.7
Indiana[c]	9,885	4,204	780	2,064	16,933	64.8	27.5	5.1	13.5	110.9
Iowa[c]	9,885	4,204	828	2,052	16,969	64.8	27.5	5.4	13.4	111.1
Kansas[c]	9,885	4,204	0	2,304	16,393	64.8	27.5	0.0	15.1	107.4
Kentucky	9,885	4,204	0	2,304	16,393	64.8	27.5	0.0	15.1	107.4
Louisiana	9,885	4,204	0	230	14,319	64.8	27.5	0.0	15.1	107.4

Maine[c]	11,996	4,204	0	1,752	17,952	78.6	27.5	0.0	11.5	117.6
Maryland[c]	9,885	4,204	0	2,304	16,393	64.8	27.5	0.0	15.1	107.4
Massachusetts[c]	12,956	4,141	0	1,500	18,597	84.9	27.1	0.0	9.8	121.8
Michigan–Washenay Cty.	9,885	4,204	0	2,304	16,393	64.8	27.5	0.0	15.1	107.4
Michigan–Wayne County	9,885	4,204		2,304	16,393	64.8	27.5		15.1	107.4
Minnesota[c]	9,885	4,204	372	3,744	0	64.8	27.5	2.4	24.5	119.2
Mississippi	9,885	4,204	0	2,304	16,393	64.8	27.5	0.0	15.1	107.4
Missouri	9,885	4,204	0	2,304	16,393	64.8	27.5	0.0	15.1	107.4
Montana	9,885	4,204	0	2,304	16,393	64.8	27.5	0.0	15.1	107.4
Nebraska	9,885	4,204	0	2,304	16,393	64.8	27.5	0.0	15.1	107.4
Nevada	9,885	4,204	0	2,304	16,393	64.8	27.5	0.0	15.1	107.4
New Hampshire	9,885	4,204	2,148	1,656	17,893	64.8	27.5	14.1	10.9	117.3
New Jersey[c]	9,885	4,204	0	2,304	16,393	64.8	27.5	0.0	15.1	107.4
New Mexico	9,885	4,204	60	2,280	16,429	64.8	27.5	0.4	14.9	107.7
New York–New York City[c]	9,885	4,204	2,112	1,668	17,869	64.8	27.5	13.8	10.9	117.1
New York–Suffolk[c]	9,885	4,204	3,624	1,212	18,925	64.8	27.5	23.7	7.9	123.9
North Carolina	9,885	4,204	0	2,304	16,393	64.8	27.5	0.0	15.1	107.4
North Dakota	9,885	4,204		2,304	16,393	64.8	27.5		15.1	107.4
Ohio	9,885	4,204	624	2,112	16,825	64.8	27.5	4.1	13.8	110.2
Oklahoma[c]	9,885	4,204	0	2,304	16,393	64.8	27.5	0.0	15.1	107.4
Oregon[c]	13,244	4,075	0	1,428	18,747	86.8	26.7	0.0	9.4	122.9
Pennsylvania	9,885	4,204		2,304	16,393	64.8	27.5		15.1	107.4
Rhode Island[c]	11,804	4,204	1,272	1,416	18,696	77.4	27.5	8.3	9.3	122.5
South Carolina	9,885	4,204	0	2,304	16,393	64.8	27.5	0.0	15.1	107.4
South Dakota	9,885	4,204		2,304	16,393	64.8	27.5		15.1	107.4
Tennesse	9,885	4,204	1,404	1,884	17,377	64.8	27.5	9.2	12.3	113.8
Texas	9,885	4,204	0	2,304	16,393	64.8	27.5	0.0	15.1	107.4

(continued)

Table 7.6 *(continued)*

State	Net[b] earnings	EIC (Federal)	TANF	Food stamps	Combined total	Net[b] earnings	EIC (Federal)	TANF	Food stamps	Combined total
Utah	9,885	4,204	936	2,016	17,041	64.8	27.5	6.1	13.2	111.6
Vermont[c]	11,996	4,204	0	1,752	17,985	78.6	27.5	0	11.5	117.6
Virginia	9,885	4,204	4,668	900	19,657	64.8	27.5	30.6	5.9	128.8
Washington	13,455	4,027	0	1,368	18,850	88.2	26.4	0	9	123.5
West Virginia	9,885	4,204	0	2,304	16,393	64.8	27.5	0	15.1	107.4
Wisconsin—Com. Service[c]	9,885	4,204	0	2,304	16,393	64.8	27.5	0	15.1	107.4
Wisconsin—W2 Transition	NA	NA	NA	NA	NA	NA	NA	NA	NA	NA
Wyoming	9,885	4,204	0	2,304	16,393	64.8	27.5	0	15.1	107.4

Sources: Table prepared by the Congressional Research Service, based on federal and state minimum wage rates, federal rules for EIC and food stamps, and state rules for TANF.

Notes:

[a]The 2003 poverty guideline for a family of three was $15,260 in the 48 contiguous states and the District of Columbia ($19,070 in Alaska and $17,550 in Hawaii).

[b]Earnings net of 7.65 percent payroll tax (for Old-Age, Survivors, and Disability Insurance–Social Security).

[c]These states have their own earned income credits, but they are not shown in this table. In all but one of these states, the credit is calculated as a percent of the Federal EIC, ranging from 5 to 50 percent of the federal credit.

minimum wage. The example is for the thirteenth month of employment because some states reduce or terminate TANF benefits after the twelfth month. Net earnings for family heads vary by state, depending on state tax rules, and, in some cases, differences in the minimum wage. EITC grants reflect net earnings, while TANF benefits are governed by state decisions about the level of support provided this type of family. Food stamp eligibility is based on the total net earnings of the family, not counting the EITC grant. Because of income disregards and the EITC, the combined cash and food stamp benefits of these families is much better than it would be if they were unemployed. Still, in almost all the states the family's combined benefits leave it below the poverty level, or only modestly above poverty. The financial situation of families is improved by the combination of benefits, but families are economically marginal, highly vulnerable, and living far below median income levels in American society.

Table 7.7 shows the composition of AFDC/TANF families between 1969 and 2001. One change over time is clear. The number of recipients in TANF families has declined quite significantly over time. A major reason is that the number of adults in TANF families, single or plural, has declined. A large percentage of all families are now children-only families, including over 37 percent of all families in 2001. These are families in which grandparents, relatives, or other adults have custody of minor children who qualify for TANF. Additionally, in all TANF households, the average number of children in the family is only one or two, significantly fewer than in the late 1960s. Last, it should be noted that only a very small percentage of all TANF families are headed by teenagers. In 2001 only 2.3 percent of all TANF families had a teenage head.

Food Stamps

Established on a pilot basis in 1964 and expanded nationwide in 1974, the food stamp program has become one of the nation's most important welfare programs. The program is designed to help low-income households purchase a nutritionally adequate diet. Participating families are expected to contribute 30 percent of countable income to food purchases. Food stamps are intended to make up the difference between the family's contribution and the estimated cost of an adequate low-cost, nutritious diet. The maximum food stamp benefit varies by family size and is based on the Thrifty Food Plan, a diet designed by the Department of Agricul-

Table 7.7

Composition of AFDC/TANF Families, 1969–2001

	1969	1979	1988	1994	1996	1998	2001
Number of family members	4.0	3.0	3.0	2.8	2.8	2.8	2.6
Number of adult recipients (percent of all AFDC/TANF families)[a]							
One adult	78.4	78.9	81.2	74.4	70.7	68.7	59.3
Two adults or more	11.9	6.2	9.2	8.3	7.7	7.4	3.5
No adults	9.6	14.9	9.6	17.3	21.5	24.0	37.2
Number of child recipients (percent of all AFDC/TANF families)[b]							
One child	26.7	42.5	43.2	44.8	45.9	44	45.8
Two children	23.1	28.0	30.7	30.0	29.9	29.7	29.1
Three children	17.6	15.5	16.1	15.6	15.0	15.7	15.1
Four or more children	32.6	13.9	10.7	9.6	9.2	10.6	10.1
Age of youngest child (percent of all AFDC/TANF families)[b]							
Less than 6 years old	NA	56.5	60.6	62.7	60.0	57.3	54.1
Six years old and older	NA	43.5	39.4	37.3	39	42.7	45.8
Average age of adult recipients	33.1[d]	28.7[d]	27.0[d]	30.8	31.1	31.3	31.3
Teen parents (percent of all AFDC/TANF families)	NA	2.2	2.2	2.4	1.9	1.6	2.3
Households containing member who does not receive AFDC/TANF							
Percent of AFDC/TANF families in households with nonrecipients	33.1	40.2	36.8	46.4[e]	50.0[e]	NA	38.6[f]

Source: Congressional Research Service (2004), table 7-29.

Notes:

[a] 1969 data for May; 1979 for March; all other data for fiscal years.

[b] 1988 tabulations exclude Utah, West Virginia, Wisconsin, Puerto Rico, and the Virgin Islands because HHS concluded that data on no-adult families for these states were unreliable.

[c] Rhode Island was excluded from 1994–98 tabulations of the percentage of families with a given number of child recipients because 1998 data were found unreliable.

[d] Median ages of mother.

[e] This item is from the HHS series of studies on characteristics of AFDC families.

[f] Percent of all adults in the household who are nonrecipients.

NA = Not available.

ture. A family with no countable income receives the maximum food stamp benefit, while a household with countable income receives a lesser amount based on a 30–cent reduction in the maximum benefit for each counted dollar of income.

Benefits are available to most households who meet income and asset standards. Households in which all members of the family are eligible for TANF, SSI, and state general assistance are normally automatically qualified for food stamps. Most noncitizens are barred from the program, along with strikers (unless eligible before the strike), most post–secondary students, most persons living in institutional settings, and anyone found guilty of committing fraud against the program or failing to comply with any program rules.

Generally, the food stamp program is administered by the same state welfare agency that runs TANF and Medicaid programs. These agencies screen applicants for eligibility, determine benefit levels, and issue food stamps. The most common form of transfer is an EBT, an electronic benefit debit card. In a few jurisdictions recipients are still given coupons redeemable at approved food stores. Generally, food stamps can only be used to purchase food. They may not be used to purchase non-food products such as soap, paper goods, tobacco, alcohol, or prepared foods intended for immediate consumption. There are a few exceptions, including seeds and plants to grow vegetables for consumption, and some prepared meals for elderly and handicapped recipients.

Households become eligible for food stamps either by qualifying for TANF, SSI, or state general assistance, or by low monthly cash income. In recognition that not all income is available for food consumption, a household's counted (or net) income is determined by use of some standard deductions. These deductions include a standard deduction of $134 a month for households of one to four persons, $149 for five-person households, and $171 for households of six or more persons. Twenty percent of earned income is deducted, and deductions are also allowed for child-support payments, child care, high shelter costs, and, in the case of elderly or handicapped applicants, some out-of-pocket medical expenses. Net income cannot exceed the poverty level for the household. Except for households with an elderly or handicapped person, the gross income of the family cannot exceed 130 percent of the poverty line. In 2004, the net monthly income limit of a three-person family was $1,272; four-person, $1,534; and five-person, $1,795. Households without an elderly member cannot have liquid assets above $2,000. The asset level for households with an elderly member is set at $3,000. The fair market value of a car above $4,650 is counted as a liquid asset.

There are work requirements for able-bodied adult recipients of food stamps. Recipients are required to register for work, accept any suitable job offered, fulfill any required job training or job search obligations, and not quit a job without good cause or reduce their work hours below thirty hours a week. If the family head fails to comply with these requirements, states have the authority to suspend the family for up to 180 days. Disqualification periods vary depending on the number of violations. If the family head is required to participate in employment or training, she or he cannot be required to work more than the minimum wage equivalent of the household benefit.

PRWORA allows the states to design experimental programs that might improve the chance that recipients will become established in the job market. Some states "cash out" food stamp benefits for the elderly, SSI recipients, and households that are part of state welfare reform efforts. Additionally, states may use food stamps as a wage supplement, and states can "cash out" benefits to working families to help them escape welfare. Some states have established workfare programs in which recipients must accept employment or training in return for food stamps.

The food stamp program is a federal program with the vast majority of costs paid by the federal government. States pay about half the administrative costs, which were about $1.7 billion in 2002 (Congressional Research Service, 2004, table 15-4). As Figure 7.7 shows, 6.7 percent of the population—about 19 million persons—received food stamps in 2002. The percentage of the population receiving food stamps has declined quite significantly since 1999. In 1994, 10.4 percent of the population—about 28 million people—received food stamps. Additionally, there has been a significant reduction in the percentage of all the poor receiving food stamps. In 2002, the percentage was 55.2 percent. In the early 1990s, on average about 70 percent of the poor received food stamps.

The food stamp program was implemented nationwide in 1974. It was a fairly large program from the beginning, serving some 13 million people a month in 1974. The program grew rather rapidly, exceeding 20 million recipients by 1980, and reaching levels that exceeded 28 million recipients by the early 1990s. Program costs also escalated over time, rising to over $25 billion in 1994. Costs and recipients have declined

Figure 7.7   **Food Stamp Participation Rates in the United States,
1975–2002** (selected years)

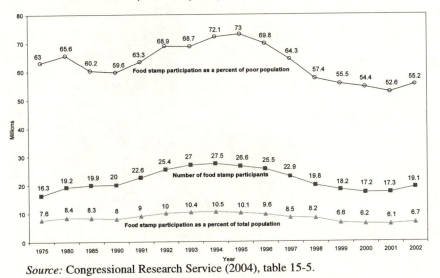

Source: Congressional Research Service (2004), table 15-5.

since the passage of PRWORA. In 2002 the average monthly per-person benefit was $79.60, with an average of $452 for a family of four. Recipient benefits are rather modest, but as Table 7.6 shows, when food stamp benefits are added to TANF and other benefits, the overall purchasing power of families is considerably enhanced.

Medicaid

The companion program to TANF and food stamps is the Medicaid program. Added by amendment in 1965 to the Social Security Act, Medicaid has become the second most expensive social welfare program. Only Social Security cost more. Each state runs its own Medicaid program, within restrictions established by federal guidelines. Costs are shared by the federal and state governments. The federal government's contribution is based on a formula that is adjusted yearly. The federal payment rate is inversely related to the per capita income of the state, ranging from 50 to 83 percent of all costs. The flexibility allowed states means that there is substantial variation among them in coverage and payment levels for services. Medicaid is an extremely complicated program that provides medical assistance to targeted low-income groups of people

Figure 7.8   **Medicaid Enrollees by Basis of Eligibility, FY 2002**

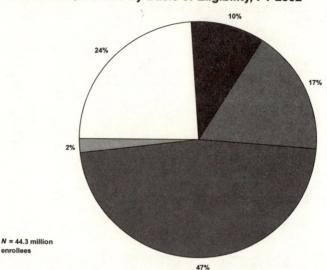

N = 44.3 million
enrollees

Source: Congressional Research Service (2004), table 15-1.

who are aged, blind, or disabled, almost all TANF recipients, some pregnant women and their children, other low-income children, and special
groups identified by legislation. In 2000, there were 44.3 million people
enrolled in Medicaid. Only about 40 percent of those individuals living
in poverty were covered, while many of those receiving assistance were
above the poverty line (Congressional Research Service, 2004, 15–31).
Figure 7.8 shows Medicaid enrollees in 2002 by basis of eligibility. These
data show that most Medicaid enrollees are nondisabled children and
adults (about 73 percent). Ten percent of enrollees are sixty-five years
of age or older, while 17 percent are blind and/or disabled.

TANF recipients automatically qualify for Medicaid. To encourage
TANF family heads to work or leave welfare for employment, Medicaid
is not immediately terminated by employment-related earnings or departure for employment. States are required to provide transitional assistance
to families made ineligible for Medicaid because of employment or earned
income. Depending on income and enrollment, states must provide full or
partial coverage for six to twelve months. States may opt to extend coverage beyond the required time period as part of their welfare reform plan.
States are also required to continue to serve individuals who would have
been qualified for AFDC in July of 1996, even if they do not qualify for

TANF. States are permitted to deny or cease assistance to low-income nonpregnant adults and heads of households who do not comply with work rules, but their enrolled children cannot be terminated.

In the late 1980s and early 1990s Congress passed a number of acts that gradually extended Medicaid to an increasing percentage of all low-income pregnant women and children. States are required to provide medical services to all pregnant women and to children under age six with family incomes below 133 percent of the poverty threshold. The mothers receive services related only to pregnancy or complications of pregnancy, while the children receive full Medicaid coverage. Since 1991 states have been required to provide services to all children under age nineteen who were born after September 30, 1983, if their family income is below 100 percent of the poverty level. States also have the option of providing services to pregnant women and infants under the age of one if the family income is no more than 185 percent of the poverty level.

Under federal rules states may opt to cover other groups with incomes above 185 percent of the poverty level, and some have chosen to do so. Normally, SSI recipients qualify for Medicaid. States may also provide Medicaid to individuals who are not receiving SSI, but instead are receiving state-only supplementary cash benefits. States have the additional option of providing Medicaid to disabled SSI recipients with incomes up to 250 percent of the poverty level. These recipients can "buy into" Medicaid by paying a sliding scale fee based on their income.

States are required to provide some Medicaid coverage to "qualified Medicare beneficiaries" (QMBs). These Medicare recipients are aged and disabled persons with incomes below 100 percent of the poverty level. States must pay Medicare part B premiums and often part A premiums for QMBs, as well as required Medicare coinsurance and deductibles. If individuals would qualify to be a QMB except for the fact that their income is between 100 and 135 percent of the poverty level, the state must pay part B premiums for them. States have the option of providing full Medicaid benefits to qualified QMBs rather than just Medicare premiums and cost sharing. States are also required to pay part A premiums for individuals who formerly received Social Security disability and Medicare and have incomes below 200 percent of the poverty level.

The law gives the states the discretion of setting a different Medicaid income limit for institutionalized persons. The income cutoff can be set at 300 percent of maximum SSI benefits for a person who is living at home. States may also provide Medicaid to individuals who would qualify for SSI if they were not institutionalized. Likewise, states may provide Medicaid to individuals who would qualify for benefits if they were institutionalized. This includes children being cared for at home, persons who are ventilator-dependent, and persons receiving hospice care. Forty states and several jurisdictions provide Medicaid services to the "medically needy." These are low-income families with limited resources who have incomes above 100 percent of the poverty level, but below a maximum of 133 percent. If a state covers any medically needy citizens, children under eighteen and pregnant women who meet income and asset requirements must be covered.

The medical services that states must provide to benefit eligible groups is comprehensive. States must provide inpatient and outpatient hospital services, physician services, nursing facilities for those over age twenty-one, home health services, early and periodic screening, diagnosis and treatment for those under age twenty-one, and family planning. States may cover other services including drugs, eyeglasses, and psychiatric care for individuals under twenty-one and over sixty-five. States have considerable discretion in the services provided to the medically needy, but if they cover any groups, they must cover children and prenatal and delivery services for pregnant women. If the state covers institutional care for any needy group, it must also provide ambulatory services for this group.

To broaden services while dealing with the very high costs of Medicaid, states are increasingly turning to managed care systems. Under managed care, providers agree to offer a contracted range of services for a fixed cost. The Balanced Budget Act of 1997 allows states more flexibility in enrolling most of their Medicaid beneficiaries in managed care systems. States now have the option of contracting with managed care organizations serving only Medicaid beneficiaries and to "lock" recipients into the same plan for up to twelve months. This new law also attempts to safeguard the quality of care provided under managed care. By 2002 about 58 percent of all Medicaid recipients were enrolled in a managed care system.

State Children's Health Insurance Program

The Balanced Budget Act of 1997 established the State Children's Health Insurance Program (SCHIP). This program offers federal matching funds to states and territories to provide medical assistance to low-income children. States may provide assistance to children under nineteen if their family's income is above the state's Medicaid eligibility standard but less than 200 percent of the poverty level. If the state was using a maximum income level that was above 200 percent before the passage of SCHIP, they may increase the SCHIP level by an additional 50 percentage points. Since states have a great deal of discretion in setting eligibility standards under SCHIP, the percentage of low-income children served varies greatly by state. In 2002, twenty-four states and the District of Columbia set the income limit at 200 percent, thirteen exceeded 200 percent, and another thirteen set maximum income levels below 200 percent (Congressional Research Service, 2004, 15–84).

SCHIP enrollments have grown quite rapidly since the program was authorized. In 1999 nearly 1 million children were enrolled. In 2002 over 5 million children received medical assistance under SCHIP. States have the option of enrolling SCHIP children in Medicaid, creating a separate program for them, or a combination of the two. Most states have created a separate program that provides comprehensive services to the youngest enrollees. In some states, a less comprehensive set of services is offered to older children.

Supplemental Security Income

The Supplemental Security Income (SSI) program was passed by Congress in 1972 and became effective in 1974. SSI is a guaranteed income program for the aged, disabled, and blind. The program was designed to establish a national minimum level of income for this select group of Americans. It is a guaranteed income program of last resort. That is, the aged, disabled, and blind are guaranteed a certain level of monthly income. If they have less income than the guaranteed amount, SSI pays the difference.

SSI has become a very important welfare program. It not only provides almost 7 million recipients a month with cash benefits, but its recipients are also frequently enrolled in Medicaid and other welfare programs such as food stamps. Table 7.8 provides an overview of the program. SSI has grown from about 4 million recipients in 1974 to some 6.8 million in 2002. In 2002 the program cost over $34 billion, with most of the costs associated with assistance to the disabled.

The income level guaranteed to SSI recipients is adjusted yearly. In 2002, for example, the guaranteed income level for a single individual was $545, and $817 for a couple. As Table 7.8 shows, the average recipi-

Table 7.8

Supplemental Security Income Summary, 1974–2002 (selected years)

Item	1974	1978	1980	1984	1988	1992	1994	1996	1998	2000	2002
Recipients[a]											
Aged	2,285,909	1,967,900	1,807,776	1,530,289	1,433,420	1,471,022	1,465,905	1,412,632	1,331,782	1,289,339	1,251,528
Blind	74,616	77,135	78,401	80,524	82,864	85,400	84,911	82,137	80,243	78,511	77,568
Disabled	1,635,539	2,171,890	2,255,840	2,418,522	2,947,585	4,009,767	4,744,470	5,118,949	5,154,044	5,233,836	5,458,671
Total	3,996,064	4,216,925	4,142,017	4,029,333	4,463,869	5,566,189	6,295,786	6,613,718	6,566,069	6,601,686	6,787,857
Annual payments (in millions of current dollars)											
Federal benefits	3,833	4,881	5,866	8,281	10,734	18,247	22,175	25,265	26,405	27,290	29,899
Federally administered State supplementation	1,264	1,491	1,848	1,792	2,671	3,435	3,116	2,988	3,003	3,381	3,820
State administered State supplementation	149	180	226	299	381	556	579	539	808	892	911
Total	5,246	6,552	7,940	10,372	13,768	22,238	25,870	28,252	30,216	31,564	34,630
Annual payments (in millions of 2002 dollars)	19,937	18,566	18,074	18,026	21,102	28,518	31,338	32,406	33,114	33,116	34,630
Maximum monthly federal benefits											
Individuals	140	177.8	208.2	314	354	422	446	470	494	513	545
Couples	210	266.7	357	472	532	633	687	705	741	769	817

Average federal SSI payments											
All recipients	95.11	111.98	143.35	196.16	227.49	329.74	325.26	339.24	359.45	378.82	407.42
Aged individuals	78.48	91.22	112.45	143.24	159.36	195.86	211.55	227.42	271.66	292.67	322.26
Aged couples	93.02	120.48	157.56	221.98	273.18	448.61	505.64	563.39	611	665.6	730.49
Percent of recipients with other income											
Social Security benefits	52.7	51.7	51	49.6	47.8	41.3	39.1	37	36.5	36.1	35.5
Other unearned income	10.5	11.5	11	11.2	12.4	14.5	13.1	12.4	11.7	11.7	11.7
Earnings	2.8	3.1	3.2	3.5	4.4	4.4	4.2	4.4	4.5	4.4	4.1
Average amount of											
Social Security benefits	130.01	156.5	196.94	250.61	286.49	335.72	345.2	382.56	374.6	378.82	407.42
Other unearned income	61.1	66.93	74.35	84.56	85.92	91.96	101.13	112.46	129.9	292.67	322.26
Earnings	80	99.32	106.95	126.47	173.09	207.55	225.01	258.42	282.52	665.6	730.49
Poverty thresholds (age 65 and over)											
Individuals	2,364	3,127	3,949	4,979	5,674	6,729	7,108	7,525	7,818	8,259	8,628
Couples	2,982	3,944	4,983	6,282	7,158	8,489	8,967	9,491	9,862	10,414	10,874
Federal Benefit as a percent of poverty											
Individuals	74.1	72.7	72.3	75.6	74.9	75.3	75.3	75	75.8	74.5	75.8
Couples	88.1	86.4	86	90.2	89.2	89.5	89.5	89.1	90.2	88.6	90.2

Source: Congressional Research Service (2004), table 3-1.

Note: [a]December data. Includes federal SSI and federally administered state supplements.

ent received less than the maximum payment because they had income from other sources. The average recipient in 2002 received $407.42. Most recipients have income of some type, often from Social Security, general assistance, and even modest earnings. In 2002, for example, 35.5 percent of SSI recipients were receiving Social Security benefits, about 12 percent had other unearned income, and 4.1 percent had earnings. Forty-three states subsidize the benefits of some SSI recipients, mostly those with high shelter costs.

SSI benefits generally push recipients closer to the poverty threshold than do TANF benefits. As Table 7.8 shows, in 2002 the SSI benefit rate for an individual was 75.8 percent of the poverty threshold, while it was 90.2 percent of the poverty level for a couple.

The Earned Income Tax Credit

The last major program that is important to understanding the combination of benefits available to assist the poor in escaping poverty is the Earned Income Tax Credit (EITC). This program is designed to make work pay better for low-wage earners (Meyer and Rosenbaum, 2001; Ellwood, 2000). Essentially, the EITC subsidizes the wages of targeted adults who work but earn low wages. As Table 7.9 shows, the program has grown from providing benefits to 6.2 million families in 1975 to assisting 19.3 million families in 2003. The number of recipients has been rather static since 1994, but the costs of the program have risen. The costs and coverage of the program were modest until Congress indexed it for inflation in 1987, and expanded its coverage in 1990, 1993, and 2001. In 2003, almost $31 billion was refunded to taxpayers. The average qualifying family in 2003 received $1,784. The EITC lifted 4.9 million people, including 2.7 million children, above the poverty level in 2002. No other federal or state program is this effective in moving children above the poverty line (Llobrera and Zahradnik, 2004, 1).

The EITC is also very effective in encouraging employment (Beamer, 2005). The EITC is designed both to subsidize low-wage workers and to encourage them to earn as much as possible. As Table 7.10 shows, childless adults and couples can qualify for a modest refundable tax credit, and there are much more generous programs for single- or dual-parent families with one or more children. The refundable credit is higher for two-parent families when they file a joint return.

Table 7.9

Earned Income Credit: Number of Recipients and Amount of Credit, 1975–2003

Year	Number of recipient families (thousands)	Total amount of credit (millions)	Refunded portion of credit (millions)	Average credit per family
1975	6,215	1,250	900	201
1976	6,473	1,295	890	200
1977	5,627	1,127	880	200
1978	5,192	1,048	801	202
1979	7,135	2,052	1,395	288
1980	6,954	1,986	1,370	286
1981	6,717	1,912	1,278	285
1982	6,395	1,775	1,222	278
1983	7,368	1,795	1,289	224
1984	6,376	1,638	1,162	257
1985	7,432	2,088	1,499	281
1986	7,156	2,009	1,479	281
1987	8,738	3,391	2,930	450
1988	11,148	5,896	4,257	529
1989	11,696	6,595	4,636	564
1990	12,542	7,542	5,266	601
1991	13,665	11,105	8,183	813
1992	14,097	13,028	9,959	924
1993	15,117	15,537	12,028	1,028
1994	19,017	21,105	16,598	1,110
1995	19,334	25,956	20,829	1,342
1996	19,464	28,825	23,157	1,481
1997	19,391	30,389	24,396	1,567
1998	20,273	32,340	27,175	1,595
1999	19,259	31,901	27,604	1,656
2000	19,277	32,296	27,803	1,675
2001	19,593	33,376	29,043	1,704
2002	19,795	35,784	31,769	1,808
2003	19,284	34,412	30,869	1,784

Source: Congressional Research Service (2004), table 13-1.

Below we provide an example of how the EITC works using the benefit levels that a two-parent family with two children would receive if the parents filed jointly. There are three earning levels for this type of family: (1) a base with a subsidy rate, (2) a plateau income range where the family would receive the maximum refundable credit, and (3) a phase-out range in which benefits would be reduced as income rises. Three examples illustrate how the EITC works at each earning level.

A Base With a Subsidy Rate

A family with two children earns less than the established base for their family size. In 2003 the base for a family with two children was $10,510 (see Table 7.10). For earnings below the base, the family receives a refundable credit equal to 40 percent of earnings. For example, if this family earned $6,000, they would have received a credit worth $2,400 (0.40 x $6,000 = $2,400). If the family owed no federal taxes (which would almost always be the case at the lowest income levels), it would receive this $2,400 in the form of a check from the federal government. This would have raised this family's total income to $8,400. The EITC credit check can be in a lump sum at the end of the tax year, or it can be prorated and paid out in monthly payments.

A Plateau

A family with two children earns above the base, but within the plateau range. In 2003 the base was $10,510 with a phase-out range beginning at $13,730. Earnings that fall within this range received a standard subsidy of $4,204. Thus, a worker with two children earning $12,000 in 2003 would have had a total income of $16,204 ($12,000 plus $4,204).

A Phase-Out Range

A worker with two children has earnings within the phase-out range. In 2003 this range started at $14,730 and ended at $34,692. The maximum tax credit of $4,204 is reduced by 21.06 cents for every dollar earned above $14,730. If earnings reached or exceeded $34,692, the credit would have been exhausted. Thus, if a worker earned $20,000, she/he would have $5,270 in income above the beginning of the phase-out range. These dollars would be taxed at the 21.06 rate (0.2106 x $5,270 = $1,109.86), reducing the maximum credit by $1,109.86. Thus this worker would have received a credit of $4,160.14, yielding a total income of $24,160 ($20,000 plus $4,160).

The EITC significantly increases the value of a low-wage job to a worker. The effect of the EITC on a minimum-wage job, for example, is substantial. In 2003 a worker with two children earning the minimum wage would have a yearly income of $10,712 ($5.15 x 40 hours x 52

Table 7.10

Earned Income Credit Parameters, 2003

Credit	Percent credit rate	Minimum income for maximum credit	Maximum credit	Percent phaseout rate	Phaseout range				
					Non–Joint filters		Joint filters		
					Beginning income	Ending income	Beginning income	Ending income	
No children	7.65	4,990	382	7.65	6,240	11,230	7,240	12,230	
One child	34	7,490	2,547	15.98	13,730	29,666	14,730	30,666	
Two children	40	10,510	4,204	21.06	13,730	33,692	14,730	34,692	

Source: Congressional Research Service (2004), table 12-13.

weeks = $10,712). The EITC would provide another $4,204, yielding a total yearly income of $14,916. With the EITC subsidy, the worker's $5.15 an hour job is turned into a job that paid $7.17 an hour, a considerable improvement (see Figure 8.10).

Conclusions

The American welfare system that was founded by the Social Security Act of 1935 developed quite slowly during its first thirty years, but grew dramatically over the next three decades. The unexpected growth in the number of families headed by single mothers fueled much of this growth, as did the nation's decision to provide better assistance to the aged, disabled, and blind, and to extend medical care to millions of low-income and poor Americans.

By the early 1990s the combined cost of welfare programs at the federal and state level was considerably in excess of $300 billion. These programs provided valuable assistance to millions of Americans, but increasingly the core cash assistance program was judged to be seriously flawed. AFDC, the nation's major cash-welfare program, failed to play a meaningful role in preventing poverty or in helping those who received benefits, even over long periods, to escape poverty. The result was a growing class of poor Americans who received welfare benefits for long periods with little or no attachment to the employment market.

AFDC's flaws led to major reforms in 1996. TANF interacting with other welfare programs has the goal of "ending welfare as we know it" by moving families headed by able-bodied adults off welfare and into the employment market. To make work a more viable option, PRWORA gives states the flexibility and much of the funding required to provide support services such as child care, job search and job training, transportation assistance, and many other services to help family heads become established in the job market. In the next chapter, we will evaluate the evidence of the impact of these programs.

8

The Impact of Welfare Reform

In Chapter 5 we reviewed the history of the welfare reform movement over the last thirty years and analyzed how the various forces for reform resulted in the passage of the Personal Responsibility and Work Opportunity Reconciliation Act (PRWORA) of 1996. We also examined the underlying philosophy and major provisions of this act. In Chapter 6 we examined how the states have opted to design their new welfare systems within the rather liberal boundaries allowed by PRWORA. In this chapter we turn to an examination of the impact of PRWORA. We review the research on how well those who have left welfare, those diverted from welfare, and those low-income families that might fall into the welfare system are faring. The outcomes of the major provisions of PRWORA, along with legislation passed to supplement or support the reform legislation, are evaluated in depth.

Impact on Welfare Rolls

Regardless of the decisions that states have made about how to design their new welfare plans, the debates and changes that have taken place since the early 1990s in state welfare systems have resulted in significant declines in welfare rolls in all states, and truly major declines in most states. In 1993 the Aid to Families with Dependent Children (AFDC) rolls contained 14.2 million recipients, or 4.5 percent of the population. By March of 2002 Temporary Assistance to Needy Children (TANF) enrollment had shrunk to 5.2 million recipients, or about 1.8 percent of the population. This represented a decline in recipients between 1993 and March 2002 of about 64 percent. As Figure 8.1 shows, the percentage of the population receiving TANF in 2002 was as low as the rates in the early 1960s, and far below the rates during the 1970s, 1980s, and almost all of the 1990s (Bell, 2001; Blank, 2001; Bartik and Eberts, 1999).

Figure 8.1   **Percentage of Population Receiving Temporary Assistance for Needy Families (TANF), 1960–2002**

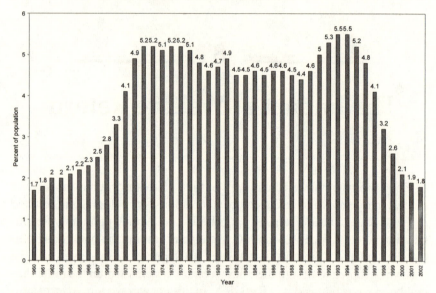

Source: Department of Health and Human Services (2004a). Data can be found at www.acf.hhs.gov/news/stats/6097rf.htm. Data for 2002 are through March 2002.

Figure 8.2 shows the declines in the TANF caseloads in each state and the District of Columbia from 1996 through 2001. The decline in most states has been very high. Only eight states have had a decrease below 40 percent. Thirty-five states had a decline of 40 to 70 percent, and eight states had a drop greater than 70 percent. Most of the states have cut their welfare rolls by at least half.

Why Have the Rolls Dropped So Substantially?

There are several reasons why the rolls have dropped so fast (Mead, 2000; Ziliak et al., 2000; Figlio and Ziliak, 1999). First, under "Work First" most adult recipients are required to move into the job market very quickly. Second, some states make it very difficult for applicants to enter the rolls. Often they require a job search before potential recipients can apply for welfare, and many states now simply deny assistance to families that would have previously qualified for cash welfare. Obvious examples include state laws that reject mothers who cannot or will not identify the father(s) of

Figure 8.2 **U.S. Average Monthly AFDC/TANF Recipients, FY 1996–2001: Percent Decrease** (fifty states and DC)

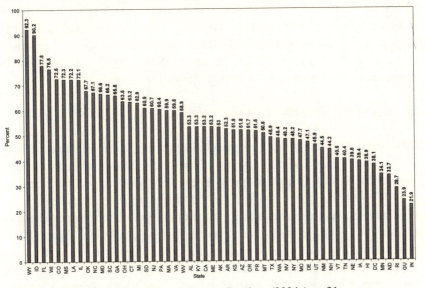

Source: Department of Health and Human Services (2004a), p. 31.
Note: During this period, 7.2 million people left the rolls.

their children, mothers who cannot prove that they have been looking for a job, or mothers who are judged to have family members they can rely on for support. Third, many states use diversion programs to give potential recipients assistance of some type in return for an agreement that they will not apply. Last, some recipients have sized up the new law in their state and decided on their own to leave the rolls. These recipients have often cited objections to work, job search, or education requirements, or they may have concluded that they can find a better job on their own. Some of these recipients may have left the rolls because they were working off the books and, therefore, not really available for job training or placement. Other recipients simply are determined not to be coached, coerced, or supervised in any fashion (Pavetti et al., 1996).

As detailed below, many recipients have left the rolls because they have been sanctioned. One study found that 38 percent of those who left welfare during one three-month period in 1997 did so because of state sanctions. The new law substantially expands the grounds for sanctioning recipients, and many states have used sanctions to remove hard-to-serve clients (Sherman et al., 1998; Kaplan, 1999; Holcomb and Ratcliffe, 1998). Of those recipients forced off the rolls for noncompliance, many return to the rolls as soon as they are eligible. Last, some legal immigrants may have left the rolls or avoided them because they mistakenly believe that welfare receipt could jeopardize their chances of becoming citizens or result in their being deported. Some legal immigrants also may have illegal immigrants in their families.

Impact of the Reforms on Employment

PRWORA has had a major impact on the employment rates of both welfare recipients and on those who have left welfare (Bryner and Martin, 2005). Since most states provide employment support services under PRWORA to some low-income family heads who are not receiving cash welfare, it may have also increased employment among these adults. Under TANF guidelines, states have relied primarily on "Work First" programs that require job search and prompt employment. States have supported employment through services such as child care, and by letting recipients keep some cash welfare for specified periods after they become employed. The data supplied by the states and numerous research projects have shown that programs mandating job search results in increased employment and reductions in welfare use.

Figure 8.3 shows the work participation rates of welfare recipients from 1992 to 2001. Under AFDC, few welfare recipients were employed. AFDC did not provide even modestly adequate support for mothers who wanted to work, and benefit reduction rates meant that work generally resulted in only modest gains in real income in most states and in no gains in a few states. In 1992 only 6.6 percent of AFDC recipients were employed, and most of them were employed part time. The emphasis of TANF on employment has significantly increased the work activities of recipients. As Chapters 6 and 7 detailed, the percentage of TANF recipients who are required to engage in work activities increases by year. Figure 8.3 shows the percentage of recipients who were engaged in work activities after the passage of PRWORA in 1996. The overall rate of work participation increased from 30.7 percent in 1997 to 38.3 percent in 1999, declined to 34.0 percent in 2000, and rose slightly to 34.4 percent in 2001. The combination of rising standards and a weakened economy seems to have combined to lower the overall employment rate in 2001. The picture is

Figure 8.3 **AFDC/TANF Work Participation Rates, FY 1992–2001**

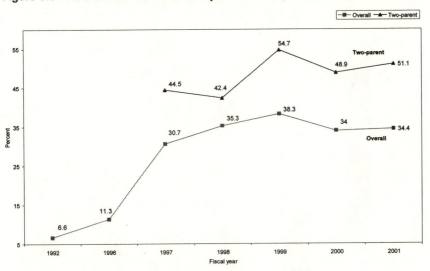

Source: Department of Health and Human Services, Administration for Children and Families, TANF, 5th Annual Report to Congress, 2003, figure 1.

similar for two-parent families, with a decline in 2000, followed by a modest recovery in 2001.

PRWORA allows states to meet employment standards in several ways. Clients may be employed, or engaged in job search, community work experience, or several types of education or training. Figure 8.4 shows the work activities of recipients in 2001. The categories are not mutually exclusive because some recipients are involved in more than one type of activity. Most of the recipients engaged in work activities were employed (59.5 percent), while another 11.0 percent were engaged in community and/or work experience programs. The other recipients were primarily engaged in education and training programs.

Impact on Employment of Low-Income Adults

PRWORA has impacted the employment market for low-income adults in a couple of other ways, but the impact is difficult to measure precisely (Bartik, 2000). First, PRWORA has limited, diverted, and even closed welfare options for many family heads, leaving them with no alternative but to seek employment. In turn, PRWORA provides employment support services to

Figure 8.4   **Weekly Work Activities of All Adult TANF Recipients, FY 2001**

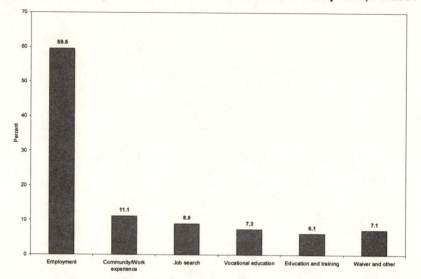

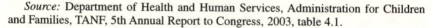

Source: Department of Health and Human Services, Administration for Children and Families, TANF, 5th Annual Report to Congress, 2003, table 4.1.

family heads and some single adults that did not exist before, making it easier for them to work. Individuals and families no longer have to be on welfare to qualify for Medicaid, and all the states provide support services such as child care, job training, and education to some individuals and families who suffer low incomes, even if they are not living below the poverty line. If these policies are having an impact, employment, particularly among women, should have accelerated since the mid-1990s.

Figure 8.5 shows the employment rate among women by marital status and presence and age of children since 1980. In 2002 the rate of employment was high for each of the groups shown, with particularly high rates for single women with and without children, and married women with children. The highest rate of employment is for single women with children under the age of six. For all household types, the rate of employment increased between 1980 and 2002. The highest rates of increase have been for single women with children under six (an increase of 61 percent) and single women without children (45 percent increase). Single women with children six to seventeen increased their rate of employment by about 21 percent. The fact that women who have a low probability of being involved with welfare (single women and married women with no children)

Figure 8.5   **Employment Status of Women by Marital Status and Presence and Age of Children, 1980–2002**

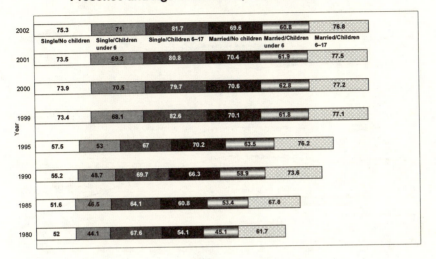

Source: Bureau of Labor Statistics, 2004, Bulletin 2307.

increased their rate of employment over time suggests that there are many forces at play. Still, those groups of women most likely to be involved with and impacted by welfare increased their rate of employment quite substantially. This is particularly true of single women with children under six. This suggests that PRWORA is doing exactly what its authors intended. It is moving women, especially single mothers, away from the welfare system and into the job market.

Figure 8.6 shows that as single women have joined the workforce, their rate of poverty and their use of welfare have declined. The percentage of single mothers who worked at any time during the year rose from 67 percent in 1992 to 83 percent in 2001. Over the same period, the poverty rate of single mothers declined from 45 percent to 32 percent. Cash welfare use also declined, from 35 percent in 1993 to 11 percent in 2001. Figure 8.7 focuses on work and cash welfare use among poor single mothers. These data show a significant increase in employment by poor mothers, increasing from 44 percent in 1992 to 59 percent in 2001. As work increased, there was a dramatic drop in cash welfare receipt. In the late 1980s and early 1990s over 60 percent of poor mothers received cash welfare. By 2001 the percentage was 23 percent. The percentage of poor mothers who received cash welfare and did not work

Figure 8.6 **Welfare, Work, and Poverty Status Among Single Mothers, 1987–2001**

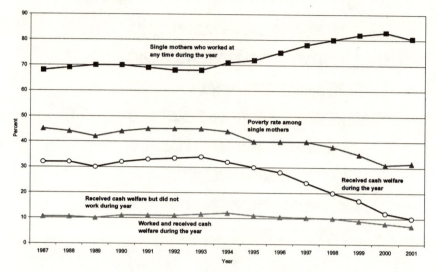

Source: Prepared by the Congressional Research Service, based on analysis of U.S. Census Bureau, March 1988–2002 Current Population Survey data.

Figure 8.7 **Poor Single Mothers, Work and Welfare Status, 1987–2001**

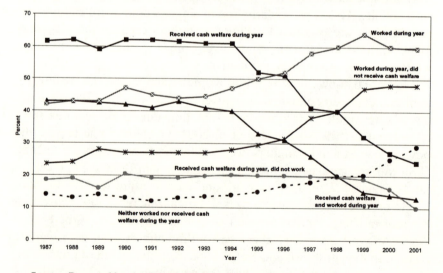

Source: Prepared by the Congressional Research Service, based on analysis of U.S. Census Bureau, March 1988–2002 Current Population Survey data.

dropped from 43 percent in 1991 to 13 percent in 2001. Poor mothers who combined work with cash welfare receipt declined from 20 percent in 1993 to 10 percent in 2001. At least in terms of moving single women into employment and reducing cash welfare, PRWORA is having its intended effect. Overall, poverty among single mothers has also declined, but the data below show that many who escape poverty do so by a very small margin.

Studies of Welfare Leavers

Adults who leave TANF for a sustained period (generally two months or more) are defined as "welfare leavers." Leavers have been monitored in dozens of studies, most of which were funded by the Department of Health and Human Services and/or individual states (Blum and Berrey, 1999; Loprest, 2001; Acs, Loprest, and Roberts, 2001; Acs and Loprest, 2001). Table 8.1 summarizes many of these studies. Findings vary, but there is a rough consistency. The studies document a rather high work rate among single-parent leavers during the first year after welfare exit. About three out of four leavers work during some period in the first year after TANF exit. About three out of five are working at any given point in time (Bloom and Michalopoulos, 2001; Devere, 2001; Brauner and Loprest, 1999). However, only a little more than one-third of all leavers were employed in all four quarters, and about 20 percent show no employment (Martinson, 2000).

Women with low skills, young children, a history of substance abuse or health problems, and those who are victims of domestic violence are the least likely to be employed (Danziger et al., 2000; Zedleweski and Loprest, 2001). Acs, Loprest, and Roberts (2001) found that the best predictors of employment were education and quality of job skills. Not surprisingly, those with the best skills were the most successful in the job market. Lemke, Witt, and Witte (2001) found that when states provide wage subsidies and quality child care, employment rates significantly improve. One study found that cohabitation improves the chances of recipients being employed (Danziger et al., 2002). Most likely this is because two adults can better balance employment and family responsibilities. Holzer, Stoll, and Wissoker (2001) found that employers rate welfare recipients as good or better than other employees. Martinson (2000) found that most employed leavers have no more than two spells

Table 8.1

Welfare Leaver Studies

Study	Employed	Hourly wages	Percent poor
Cancian et al. (1999)	61% to 64% employed two years after welfare exit	$6.50 to $7.50	55/42 after five years
Loprest (1999)	55% to 71%	$6.28 to $8.05	Almost all
Moffit and Roff (2000)	63%/Three surveyed metropolitan areas	$7.50	74
Acs and Loprest (2001)	75%	$7.00 to $8.00	58
Loprest (2001)	50%	$7.72	48
Devere (2001)	55% to 64% within three months of leaving welfare	$5.50 to $8.50	
Danzier (2001)		$7.00	
Richer, Savner, Greenbery (2001)	50% all four quarters	$7.00 to $8.00	50 to 63
Loprest (2003)	Declined from 50% in 1999 to 42% in 2002	$8.06	50
ACS and Loprest (2004)	60%		
Martinson (2000)	About 20% never work among workers, no more than two spells of unemployment		
Holzer, Stoll, Wissoker (2001)	Employer rate welfare recipients as performing as well or better than other employees		
Danziger et al. (2000)			
Zedloweski and Loprest (2001)	Women with health problems, substance abuse, low skills, domestic violence work less		
Lemke, Witt, Witte (2001)	Wage subsidy and child care improve chances of employment		
Johnson (2003)	Quality of job skills best predictor of economic success		
Danziger et al. (2002)	Those who leave for work or combine work and welfare, better off than those who stay on TANF		
Cancian and Meyer (2000)			
Cancian et al. (2002)			
Coulton et al. (2003)	Families heads with younger children less likely to work		
Danziger et al. (2002)	Cohabitation improves the chances of adults being employed		

of unemployment, suggesting that their employment patterns are not too volatile.

Unfortunately, the income of leavers, and their cumulative family income, remain very low, and between one-quarter and one-third of leavers return to TANF within the first year after exit (Harknett and Gennetian, 2001; Haskins, 2001). The majority of employed leavers report that their income is the predominant source of income in the family (Corcoran and Loeb, 1999). The most recent studies find that the mean earnings of employed leavers is about $3,000 per quarter. The income of leavers with sustained employment shows an increase of a few hundred dollars between the first and fourth quarter after exit. Acs, Loprest, and Roberts (2001) reviewed fifteen studies and found that in the fourth quarter after exit the mean income ranged from a high of $3,934 to a low of $2,327. The studies summarized in Table 8.1 generally find that wages of working leavers average between $7 and $8 an hour, and employed leavers work about thirty-five hours a week.

The cumulative income of leaver families from all sources is often either below or just above the poverty line. In four studies funded by the Department of Heath of Human Services (DHHS) that explicitly examined the poverty rate of leaver families, on average over half of all the families lived in poverty (Acs, Loprest, Roberts, 2001, 9). In the studies summarized in Table 8.1, those that addressed the issue found a range of about 50 to near 60 percent of leavers living below the poverty line. Still, the data show that leavers who are employed or combine welfare with work have significantly higher incomes than they did while on welfare (Danziger et al., 2002). Employed leavers, in other words, tend to be financially better off than they were while on welfare, but most remain poor or live just over the poverty line.

Have the job supports built into TANF significantly improved the after-welfare employment and earning potential of welfare leavers? A considerable body of research shows that TANF leavers compared to AFDC leavers are more likely to work, and more likely to work full time, stay employed longer, have better earning power, and use means-tested programs less (Cancian et al., 1999, 1998a, 1998b, 1998c; Pavetti and Acs, 1997; Gritz and MaCurdy, 1991; Cheng, 1995; Burtless, 1995; Harris, 1996; Bane and Ellwood, 1983). TANF leavers are struggling, but they are doing much better than AFDC leavers.

The evidence also suggests that post–1996 reform leavers are doing somewhat better than those recipients who left welfare under waiver programs implemented in the early 1990s. A series of studies suggests marginally better outcomes for the most recent TANF leavers, probably because support services have improved to some extent and the work ethic the reform is based on is becoming more institutionalized and accepted. Meyer and Cancian (1999) and Cancian and Meyer (1998) found that about two-thirds of waiver leavers worked each year, with the proportion working full time year round increasing from 13 percent in year one after exit to 25 percent in year five. Less than 5 percent of the ex-recipients worked full time full year in all five years, but most worked. Among those who worked, annual earnings increased from $6,059 to $9,947 over the five-year period. Poverty rates declined over time, especially when all income in the family (not just the recipient's earnings) was considered. If only the income of the recipient was considered, 79 percent were poor in the first year after exit, declining to 64 percent in the fifth year. However, when all family income was calculated, only 19 percent were poor in all of the first five years, while only 22 percent escaped poverty in all five years. Some 60 percent of former recipients received means-tested benefits in the first year after leaving AFDC, declining to 40 percent in the fifth year. Women who were the most economically successful were better educated, had better job skills, were married, had fewer children, were more consistently employed, and received job promotions.

Are the Food Stamp and Medicaid Programs Playing a Supportive Role?

As PRWORA has lead to reductions in TANF recipients, there has been concern that the supportive role that food stamps and Medicaid play in helping transitioning and low-income families would also decline (Greenstein and Guyer, 2001). Recipient rates for food stamps have always been much lower than qualification rates (Blank and Ruggles, 1996). Some people qualified by income decline to apply; others may not be able to for one reason or another. Potential recipients report that they pass because they do not want to do the paperwork, cannot understand the paperwork, find the thought of using food stamps embarrassing, or cannot get to the application offices (Department of Health and Human Services, 2004a, 13). Figure 8.8 shows enrollment data for the food stamp program since 1975. At its highest rate of usage in 1994, almost 70 percent of qualified recipients received food stamps. As some

Figure 8.8 Percentage of Total Population Receiving Food Stamps, 1975–2004

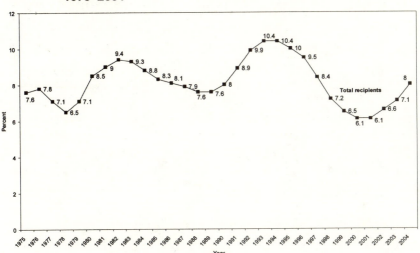

Source: U.S. Department of Agriculture (2004). Characteristics of Food Stamp Households, FY 2001, figure 3, *State of the States*, 2004, table 1.

Note: Figure for 2004 is for August.

feared, after 1994 there was a rather steep decline in food stamp use. Almost half of TANF leaver families did not apply (table IND 4b). However, because of a serious slump in the economy, enrollments for TANF leavers and other qualified families increased considerably from 2002 through 2004. By fall 2004 there were some 6 million more recipients than in 2001. In 2004 about 59 percent of all qualified families received food stamps, slightly higher than the percentage that received assistance in 1997. TANF recipients, as opposed to TANF leavers, have maintained high enrollment rates. In 2001, 81 percent of all TANF recipients received food stamps. Some 74 percent of those leaving TANF in 2001 continued their enrollment. Rates for TANF recipients have not varied much over the last decade (table 10.13).

TANF families also have a very high rate of enrollment in the Medicaid program. In 2001 about 97 percent of all TANF recipients were enrolled in Medicaid. A small percentage of TANF families also received help with housing (7.2 percent in public housing, 12.8 percent in subsidized housing). A very modest percentage (8.8 percent) received subsidized child care (Department of Health and Human Services, 2004a, table 10.13). Figure 8.9 shows enrollment in the Medicaid program and

Figure 8.9   **Medicaid Costs and Recipients, FY 1985–2000**

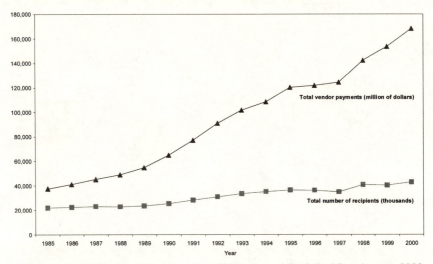

Source: Social Security Administration (2004), Annual Statistical Supplement, 2003, table 8.E1.

expenditures since 1985. The number of Medicaid recipients declined slightly in 1997, but increased again in 1998 and rose to 42.8 million in 2000. The cost of the Medicaid program continues to increase at a rate higher than inflation because the population is aging, more people are being classified as disabled, and because many employees lost their private health-care coverage in the economic downturn that began in 2000. If not for Medicaid coverage, about 1 million adults and 2 million children would have joined the ranks of the uninsured in 2000 (Ku and Broaddus, 2003, 3–4; see Appendix C).

The data show, then, that most TANF recipients and TANF leaver families benefit from food stamps and Medicaid, and some receive benefits from other social welfare programs as well. Figure 8.10 provides examples of how the food stamp and Earned Income Tax Credit (EITC) programs combine to assist low-income earners. The data show that even at minimum wages, a family of three with one worker can escape poverty with thirty-five to forty hours of employment per week. In 2003 if the head of a three-person family worked twenty hours a week at the minimum wage, she/he would earn $5,150 in wages. This family would qualify for $4,452 in food stamps, and receive $2,070 from the EITC program. The combined cash and food stamp benefits for this family

Figure 8.10   **Contributions of Food Stamps and Earned Income Tax Credit (EITC) to Family Economic Security at Different Levels of Minimum-Wage Work, FY 2003**

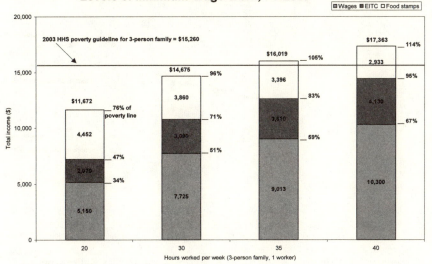

Source: U.S. Department of Agriculture (2004), chart 1.

would be $11,672, about 76 percent of the poverty line for this family. As the family head works more hours a week, food-stamp benefits decline, but EITC benefits increase. At thirty-five hours of work per week the combined benefits barely push the family over the poverty line, and at forty hours per week the family has combined earning and purchasing power that is $2,103 above the poverty line. At thirty-five to forty hours of work per week, the family is not well off, but it escapes poverty and is much better off than it would be on TANF without earnings. The data reviewed on leavers suggest that steady work translates into better wages over time. But the same data suggest that without increased education and/or training, income gains are usually modest.

One last major program that assists some TANF recipients and leavers is the Supplemental Security Income (SSI) program. Notice in Figure 8.11 that the number of SSI recipients reached record levels by the mid-1990s, but declined just after the passage of PRWORA. The reduction in recipients was mostly among children. As Chapter 6 details, PRWORA tightened the definition of childhood handicaps, reducing the number of children who qualified for SSI. Recipiency rates for children declined after 1996, but leveled off in the late 1990s and early 2000s. The number

Figure 8.11   **Percentage of the Total Population Receiving SSI by Age, 1975–2001**

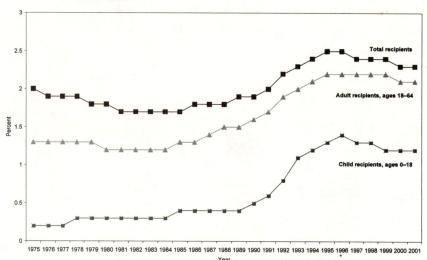

Source: Social Security Administration (2002), Social Security Bulletin, table 4.

of adults aged eighteen to sixty-four qualifying for SSI declined less substantially after 1996, and has remained much higher than rates in the 1970s and 1980s.

Is Child Care Available and Adequate?

The central goal of PRWORA is "supported work." Healthy adults are expected to leave or bypass welfare by entering the job market. Employment is to be made possible by supportive services such as child care, medical coverage, transportation assistance, and other services. Quality child care has always been a major challenge because it is an expensive but critical need of poor and low-income households. PRWORA recognizes the importance of expanding the national inventory of affordable, quality child care (Anderson and Levine, 2000). PRWORA provided two new sources of income that states could use to increase and improve child-care services. PRWORA consolidates four child-care funding programs into one Child Care and Development Fund (CCDF), increases funding for child care, and allows the states the option of transferring funds from the TANF block grant to CCDF. In FY 1996 about 1 million children were being served by existing programs. CCDF funds increased from $2.3 bil-

Figure 8.12   **Federal CCDF Allocations and TANF Used for Child Care, 1992–2001**

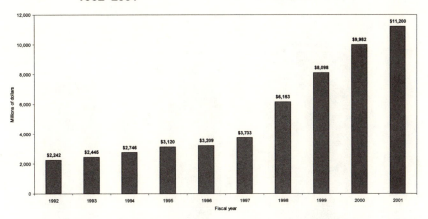

Source: Department of Health and Human Services (2004), Administration for Children and Families, *Child Care and Development Fund*, Report to Congress, 2003, p. 4.
Note: FY 2001 includes SSBG funds spent on child care.

lion in FY 1996 to $4.6 billion in FY 2001. All the states also opted to transfer TANF funds to CCDF. As TANF rolls declined, freeing up money, the states increasingly transferred funds to CCDF, reaching $3.7 billion by FY 2001. Total spending on child care for both poor families and low-income families increased quite dramatically. Figure 8.12 shows the increase in expenditures from 1992 to 2001, an increase from about $2.3 billion to more than $11 billion.

The states used these dollars to increase the number of families served, to lower co-payments, and to fund improvements in the quality of child care. By FY 2003, the number of children being served had increased from 1 million in FY 1996 to 2.5 million (Figure 8.13). Research has confirmed that families receiving child-care assistance are more likely to leave or avoid welfare, become settled in the job market, and work more hours (Fremstad, 2004). While the basic evidence on the impact of child-care spending is positive, there are two negatives. First, only about one in seven children qualified for child-care assistance is being served (Mezey, Greenberg, and Schumacher, 2002, 2). Second, funding for child care has stopped expanding. Welfare rolls have not continued to fall, thus there is less new money to support child care, and states have faced increasing fiscal challenges in a weak economy. The General Accounting Office (GAO) found that since 2001, twenty-three states have re-

Figure 8.13 **Children Projected to Receive Child-Care Assistance, FY 2005 Budget**

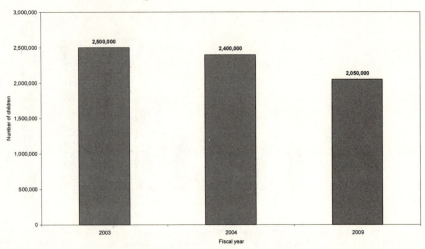

Source: Mezey et al. (2004).

duced child-care services, while nine states increased the availability of assistance, and three states made mixed changes (General Accounting Office, 2003, 8). In 2003, the GAO found that twenty-five states were serving all families who met eligibility requirements, while another twenty-five states and the District of Columbia do not meet the need (p. 19). Some states have a very large waiting list, including California (200,000 children), Florida (48,000), Georgia (22,000), and Texas (29,900) (Greenberg, Mezey, and Schumacher, 2003, 11).

The available data are not clear on the impact of child-care shortages. Employment rates for TANF recipients are probably lowered since families that cannot obtain child-care assistance are sometimes exempted from work requirements. Other families clearly rely on alternatives, such as relatives and friends and informal networks. Since the larger goal is not just child care, but quality child care that helps children make educational and social gains, the losses to children are impossible to quantify.

The federal budget being debated in the fall of 2004 projected a flat or even declining budget for child care through FY 2009. Using congressional budget estimates of anticipated future spending, Figure 8.13 shows a decrease in children served from 2.5 million in 2004 to 2.05 million in 2009. This would be a reduction of almost a half million children served. Thus, rather than grow to meet the unmet need, this critical service is projected to shrink. This is a serious negative for welfare reform.

How Well Are Sanctions Being Used?

To help the states implement PRWORA, they are given much stronger sanctioning powers. States vary significantly in how they use this authority. The way sanctions are being used in many states raises troubling issues (Bloom and Winstead, 2002). PRWORA allows the states to apply three types of sanctions: (1) adult-only sanctions, (2) pay-for-performance sanctions, and (3) full-family sanctions (Holcomb et al., 1998). Full-family sanctions result in the elimination of all cash assistance to the family unit. Sanctions may be lifted in return for compliance, or after some specified period, but they may also be permanent. Over thirty states impose full-family sanctions, generally only after less severe sanctions have failed to produce a desired change (Pavetti, Derr, and Hesketh, 2003; Pavetti and Bloom, 2001; Derr, 1998; Holcomb and Ratcliffe, 1998; Kaplan, 1999).

State officials generally believe that sanctions are necessary to convince recalcitrant recipients that they must comply with program guidelines or leave the rolls. In some states as many as half of all recipients have received one or more sanctions (Wu et al., 2004; Kalil et al., 2003; General Accounting Office, 1997; Fein and Karweit, 1997). Many recipients seem to be sanctioned because of barriers such as lack of transportation or child care or illness in the family that were undetected during initial interviews. Agency errors also account for a significant percentage of all sanctions. In Milwaukee County, Wisconsin, supervisors reversed 44 percent of the more than 5,000 sanctions issued through August 1996. In Massachusetts, some 47 percent of sanctions appealed through December 1996 were decided in the family's favor (Sherman et al., 1998). In Tennessee over 30 percent of all sanctioned cases were found to be in error (pp. 11–14).

By contrast, Oregon has designed its program to avoid inappropriate sanctions and to safeguard children in families when benefits are terminated. Before full-family sanctions can be imposed, a caseworker must meet with the noncompliant adult to determine if there are legitimate barriers to employment that can be addressed. Additionally, the caseworker must visit the home and develop a plan with other community agencies that addresses the safety of the children in the family. The plan has to include follow-up home visits. Last, a decision to impose a full-family sanction must be reviewed and approved by management (Holcomb et al., 1998).

Not surprisingly, families suffering full sanction are often in dire straits. In Michigan a study of sanctioned families found that before termination of benefits 85 percent had an income of at least $400 per month, and none had an income of less than $250 per month. After sanction, only 47 percent had an income of more than $400 per month, while 15 percent had no known income or employment (Pavetti et al., 1997). A significant percentage of the sanctioned families reported problems providing sufficient food for the family, insufficient income, and receipt of utility shutoff notices (Colville et al., 1997). A study of sanctioned families in South Carolina reported similar findings (Sherman et al., 1998).

The evidence also suggests that many sanctioned families are having difficulty paying for housing. In an Atlanta survey of families in shelters or other facilities for the homeless, 46 percent had lost TANF in the last year. An Idaho study found a similar problem, but at a lower rate. Sanctioned families also frequently report having trouble obtaining medical care (Sherman et al., 1998). Last, a study of sanctioned families found a much higher rate of referrals to child protective services for child abuse and neglect than in nonsanctioned families (Colville et al., 1997). While sanctions may or may not have contributed to abuse and neglect, it is clear that these families needed to be under supervision.

Significant barriers are rather common in welfare families. Sanctioned families seem to be those with the most severe barriers to employment (Cherlin et al., 2002; Kalil et al., 2003; Sherman et al., 1998). Olson and Pavetti (1996) have identified eight major personal and family challenges capable of hindering a recipient's transition from welfare to the workforce: physical disabilities and/or health limitations; mental health problems; health or behavioral problems of children; substance abuse; domestic violence; involvement with the child welfare system; housing instability; low basic skills and learning disabilities (see also Pavetti, 1999). Based on an analysis of the National Longitudinal Survey of Youth (NLSY), Pavetti and Olson concluded that some 90 percent of twenty-seven to thirty-five-year olds on welfare exhibit one or more potential challenges to employment (low basic skills, substance abuse, health problems, depression, domestic abuse, or a child with medical problems). About 50 percent of recipients suffer a more serious form of these barriers (alcoholism, abuse of crack or cocaine, extremely low basic skills, health problems that prevent work) (Pavetti et al., 1997).

These findings suggest that most states are not using sanctions, especially full-family sanctions, in a thoughtful manner. Sanctions clear the rolls of difficult and uncooperative recipients, but unless they are used carefully, they do not bring about desired behavioral responses, and the consequences for the family, especially children, are often far too high. Children are often punished simply because they had the misfortune of being born into a troubled family. Sanctions also frequently seem to result from poor assessments of the family's needs. The Oregon model of careful case management, home visits, intra-agency coordination, safeguards for children, and administrative review and approval is a much sounder policy.

Summary: What We Know About TANF Recipients and Leavers

The various studies of TANF recipients and leavers provide a number of important insights:

1. Employment among TANF family heads has greatly increased. Employed TANF heads have higher incomes and often are gaining employment skills. TANF families receive a great deal of support from the food stamp and Medicaid programs. They sometimes receive support from SSI, housing programs, and child-care and school-based meals programs.
2. When family heads leave cash welfare for employment, work pays. The incentive to move from no work to work is particularly clear. When leavers work, especially full time, their incomes modestly improve over time and their reliance on welfare programs declines. Still, although work pays better than welfare, family incomes tend to be below the poverty level or marginally above it. One major reason is that former welfare recipients often have very low skills, and most receive little in the way of education or skills training. Most earn wages that are above the minimum wage, but generally in the $7 to $8 range. A significant percentage has periods of unemployment or part-time employment. Because support services such as child care are often deficient or not available, many struggle to balance work with family responsibilities and the opportunity to assist low-income children is often lost.

3. States can design programs to help poorly educated and low-skilled recipients find a decent job and stay employed, but it is not easy (Gueron and Pauly, 1991; Blank, 1994; Pavetti et al., 1997). Considerable research has found that programs that only provide basic education and/or job skill training generally have only a modest impact on either employment or earnings. When earnings do increase for recipients who have received these services, most often it is because the recipients work longer hours, not because they find better jobs (Pauly and DiMeo, 1996). By contrast, programs that focus only on moving recipients into jobs as quickly as possible increase employment, but leave most recipients living in poverty. Portland's Steps to Success program (Scrivener et al., 1998) and several other similar projects suggest that the most promising strategies are those that move recipients into work and then provide them with help in pursuing education and building job and basic skills (Strawn, Greenberg, and Savner, 2001; Strawn, 1999; Cancian and Meyer, 1998; Rangarajan, Schochet, and Chu, 1998; Friedlander and Burtless, 1995; Freedman et al., 1996). Training and education produce the best results when they are directed at helping recipients gain the skills required to advance in their current jobs or obtain better-paying jobs. The training must provide skills that are in demand and employers must be willing to hire or promote people with those skills. Several states have developed promising initiatives to provide education and skill training to recipients on-site during work hours (Strawn, 1999, 10).

4. Programs that combine mandated work requirements with incentives have often produced very positive results, especially with the least-skilled workers. Both Minnesota and Connecticut have designed and implemented programs that have produced positive results (Bloom et al., 2000; Bos et al., 1999; Miller et al., 2000).

5. When poor and low-income family heads work, the EITC program, combined with food stamp and Medicaid benefits, greatly improves the income and security of recipient families. As Figure 8.10 shows, this combination of programs moves most families with one member working thirty-five or more hours a week over the poverty line.

6. Many family heads who leave welfare are not finding any type

of steady work. Estimates vary, but somewhere between 20 and 30 percent all welfare leavers have no steady employment. There is little evidence on what happens to these ex-recipients.

7. As detailed below, a significant percentage of those who have left welfare are having serious food and nutrition problems. However, the rates do not seem to be higher than pre–1996 levels.

8. A few states are doing a good job of subsidizing wages to make work pay (Sherman et al., 1998, 4). However, most states need to improve their effort. States have many options to help the working poor. States can improve the value of work by lowering the tax burden on low-income workers, by better designing income disregards, and by raising the eligibility levels for services such as child and health care. The federal government could make work pay better by raising the phase-out range of the EITC and by doing a better job of informing recipients that EITC benefits are available on a monthly rather than only on an end-of-year, lump-sum basis.

9. The broad discretion that PRWORA gives states to use sanctions to discipline TANF recipients is used badly by many states. While some states use this authority to encourage recipients to take corrective actions, other states seem to use it in a heavy-handed fashion to clear the rolls of recipients who need help the most. Children are often the victims of these policies. A number of states, including Oregon, demonstrate a much more enlightened and productive approach.

Reducing Out-of-Wedlock Births

An important focus of PRWORA is to bring about a significant reduction in out-of-wedlock births (Grogger and Bronars, 2001; Horvath-Rose and Peters, 2001; Fein, 1999; Bachrach, 1998). The legislation seeks to achieve this goal in several ways. The states are required to review and update their programs designed to reduce teen pregnancy and out-of-wedlock births. The act also attempts to reduce the chances of an additional pregnancy and improve the skills of teen mothers by giving them assistance only if they stay in school and live at home or in an adult-supervised setting. The law also provides funding for abstinence education, with high-risk groups being the target population. As an incentive, each year up to five states receive bonuses for having the largest declines in out-of-wedlock births without raising abortion rates above the state's 1995 level. If four or fewer states qualify for the bonuses, the bonus is $25 million per state. Improved child-support enforcement is also designed to encourage responsibility among teens and adults of both sexes.

Several provisions of the new law are implicitly and explicitly designed to lower the birth rate of adult women. First, most adult women are required to join the workforce, and working women generally have fewer children. Second, the law allows states to cap welfare benefits, with the hope of convincing single women that they should not take on additional financial responsibilities. The few well-designed studies of family caps have found no consistent impact on births (Congressional Research Service, 2004, L-3). Third, the emphasis on child support is designed in part to convince men to take more responsibility for birth control. The expectation over time is that both teen births and out-of-wedlock births to adult women will decline.

The emphasis of PRWORA is still more direct where teen births are concerned. PRWORA created a new section 510 of Title V, the Maternal and Children Health Block Grant of the Social Security Act. This section establishes a separate program for abstinence education. For each fiscal year between 1998 through 2004, $50 million a year is available for abstinence education.

The DHHS also attempted to give the states guidance in setting up effective antipregnancy programs by offering several models that have shown some successes, and by publicizing some of the characteristics of programs that have been judged to produce positive results. Although funding is provided only for abstinence programs, some of the models are considerably more comprehensive. DHHS has spread the message that effective antipregnancy policies include: (1) active involvement of parents and adults; (2) clear messages stressing abstinence and personal responsibility for one's actions; (3) strategies to help teens understand career options available to those who avoid pregnancy and obtain an education; (4) community involvement to help teens understand how to achieve worthy life goals; (5) strategies to enhance the self-worth and self-esteem of teenagers, ranging from community service to apprenticeships; and (6) sustained commitment (Department of Health and Human Services, 1998).

If a state decides to accept funding to promote abstinence, the guide-lines the state must follow are quite specific. Additionally, the secretary of the Department of Health and Human Services is required to rank the participating states on out-of-wedlock birth rates and changes in those rates over time. The secretary must prepare a report ranking the five best and the five poorest performing states. This provision is designed to share knowledge and pressure poorly performing states.

The DHHS also launched the National Strategy to Prevent Teen Preg-nancy campaign. This campaign is designed to help teenagers make bet-ter life choices, including avoidance of sexual activity. The strategy places special emphasis on encouraging abstinence, especially among nine- to fourteen-year-old girls. The campaign is called Girl Power! It includes a national media campaign designed to send a strong abstinence message to young girls.

Many of the states and some private organizations are also carrying out programs that go beyond abstinence education. Safer-sex programs are designed to provide unbiased information about sexuality, human development, and positive relationships. Interactive skills are often stressed, especially how to resist pressure to use drugs and alcohol or to have sexual intercourse. These programs generally include mentors and a support system that teens can turn to when in crisis.

Often another component of safer-sex programs is education about contraceptive use. These programs offer information regarding proper and consistent use of contraceptives, counseling about contraceptive availability, and follow-up care. Data show that teen access to contra-ceptives is often crucial to preventing adolescent pregnancy, but there are many obstacles. These include fear of family members becoming aware, high costs, lack of knowledge about where to go to get birth control services, the belief that contraceptives are dangerous, and a lack of transportation to clinics. Many programs try to overcome these barriers. The School/Community Program for Sexual Risk Reduction Among Teens is a program in current use in some states. This program provides free and confidential information and services to teens. The Self Center and Smart Start are similar programs. These programs pro-vide contraceptive information and services and also address the im-portance of monogamy.

There are clear advantages of safer-sex programs. They help teens learn about their bodies and their developing sexuality in a nonjudgmental man-ner. Adolescents are taught basic facts, along with information about the possible emotional and physical consequences of early sexual activity. They are given information about contraceptives, how to obtain them, and how to use them to protect themselves from unplanned pregnancies and the spread of sexually transmitted diseases (STDs) and AIDS. This type of program tells teens to think for themselves, ask questions, gather all the facts, and then make a rational decision based on the facts rather than yield to pressure from others teens or rely on misinformation. Safer-sex programs that rely on Norplant and Depo Provera birth control drugs have proven to be quite effective in reducing pregnancies (Donovan, 1998, 4).

There are also a large number of programs that go beyond abstinence and safer sex. These hybrid programs are much more holistic, focusing on the "whole person." Programs of this type teach sex education only as part of a more comprehensive approach. A broad range of services is offered, designed to enhance the education, self-esteem, career vision, and goals of the student. Typical services include vocational training, academic tutoring, career counseling, part-time employment, community service, and mentors. Generally, a life-options curriculum is offered as part of the program. Hybrid programs are offered under a variety of names, including the Teen Outreach Program (TOP) and the Children's Aid Society's Family Life. Programs of this type are fairly sophisticated and expensive, but they tend to be particularly effective for high-risk youth.

Figure 8.14 shows the percentage of all births to unmarried women from 1940 to 2001. Clearly, in recent years there has not been a major change in the overall rate of out-of-wedlock births. The overall rate of out-of-wedlock births rose slowly but steadily until 1994, and has changed little since then. In 2001, 33.5 percent of all children were born out of wedlock. If PRWORA-improved parent identification and child-support collections have had any impact, it has been to reduce the rate of growth in out-of-wedlock births rather than significantly reverse directions. The percent of all births to women twenty to twenty-four years of age that were out of wedlock actually increased over the 1990s and into the early 2000s. In 2001, 50.4 percent of all births to women twenty to twenty-four were out of wedlock, the highest recorded rate. In 1970, only 8.9 percent of all births to this age group were to unwed mothers.

The only group showing a decline in unwed births is teens, a major target of the reform policies. With the exception of black teens, the rate of decline for teens has been modest (Figure 8.15). In 1996, 9.6 percent of all births were to unwed teens. In 2001, the percentage had dropped

Figure 8.14   **Percentage of Births to Unmarried Women by Age Group, 1940–2001**

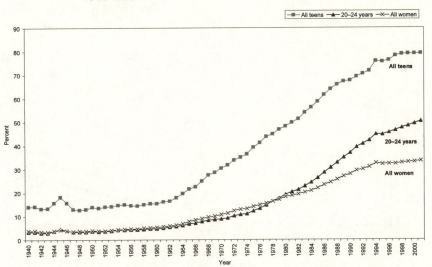

Sources: National Center for Health Statistics, "Nonmarital Childbearing in the United States, 1940–1999," *National Vital Statistics Reports*, vol. 48(16), 2000; "Births: Final Data for 2001," *National Vital Statistics Reports*, vol. 51(2), December.

to 8.7 percent. For white teens, the decline was extremely modest, declining from 7.7 percent to 7.3 percent. For black teens the drop was much more substantial. In 1996 almost 21 percent of all black births were to teens. By 2001 the rate had dropped to 17.5 percent.

Although it is too early to determine if PRWORA will accelerate the downward trend in teen pregnancy, it will not be surprising if it has that effect. None of the existing programs seems to have an overwhelming impact, but many of the more sophisticated programs lower teen pregnancies in a meaningful manner. The emphasis on reducing teen pregnancy found in PRWORA should stimulate enough attention and effort to produce even more gains. Of course, reform policies are only part of the social dynamic involved. With improved educational systems, changing cultural and peer messages, and better contraceptives, a combination of factors may contribute to a declining teen birth rate (Argys, Averett, and Rees, 2000).

The impact of PRWORA and improved child support on adult women may be more limited, but the combined impact of several factors may lower the out-of-wedlock birth rate. As low-income and poor mothers are moved into the job market, birth rates, including out-of-wedlock

Figure 8.15   Percentage of All Births to Unmarried Teens, Ages 15–19, by Race, 1940–2001

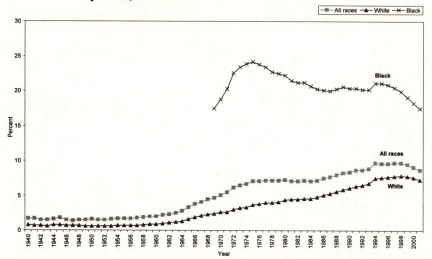

Sources: National Center for Health Statistics, "Nonmarital Childbearing in the United States, 1940–1999," *National Vital Statistics Reports*, vol. 48(16); "Births: Final Data for 2001," *National Vital Statistics Reports*, vol. 51(2), December.

births, should decline, and aggressive enforcement of child-support orders may convince many more men to take fatherhood more seriously.

Child-Support Collections

The emphasis of PRWORA on requiring both parents to support their children is resulting in significantly higher child-support collections. In 2001 almost $19 billion in child support was collected, an increase of 42 percent since FY 1997 (Figure 8.16). Of the more than 17 million cases in 2001, some 43 percent had a collection. This is almost double the FY 1997 rate. As Figure 8.16 shows, most of the collections go to non-TANF families. In 2001, 18 percent of the collections went to TANF families, while 36 percent went to families that never received public assistance, and 46 percent to families that were formerly on assistance. As TANF moves families off welfare, the trend will continue to move in the direction of non-TANF collections. The policy goal is to use child-support payments to help single-parent families obtain improved economic viability, along with a better chance of becoming established in the workforce.

Figure 8.16   **Total Child-Support Collections, 1978–2001**

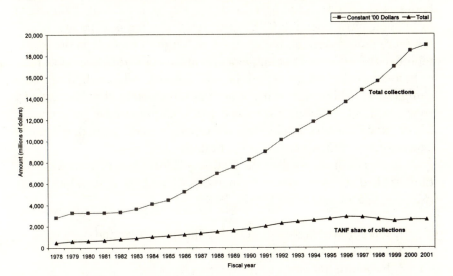

Source: Department of Health and Human Services (2004), Administration for Children and Families, *Child Support Collections*, 2003.

A PRWORA provision designed to improve child-support collections is the National Directory of New Hires, which started operation on October 1, 1998. This program requires employers to report all new hires to a state agency. The state agency consolidates all statewide data and sends them to the National Directory (Meyers, Glaser, and MacDonald, 1998). The data accumulated by the National Directory allow the federal Office of Child Support Enforcement (OCSE) to track absent parents across state lines. Almost one-third of all child-support cases involve parents living in different states. The goal of OCSE is to compile records on all noncustodial parents who, in total, owe support to over 30 million children. Once noncustodial parents are identified, child-support payments are withheld from their wages. In turn, noncustodial parents can use the registry to gain access and visitation to their children and for custody arrangements.

States use a variety of techniques to improve child support (Meyer, 1998). Many states have separated child-support enforcement (CSE) from the primary state child welfare agency. This allows caseworkers to handle a larger caseload, and it puts enforcement into the hands of an agency with more enforcement power. States are also running ad campaigns (often involving celebrities) designed to stress enforcement and "shame" parents into compliance. Wanted posters and newspaper lists are also being used. Colorado and Maryland consider their publicity campaigns to be their most effective CSE measures, reporting collections of $48 for every dollar spent on the campaigns. Virginia uses car boots to immobilize the vehicles of delinquent parents, color coding the boots pink or blue depending on the sex of the unsupported child or children. This campaign is designed to achieve both enforcement and public support (www.ncsl.org). Massachusetts and North Carolina have programs to honor "good" fathers, while Massachusetts also has a team that handles exceptionally difficult cases (www.ncsl.org).

A study commissioned by the National Conference of State Legislatures ranked the most effective methods of CSE in descending order (Meyers, Glaser, and MacDonald, 1998):

1. Income withholding (including income tax refunds)
2. License revocation
3. New hire tracking
4. Shared data for locating parents
5. Paternity establishment
6. Asset seizure

The partnership between the federal government and the states has clearly resulted in better enforcement. A supportive policy that seems to be working is the establishment of paternities. In 2001 the OCSE established 1.6 million paternities, over three times the 1992 figure of 510,000. This included paternities established under an in-hospital program that encourages fathers to voluntarily acknowledge paternity at the time of the child's birth.

The success of CSE depends at least in part on three strategies. First, child-support orders must exist. Paternity must be established, judicial access must be available for the custodial parent, and information on the employment and assets of the noncustodial parent must be available. Second, the absent parent must be located and targeted for compliance. Many states have established job search and training programs to help absent parents improve their ability to pay. Third, enforcement mechanisms must have real teeth. CSE enforcement techniques must be effective, and it must be known that they work. Publicity seems to be able to produce compliance rates beyond the actual work of the program or agency.

Over time, the expectation is that improvements in the establishment of paternity and better child-support enforcement will increasingly encourage men to take parenthood seriously. As a popular child-support enforcement ad says: "If you play, you pay."

Food Insecurity and Hunger

With rapid declines in TANF rolls, and less opportunity for many families to obtain public assistance, there has been considerable concern that food insecurity and hunger would increase (Figlio, Gundersen, and Ziliak, 2000). Figure 8.17 shows the results of annual surveys conducted in the Current Population Survey on household food resources. Based on ten questions for households without children, and eighteen for households with children, households are classified as food secure, food insecure without hunger, and food insecure with hunger (Nord, Andrews, Carlson, 2003, 2). The questions asked of household heads include whether they worry about not having enough food, sometimes cannot obtain enough food, cannot afford to eat balanced meals, sometimes skip preparing meals because food is not available, and if they or other family members are sometimes hungry because of a lack of food. Figure 8.17 shows that in recent years about 11.0 percent of households have been classified as food insecure, a very severe condition. These families have a substantial number of serious problems that keep them from having adequate food supplies. More than 3 percent of households are classified as suffering actual hunger. Children within these households suffer a lower rate of hunger, ranging in recent years from a high of 1 percent of all children in 1998, to 0.8 percent in 2002 (table 1). Adults report that they take care of children's needs before their own, that charities help, and that school feeding programs provide needed assistance.

Although the problems are very serious, one obvious fact about the data in Figure 8.17 is that while food insecurity and hunger vary somewhat by year, the problems have not become measurably worse since welfare reform. A major reason is that private charities play a critical role in helping those who have not been able to turn to government programs for help, or who need more help than they can obtain from public programs (Food Research and Action Center, 2004, News Digest #30, 6–9). Since the mid-1990s private charities have reported greatly increased demands on their resources. Additionally, in the last decade, over 50,000

Figure 8.17   **Prevalence of Food Insecurity and Hunger, 1998–2002**

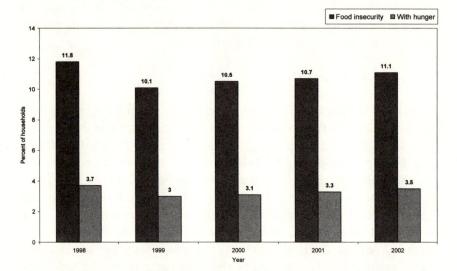

Source: U.S. Department of Agriculture (2004), Economic Research Service, *Household Food Security in the United States*, 2002, table 1.

new charities have sprung up to help the needy. Without the expanded role of private sector assistance, many more families would be struggling with food insecurity or even hunger (News Digest #27, 4–9).

Another issue is that the data in Figure 8.17 do not provide insight into the vulnerability of various high-risk households. Figure 8.18 examines food insecurity and hunger in different types of households in 2002. For some household types rates of food insecurity and even hunger are very high. Female-headed families suffer high levels of food insecurity, as do black and Hispanic households. Families below 185 percent of the poverty level suffer both high rates of food insecurity and hunger. Households with children living below the poverty level have very high rates of food insecurity (45.5 percent), but rather low rates of hunger. Again, adults are clearly skimping to help their children, many charities focus on helping children, and school feeding programs most likely play a major role in shielding children.

Food insecurity and hunger are clearly very serious problems. They are also problems that improved public policies could greatly alleviate. The fact that private charities have enhanced their role over the last decade has clearly kept these problems from being much worse.

Figure 8.18   **Prevalence of Food Insecurity and Hunger by Household Characteristics, 2002**

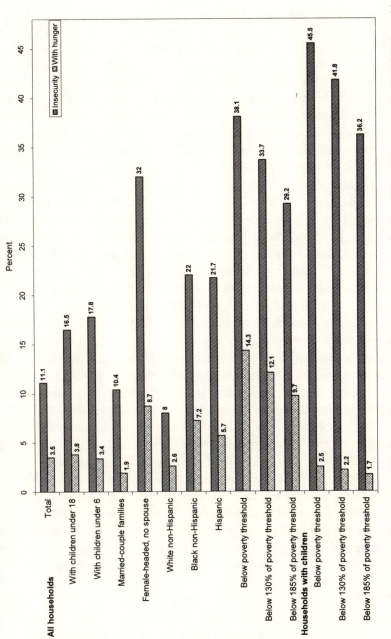

Source: U.S. Department of Agriculture (2004), Economic Research Service, *Household Food Security in the United States*, table 3.

Conclusions

PRWORA has had a major impact on America's welfare system and the low-income population. To a very significant extent, American welfare is becoming a system that is primarily focused on moving able-bodied adults into the job market while providing support services to help them remain employed. Welfare rolls across the nation have dropped dramatically since the early 1990s, and employment rates for adults receiving TANF are much higher than the rates under AFDC. Former recipients, and those diverted from welfare, have entered the job market in large numbers. Employment patterns among leavers vary substantially, but the evidence suggests that most work after leaving welfare, and many are working thirty to forty hours a week. Those who have left welfare for employment are financially better off than they were on welfare. A major reason is the financial support low-income earners receive from the EITC program, frequently supplemented by food stamps, school meal programs, and sometimes other assistance to help with housing and medical costs. Still, even leavers who work thirty to forty hours a week have incomes that barely push them over the poverty line for their family size, or incomes that leave them below the poverty line.

A great deal needs to be done to help TANF leavers and other low-income workers enjoy more success in the job market. Opportunities for continuing education and job training need to be significantly expanded. States can make work pay better by reducing taxes on low-income families, raising income disregards, lowering benefit reduction rates, and supplementing the EITC. States that do not supplement the EITC are missing an obvious way to help workers be more successful. Support services such as child care need to be substantially improved in almost every state. Child care is critical to working household heads, but it is the most deficient of the various support services promised by PRWORA. The federal government can also play an important role in making work pay better. The EITC can be amended to improve assistance to low-income families and to make more families aware of the program.

A substantial shortcoming of PRWORA is that states can meet employment goals by reducing their welfare rolls. The effect is to allow states to focus on moving recipients off the rolls, with little interest in what happens to them once they depart. If states had to meet real employment goals, they would focus more on continuing education and job training for leavers and much improved support services. States would also be less likely to use heavy-handed sanctions, which often do little other than remove the most troubled and needy recipients from the rolls.

Food insecurity and hunger are serious problems with low-income and poor households, especially those headed by single women and minorities. Private charities have worked feverishly to reduce these problems, but far too many families and children are without the food resources they require. This is a problem that requires increased federal involvement.

On the positive side, child-support collections are improving quite substantially. Whether energetic enforcement will lead to better parenting and more thoughtful decisions about parenthood is still an open question. Teen pregnancy rates have been headed in the right direction throughout the 1990s, and PRWORA may accelerate or at least maintain this trend.

In Chapter 9 we will examine the positives and negatives of welfare reform in more depth and suggest policy changes that will be required to better realize the goal of improving the lives of poor and low-income families through supported work.

9

Refining American
Social Welfare Policy

PRWORA has fundamentally changed the American approach to poverty, both philosophically and in policy design. The philosophical change is more important than the specific policies that have been passed to implement the new approach (Kaushal and Kaestner, 2001; Jones, 2001). The model PRWORA is based on—supported work for able-bodied adults—is in harmony with the American public's belief in self-reliance, equal opportunity, and limited government (Figure 1.3). Substituting employment for cash aid is likely to be the future of American welfare. It is unlikely that America will return to policies that allow large numbers of unemployed able-bodied adults to receive cash assistance for extended periods. The central question is: can this new approach be refined to do a better job of preventing poverty and helping the poor become economically independent?

The state policies that have been passed to implement the new welfare philosophy (that is, PRWORA, its amendments, and supplemental legislation) vary in imagination, energy, details, and success. The intent of Congress was to revamp the nation's welfare system in a short time, but the flexibility that states are given has resulted in mixed outcomes. Given the magnitude of the changes that states face to design and implement sophisticated reform, the short deadlines allowed by PRWORA, and the slackness of federal guidelines, it is not surprisingly that state results have been mixed. Some states are carrying out effective supported-work plans, and other states have shown considerable success, but most states are lagging. Welfare rolls have declined dramatically and welfare spending has shifted from cash assistance to support services for working families and the financing of some programs designed to reduce future poverty. Poverty rates declined modestly after PRWORA was passed, but the healthy economy of the late 1990s has vanished and poverty rates are rising. Families who have left welfare for full-time work are generally better off financially than they were on welfare, but many are still living in poverty or just above the poverty line. Many other ex–welfare families seem to be struggling with part-time or intermittent employment. To help the poor escape poverty through work, and to reduce the number of Americans who are likely to find themselves facing poverty, considerable policy innovation is still needed. To make welfare reform a serious and sincere national policy designed to help people escape poverty through supported employment, Congress will have to focus remedial attention on the lagging states.

The Pros and Cons of PRWORA

Below we will examine the best and worse characteristics and outcomes of PRWORA and its supporting legislation. This analysis provides insights into the policy changes required to make the reform approach work better.

The Positives

On the positive side PRWORA significantly improves the approach to welfare by:

Emphasizing Supported Work Over Welfare

Helping the able-bodied poor become employed significantly improves the chance that they will escape poverty, that their children will be in a positive environment, and that the next generation of poor will be smaller. Over the last fifty years, almost all cash welfare recipients have lived in poverty, regardless of the state in which they have resided. While cash welfare for the unemployed will continue to leave almost all recipients in poverty, employment, especially full-time, supported employment, improves the chances that families can escape poverty. This is particularly true over time as employees gain job experience and improved skills. The American public can be expected to be much more sympathetic and supportive of families that are members of the workforce, and the working poor are much more likely to be active in the political system (Mettler and Soss, 2004; Soss, 1999).

Placing the Obligation of Support on Both Parents

Because of badly designed laws and poor enforcement, millions of parents, mostly fathers, have abandoned their families and their duties to their children. PRWORA makes strides toward ending this abusive behavior. Holding both parents responsible for their children will not only improve the financial situation of millions of families, it will also force men to take parenthood or the potential of fatherhood more seriously. Hopefully, this will lower the number of children who grow up with only one parent.

Emphasizing Reducing Teen Pregnancy

Teen pregnancy is the superhighway to poverty. When teens have children out of wedlock the chances the family will be poor and that the children will be at risk are very high. Therefore, lowering the teen out-of-wedlock birthrate is essential to reducing the size of the next poverty generation. PRWORA's exclusive emphasis on abstinence is not a practical policy, but many states are experimenting with a wide range of more sophisticated policies and teen culture is increasingly less supportive of single parenthood.

Supporting Innovation

PRWORA's recognition that the causes of and solutions to poverty vary by state and even within states has to be applauded. States have the flexibility to test innovative policies and adopt policies designed to deal with specific types of poverty. The states are testing many innovative welfare experiments, and these trials are yielding a great deal of valuable information.

Stressing Individual Responsibility

Welfare reform is much more likely to be successful if the poor are required to become full partners in overcoming their problems. By making them understand that government cannot solve their problems but can help them do so, reform is much more viable.

Emphasizing People Helping People

PRWORA, and its supporting legislation, substantially increase the number of people and organizations that have accepted the challenge of helping the poor escape poverty. The Welfare to Work Partnership, a private sector initiative stimulated by PRWORA, has expanded the number of corporations actively involved in helping the poor make the transaction to independence through employment. Faith-based organizations are being allowed to contract to help the poor through counseling, education, and job training. Community support groups across the nation have been recruited to help the poor with everything from child care to transportation to job training. Hundreds of community groups have joined to make teen antipregnancy programs work better. The federal and many state governments have accepted responsibility for finding good jobs in their agencies for ex–welfare recipients. The cumulative impact of all these efforts is impossible to measure, but clearly positive.

The Negatives

Despite these positive features of PRWORA, there are some provisions in need of amendment or improvement. The most obvious problems that need attention include the following:

Work Does Not Pay

One of the most significant problems with PRWORA is that almost all of the ex-recipients who have joined the workforce tend to be living in poverty or close to the poverty line. Ex-recipients who are employed full time are usually much better off than they were on welfare, but they are still poor or near-poor. One major reason is that the jobs welfare leavers obtain pay low wages. Income disregards and state tax exemptions can improve the incomes of ex-recipients, but if recipients remain on TANF while working they soon exhaust their five years of benefit eligibility. Better options include education and job training programs for the employed, and improvements in state and federal EITC programs. Another reason many ex-recipients earn low wages is that they either do not work full time, or they go through periods of unemployment. Whether these problems are caused by a shortage of full-time jobs, skill deficiencies that might be corrected by on-the-job training, a lack of critical support services, a lack of will, or some combination of these factors, is not clear. In 1999 the Clinton administration issued rules that allow states to use TANF funds to subsidize services and underwrite private sector jobs for families that are employed but earning low wages. As long as these dollars are not used as cash aid, they do not count against the five-year time clock for TANF eligibility. This is a promising strategy that few states are using.

Lack of Employment by Many Who Leave Welfare

Many ex–welfare recipients who have left the rolls are not working. The numbers are not certain, but as many as 25 to 40 percent of all ex–recipients are not reporting any employment. Some of these families may not need assistance, but many probably rely on relatives, friends, and private charities. When families in need follow this path, it is not a solution. A well-designed reform system should help able-bodied adults find employment and then make every reasonable effort to help them have a real chance to prosper through viable employment.

Too Little Emphasis on Human Capital Development

Almost all the states have dramatically reduced their welfare rolls by simply requiring welfare recipients to leave the rolls as soon as possible for any job they can find. The "Work First" approach used by almost all the states may be justified by studies that show that education and job programs play only a modest role in helping welfare recipients find a better job or earn a higher wage. However, research indicates that once employed, combining work with education and training does result in improved wages and often in promotions (Scrivener et al., 1998). Most of the states are ignoring the benefits of this approach.

Support Services Are Weak

One of the most substantial challenges faced by states in carrying out reform is the obligation to provide the support services that millions of ex-recipients and low-income citizens need to enter the workforce. This includes providing all their qualified recipients with quality child care, transportation, short-term loans, and many other services. Some states have done this very well, but most states have struggled and many have done the absolute minimum (Mead, 2004; Gais et al., 2001; Meyers, Glaser, and MacDonald, 1998). The available data suggest that the most pressing need is high quality, affordable child care at flexible hours. To make PRWORA work better, support services will have to be significantly improved in most of the states.

The Twenty Percent Exemption May Leave Many Families in Need

Some poor adults are not employable and others cannot realistically work full time. Because of age, health, or the role they play in caring for children or others, some adults will never be able to join the workforce, and others will only be able to work part time. PRWORA allows states to exempt up to 20 percent of their recipients from time-limited aid. Although the basic idea is sound, this provision is being abused by some states. States often use this provision to ignore families that are the most difficult to help. A clear distinction needs to be made between difficult cases and impossible cases. Families that have significant but not insurmountable barriers (for example, low education and/or job skills, substance abuse problems, domestic violence, etc.) should be given the support they need to make the transition to work, even if it is part-time work. There are many reasons for helping these adults, but an important one is that families that remain on welfare almost always live in poverty. This means that children in these families grow up in poverty, often without the preschool help or other services that could enhance their futures. The only real hope that most of these families have to escape poverty and improve their lives is through employment. Of course, that small group of poor adults who cannot work should be given the support they need to escape poverty.

PRWORA's Deadlines Need Reassessment

The intent of reform was to transform the welfare system quickly (Grogger, 2002, 2000). The deadlines requiring recipients to enter the workforce after receiving cash assistance for twenty-four or fewer months (at state option), and the lifetime limit of five years for adults to receive assistance paid with federal dollars, probably account for the responsiveness of states in designing new plans. Still, the evidence shows that most ex-recipients are financially marginal even when they work full time, and that in most states a relatively small percentage of TANF adults are employed. These data suggest that states are under so much pressure to meet deadlines that they are focusing more on reducing the rolls than on helping recipients succeed in the workforce. The "sink or swim" mentality results in casualties. States can exempt some of the poor from time limits if services are unavailable, but generally they do not. Thus, the poor are held to the deadlines regardless of the quality of the support services available to them.

The nation's healthy economy during the first few years of PRWORA helped the new law get off to a good start. With a rapidly expanding job base, states were able to require recipients to quickly leave the rolls for available jobs. But, most of these jobs paid low wages, many were part time, and many provided either no benefits or very limited benefits and little chance of advancement. Since 2000 the economy has been performing less well, and poverty rates, unemployment rates, and welfare use have started to climb. A more thoughtful long-term approach will require the states to do a better job of preparing recipients for employment and then providing them and their families with quality support services and opportunities to improve their education and job skills. This approach is slower and more expensive, but the long-term outcome will be much better.

The deadline that would advance welfare reform would be one requiring the states to provide quality support services for their low-income citizens. If states were obligated to provide viable child care, preschool programs, extended care programs for the children of working parents, transportation options to jobs, and on-the-job training and education to all low-income families, employment rather than welfare would be a much more attainable goal for many poor adults and low-income families. Without deadlines for these services, and realistic measures of success, many states will continue to approach welfare reform in a half-hearted fashion.

Sanctions Are Often Not Being Used Thoughtfully

Sanctions, thoughtfully applied, can play an important role in convincing welfare recipients that they must accept responsibility for their successful transition to employment. However, the evidence reveals that many states are using sanctions in a careless and even harsh fashion (Pavetti, Derr, and Hesketh, 2003). This approach to sanctions does not produce compliance; it simply results in many families being dropped from the rolls. When these sanctions are permanent, and especially when the whole family loses benefits, both the adults and children end up in real jeopardy. The short deadlines allowed by PRWORA may be the primary reason that so many states have not used sanctions more thoughtfully. Several states, including Oregon, have adopted well-designed policies that apply full-family sanctions only after careful review and the development of a plan to protect the children in the family. The Oregon model should be adopted by all the states (Scrivener et al., 1998).

Limited Emphasis on Case Management

Helping many of the poor may require very active case management. Wisconsin's innovative welfare plan was initially based on the philosophy that recipients should be given "a light touch." The idea was that recipients should shoulder responsibility for themselves and learn that they had to take the initiative to solve most of their problems. Wisconsin officials quickly decided that this approach did not work (Mead, 2004, 111). Poor adults often needed considerable help and encouragement to resolve family and work problems, and to meet work requirements such as being on time and being prepared for work. Strong case management has significantly improved the success rate of the Wisconsin plan (Mead, 2004). The state of Oregon has also adopted strong case management, with excellent results (Scrivener et al., 1998).

The laissez faire approach of many states is unlikely to produce quality results, especially with the most troubled families. The next stage in positive welfare reform will require the states to accept the fact that many families need more guidance and support than initially thought. This will require better managed and more sophisticated welfare plans than most states have today.

The Data Available for Assessing State Programs Are Inadequate

PRWORA requires the states to collect and report a considerable amount of data on welfare reform. They must report state spending on welfare, TANF enrollments, the percentage of TANF recipients and leavers engaged in work activities, job retention rates, child-support funds collected, out-of-wedlock births, abortion rates, number of fathers identified when the mother is unmarried, and many other statistics. Yet, because of the way these data are collected and used, it is not possible to evaluate state performance with any precision.

There are two problems. First, some key performance measures do not take into consideration a state's previous progress on the indicator. For example, states are ranked on the percentage of their unemployed adult TANF recipients who enter employment during a particular year. Lagging states are advantaged by this approach. Those states that have made the most progress have the lowest potential to put an additional large percentage of their recipients into employment. In fact, the TANF recipients in the most successful states might be those who are the most difficult to place. The high-performing states are the least likely to show large advances in job entry, job retention, and earning gains for recipients and leavers.

Table 9.1 shows the high-performance bonuses awarded to states for FY 2000. The states are ranked on job entry of recipients, job retention over three quarters, earning gains over four quarters, and improvement over the preceding year. The states that rank high on these measures are generally those that have been making the least progress. The bonuses do not award high performance; they primarily serve as incentives to prod the poor performing states to do a better job. Giving incentives to lagging states is good policy, but these data cannot be used to rank states by their success in implementing PRWORA.

A second problem is that some of the data required to rank state performance are not collected. The missing indicators include data on the quality of case management and support services in each state. States report waiting lists for support services, but do not report on the quality of services provided or the number of potential users who avoid or give up trying to obtain help. Data on those who are diverted from welfare for a job are modest. Leaver data are often unexceptional and based on inadequate sampling procedures. Numerous studies focus on selected groups of leavers, but these studies are based on small samples and are often of questionable quality. Leaver data cannot be used to evaluate the quality of services being provided or changes required for better progress. Except for poverty rates and food adequacy, we know far too little about poor and low-income children.

Because the data are so inadequate, the federal government does not rank states by overall success. Scholars who try to do so either focus mostly on case studies and one or two indicators (Mead, 2004), or classify states by their adoption of various policy options (Meyers, Glaser, and MacDonald, 1998). Since states often adopt options but then fail to implement them, and implement options in very different ways, state plans provide an inadequate picture of reform quality.

Better data would provide a much clearer picture of the quality of state

Table 9.1

High-Performance Bonus Awards, FY 2000

	2000 Performance		2000 Improvement	
Rank	Job entry	Success in the workforce	Job entry	Success in the workforce
1	Montana	Arizona	Iowa	Nevada
2	Louisiana	Wisconsin	West Virginia	Iowa
3	New Mexico	Nebraska	Louisiana	North Dakota
4	Wyoming	Connecticut	Dist. of Columbia	South Dakota
5	Indiana	Iowa	Connecticut	West Virginia
6	Missouri	Minnesota	Hawaii	Washington
7	Nevada	New Hampshire	Kentucky	Hawaii
8	Texas	Indiana	Montana	Idaho
9	North Dakota	Rhode Island	Vermont	Montana
10	Utah	California	Rhode Island	Wisconsin
11	Virginia	Hawaii	New Hampshire	Louisiana
12	Alabama	Idaho	California	New Jersey
13	Kentucky	Illinois	North Carolina	Vermont
14	Michigan	Florida	Indiana	Tennessee
15	Delaware	Nevada	Michigan	Indiana
16	Tennessee	Washington	Arizona	Rhode Island
17	Idaho	Tennessee	Georgia	Alaska
18	North Carolina	Georgia	New Jersey	New Hampshire
19	Vermont	Alaska	Minnesota	Texas
20	Nebraska	Oregon	Utah	Missouri
21	Rhode Island	South Carolina	Missouri	Kansas
22	Alaska	Vermont	Nebraska	California
23	Pennsylvania	Missouri	Pennsylvania	Nebraska
24	Illinois	Kansas	Wyoming	Arizona
25	Arizona	North Carolina	New Mexico	Minnesota
26	Mississippi	Michigan	Alaska	Michigan
27	New Hampshire	Virginia	North Dakota	Mississippi
28	Minnesota	West Virginia	Oregon	Oregon
29	Iowa	New Jersey	Texas	Arkansas
30	Kansas	North Dakota	Kansas	Connecticut
31	Connecticut	Texas	Nevada	North Carolina
32	Oklahoma	Utah	Virginia	Massachusetts
33	Ohio	Arkansas	Illinois	Florida
34	New Jersey	South Dakota	Delaware	Pennsylvania
35	South Carolina	Maryland	Maryland	South Carolina
36	Georgia	Ohio	South Carolina	Wyoming
37	Hawaii	Pennsylvania	Mississippi	Illinois
38	California	Wyoming	Alabama	Utah
39	Arkansas	Montana	Tennessee	Georgia
40	Wisconsin	Colorado	Washington	Kentucky
41	Washington	Delaware	Ohio	Ohio
42	Massachusetts	Mississippi	Florida	Colorado
43	Maryland	Massachusetts	Maine	Maryland
44	Dist. of Columbia	New Mexico	Colorado	Delaware
45	West Virginia	Louisiana	Massachusetts	New Mexico

Table 9.1 *(continued)*

	2000 Performance		2000 Improvement	
Rank	Job entry	Success in the workforce	Job entry	Success in the workforce
46	Florida	Dist. of Columbia	Oklahoma	Oklahoma
47	Maine	Maine	Idaho	Maine
48	Colorado	Oklahoma	South Dakota	Dist. of Columbia
49	South Dakota	Kentucky	Wisconsin	
50	Oregon	Arkansas		

Source: Department of Health and Human Services (2004). Administration for Children and Families. TANF 5th Annual Report to Congress, 2003, table 5-5.

reform, but they would also create a dilemma for the federal government. PRWORA rests on the philosophy that states should be given considerable discretion in designing and implementing reform. The available evidence is inadequate, but strongly suggests that many states are not doing a very good job. Congress could require the states to meet higher standards for support services without requiring a uniform national policy or impeding state efforts to be creative. If the national conscience is that the path to stronger families, healthy environments for children, and a more prosperous nation is through supported employment, then reform is as important in laggard Texas as it is in progressive Wisconsin.

Hunger and Food Insecurity

As Figures 8.17 and 8.18 show, there is a great deal of food insecurity in low-income households. Almost half of all poor families struggle with food insecurity. Among poor children there is also some hunger. Figure 8.17 suggests that these problems have not become worse in recent years, but PRWORA certainly has not helped alleviate this problem, and food inadequacies remain unacceptably high. The intervention of private charities has clearly played an important role in keeping these problems from deepening. The continuation of these problems strongly suggests the need for improved ways to help low-income and poor families meet basic needs for adequate nutrition.

Reform Falters in a Weak Economy

Capitalist economies always have ups and downs. PRWORA was launched during a very strong economy, which promoted a great deal of success.

However, since the early 2000s, the economy has struggled. The result is that progress has lagged, poverty rates have increased, and welfare rolls have started expanding. These reversals suggest that states have to be better prepared to help ex-recipients and other low-income workers during weak economies. Low-income, low-skilled men are almost totally ignored by welfare reform. Large numbers of low-skilled men are completely unprepared to support their children or become partners in raising a family. A solution that could help ex-recipients and low-income men that is compatible with the spirit of reform would be increased reliance on a combination of options designed to subsidize employment. Private employers could be given tax credits for each low-income employee hired, trained, and retained for twelve to twenty-four months. In a weak economy these credits might have to be more favorable than those that were made available under the Work Opportunity Tax Credit (WOTC) and the Welfare to Work Tax Credit (WWTC) programs (Greenberg, Robins, and Walker, 2005; Blank, Card, and Robins, 2000; Blank and Schmidt, 2001). Also, state and federal funds might underwrite on-the-job education and skill training. The expense of this approach would be justified if the result was a significantly larger percentage of all ex-recipients being able to escape poverty through decent jobs.

Another alternative would be increased reliance on community service jobs (CSJ). As noted above, two of the most serious problems with PRWORA are that ex-recipients are finding that work does not pay and that many ex-recipients are not in the workforce. Community service jobs offer a viable way to address both of these problems. PRWORA gives states the latitude to use CSJs, but most states have not made significant use of this option. CSJs are complicated to set up and manage, but they offer some benefits. The research reviewed in Chapter 8 shows that many ex-recipients are not able to work their way out of poverty because they do not work full time, or because they have low skill levels. CSJs can address both of these problems (Poglinco, Brash, and Granger, 1998). CSJs can provide full-time employment and be designed to provide education and skills training on the job. A full-time job would season ex-recipients to a forty-hour workweek and provide a better weekly wage. It is important the CSJs provide a real service to the community. The public will not be sympathetic of CSJs that are make-work, and recipients can only gain real skills by doing work valuable to the community. CSJs should be transitional, but the time that recipients can be employed in a CSJ should vary depending on the characteristics and problems of the recipients and opportunities in the private sector.

Another advantage of CSJs is the success of this approach would depend substantially on the states significantly expanding quality child care and after-school care. The value of an excellent system of programs for children extends far beyond its role in allowing parents to enter the workforce. A major study conducted in Wisconsin shows the importance both of providing services and supplements to help ex-recipients become settled in the workforce and the impact of programs for children (Bos et al., 1999). Known as New Hope, this project shows that well-designed services and supplements can help ex-recipients and other low-income families increase their work effort and earnings and improve their chances of escaping poverty through work. These changes were significant but moderate, probably because this project did not involve any education or training for recipients.

One of the most important impacts of New Hope has been on the children of the recipients who have been placed in programs designed to free up their parent(s) for work. The New Hope project substantially increased the exposure of children in the project to formal child care, after-school care, and other organized activities. All the children receiving care benefited and their parents reported increased parental warmth and better monitoring of their children's activities (Bos et al., 1999, table 8). The designers of the New Hope project had expected better employment, improved material resources, and improved emotional well-being to result in better relationships between parents and children. This turned out to be true, especially for parents who could make a decent wage without having to work more than forty hours a week.

The study included surveys of the teachers of the children whose parents were enrolled in New Hope. Compared with a control group, boys in these families scored much better on academic performance, classroom skills such as the capacity to work independently, and social competence. The boys also had fewer behavior problems. Also, boys whose parents were in New Hope reported higher educational expectations and higher occupational aspirations and expectations than controls, signaling the program strengthened their ambitions for future study and careers. The daughters of parents in the program did not make educational gains, and it is not clear why. While the girls displayed few behavioral problems, they continued to score low on achievement tests (Bos et al., 1999, table 10).

The impact of New Hope on both parents and children, then, was positive, if incomplete. The boys make important gains, and the relationship between parents and children improved for both sexes. This study and others suggest that welfare reform could be substantially improved by full-time CSJs and by an expanded base of quality programs for children in poor and low-income families. Policies of this type not only can lift more of the poor out of poverty through viable employment, but they can also play a major role in reducing the size of the next generation of Americans who are unprepared to compete in the American economy.

The Future of American Social Policy: Ending Poverty as We Know It

If the United States is successful over the next few decades in reducing poverty and poverty rolls permanently, what options would this open for the design and evolution of social policy? Imagine, for example, that the number of cash welfare recipients could be reduced to 3 or 4 million, less than 2 percent of the population. This would be a huge decline from the record enrollment levels of the early 1990s when the number of cash welfare recipients was over 14 million, or about 5.5 percent of the population. Given the changes that have taken place over the last few years, a drop of this size is realistic.

If welfare policy is refined to really help the able-bodied succeed in the workplace, not only enrollments, but poverty would be significantly lowered. A lower poverty rate would reduce social welfare spending while increasing tax revenues. How much social welfare outlays would be lowered is impossible to calculate because reducing poverty may require significant expenditures on support services, community service jobs, training, and subsidies. Still, overall welfare spending should decline. As ex-recipients become settled in the job market, spending on programs such as TANF, food stamps, and most importantly, Medicaid, should decline. At the same time, refined welfare programs should be able to help many ex-recipients earn incomes high enough to contribute to the tax base and become active participants in the political process (Mettler and Soss, 2004; Soss, 2000; Soss, 1999, Esping-Anderson, 1999). Effective social welfare programs should also be able to further lower the teen out-of-wedlock birthrate, improve child-support levels, lower the size of the next poverty generation through pre-school and after school programs, and even reduce the size and costs of serious social problems such as crime.

The sum total of all these changes should provide the United States with the option of reducing the emphasis on welfare policy in favor of a more fully conceptualized family policy. Family policies, simply, are programs designed to strengthen all families. If Americans want to permanently reduce poverty, antipoverty policy cannot be focused only on the poor. To greatly reduce poverty, America needs a comprehensive and thoughtful set of policies that strengthen all families. Quality, universal health care, day care, and preschool programs have proved valuable in many western European and Scandinavian nations (Garfinkel, Hochschild, and McLanahan, 1996; Garfinkel and McLanahan, 1994; Kamerman, 1991; Kamerman, 1988). Additionally, educational programs for low-income students are credited with improving productivity and reducing dependency in these nations (Ravitch, 1996). The result is that poverty rates are much lower in many of these nations, and this is especially true for children, female-headed families, and the elderly (Smeeding, 2002; Rainwater and Smeeding, 2003; Smeeding et al., 1993; Smeeding, 1992b; Wong, Garfinkel, and McLanahan, 1993). These nations also suffer less violent crime, and educational achievement levels are higher for students in low-income families (Ravitch, 1996).

American social policy needs to evolve in this direction. The most significant change in American families in the twentieth century has been the growth of single-parent families, the movement of women into the job market, and the marginalization of many jobs (Hacker, 2002; Ellwood and Jenks, 2001). Today the majority of all American families are headed by a single parent or two working parents. But American social policy has not kept pace with the changes in family demographics (Hacker, 2004; Hacker, 2002). The result is that millions of families have little or no health insurance, millions of children do not receive quality child care and preschool education, millions of children do not have proper after-school care, and millions of parents struggle (often unsuccessfully) to balance parenthood with employment (Katz, 2001; Skocpol, 2000). Thoughtful policies can give American families the support they need to be viable, productive, competitive members of American society and the global economy. The result would be a healthier, safer, more competitive America.

Appendix A

Internet Sources

To keep abreast of the topics covered in this book, here are some excellent Web sites.

I. **Poverty in the United States**. Published annually by the Bureau of the Census. Go to www.census.gov and click on *poverty*. The latest report will be posted, along with valuable supplemental data. For 2003, the report is titled: "Income, Poverty, and Health Insurance Coverage in the United States: 2003."

II. **Supplemental data on poverty**. www.census.gov/hhes/poverty/histpov.

III. **Income in the United States.** Published annually by the Bureau of the Census. Go to www.census.gov and click on *income*.

IV. **America's Families and Living Arrangements.** Published biannually by the Bureau of the Census. www.census.gov/hhes/www/poverty.

V. **Children's Living Arrangements and Characteristics.** Published biannually by the Bureau of the Census. www.census.gov/hhes/www/poverty.

VI. **Supplemental data on families and living arrangements.** www.census.gov/population/www/socdemo/hh-fam.html.

VII. **Births, Marriages, Divorces, and Deaths.** Data published annually by the Centers for Disease Control. Go to www.cdc.gov and click on *births*.

VIII. **Child statistics.** The Web site **Childstats** is maintained by a number of federal agencies that collect data on American children. www.childstats.gov.

 IX. **Trends in the Well-being of America's Children and Youth**. Published annually by the Department of Health and Human Services. http//aspe.hhs.gov/hsp/03trends/.

  X. **Temporary Assistance to Needy Families**. The Department of Health and Human Resources provides Congress with regular updates on state implement of TANF provisions. www.acf.hhs.gov/programs/ofa/indexar.htm.

 XI. **Indicators of Welfare Dependency.** The Department of Health and Human Services provides Congress with studies of welfare use. http://aspe.hhs.gov/hsp/indicators.

XII. *Green Book*. A publication commissioned by the House Ways and Means Committee and conducted by the Congressional Research Service. It is a comprehensive review of social welfare programs and expenditures. http://waysandmeans.house.gov/documents.asp?

XIII. **Luxembourg Income Study.** A major research center in Europe that does comparative analysis of income and poverty in dozens of nations.www.Lisproject.org.

XVI. **World Value Survey.** A continuing study of public values across the world, including attitudes about the role of government, obligations to the poor, and social values. www.wvs.isr.umich.edu/pub.shtml.

If Addresses Fail

Web addresses change over time, but Google is an excellent tool for running down these reports. In Google, type in topics that you are interested in finding information about. For example, type in "TANF Annual Report to Congress," "Indicators of Welfare Dependency," or "Ways and Means: *Green Book*," and it will take you to the new address.

Appendix B

State Poverty Ranges
Using Three-Year Average, 2001–3

	Three-year average, 2001–3		Three-year average, 2001–3
United States	12.1		
Alabama	15.10	Montana	14.00
Alaska	9.00	Nebraska	9.90
Arizona	13.90	Nevada	9.00
Arkansas	18.50	New Hampshire	6.00
California	12.90	New Jersey	8.20
Colorado	9.40	New Mexico	18.00
Connecticut	7.90	New York	14.20
Delaware	7.70	North Carolina	14.20
District of Columbia	17.30	North Dakota	11.70
Florida	12.70	Ohio	10.40
Georgia	12.00	Oklahoma	14.00
Hawaii	10.70	Oregon	11.70
Idaho	11.00	Pennsylvania	9.90
Illinois	11.80	Rhode Island	10.70
Indiana	9.20	South Carolina	14.00
Iowa	8.50	South Dakota	10.90
Kansas	10.30	Tennessee	14.30
Kentucky	13.70	Texas	15.80
Louisiana	16.90	Utah	9.80
Maine	11.80	Vermont	9.40
Maryland	7.70	Virginia	9.30
Massachusetts	9.70	Washington	11.40
Michigan	10.80	West Virginia	16.90
Minnesota	7.10	Wisconsin	8.80
Mississippi	17.90	Wyoming	9.10
Missouri	10.10		

Source: Bureau of the Census (2004a), p. 68.

Appendix C

Percentage of People Without Health Insurance Coverage by State Using Three-Year Average, 2001–3

	Three-year average, 2001–3		Three-year average, 2001–3
United States	12.1		
Alabama	13.3	Montana	16.1
Alaska	17.8	Nebraska	10.3
Arizona	17.3	Nevada	18.3
Arkansas	16.6	New Hampshire	9.9
California	18.7	New Jersey	13.7
Colorado	16.3	New Mexico	21.3
Connecticut	10.4	New York	15.5
Delaware	10.1	North Carolina	16.1
District of Columbia	13.3	North Dakota	10.5
Florida	17.6	Ohio	11.7
Georgia	16.4	Oklahoma	18.7
Hawaii	9.9	Oregon	14.8
Idaho	17.5	Pennsylvania	10.7
Illinois	14.0	Rhode Island	9.3
Indiana	12.9	South Carolina	13.1
Iowa	9.5	South Dakota	11.0
Kansas	10.9	Tennessee	11.8
Kentucky	13.3	Texas	24.6
Louisiana	19.4	Utah	13.6
Maine	10.7	Vermont	9.9
Maryland	13.2	Virginia	12.5
Massachusetts	9.6	Washington	14.3
Michigan	11.0	West Virginia	14.8
Minnesota	8.2	Wisconsin	9.5
Mississippi	17.0	Wyoming	16.5
Missouri	10.9		

Source: Bureau of the Census (2004a), p. 69.

Appendix D

Marriages and Divorces, 1950–2001

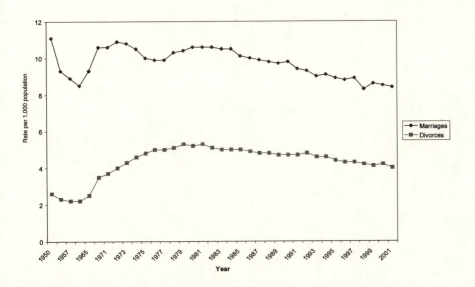

Source: National Center for Health Statistics, *Vital Statistics of the United States,* table 83.

References

Abramovitz, M. 1988. *Regulating the Lives of Women: Social Welfare Policy from Colonial Times to the Present.* Boston: South End Press.

Acs, G. 1996. "The Impact of Welfare on Young Mothers' Subsequent Childbearing Decisions." *Journal of Human Resources* 31(4): 898–915.

Acs, G., and Loprest, P. 2001. *Initial Synthesis Report of the Findings from ASPE's "Leavers" Grants.* Washington, DC: Urban Institute.

Acs, G., Loprest, P., and Roberts, T. 2001. "Final Synthesis Report of Finding from ASPE 'Leavers' Grants." Washington, DC: Urban Institute.

Acs, G., et al. 1998. "Does Work Pay? An Analysis of the Work Incentives under TANF." Occasional paper 9, Assessing the New Federalism. Washington, DC: Urban Institute.

Adams, T., Duncan, G., and Rodgers, W.L. 1988. "The Persistence of Urban Poverty." In *Quiet Riots: Race and Poverty in the United States,* eds. F.R. Harris and R.W. Wilkins, 212–41. New York: Pantheon.

Allard, S. 2004. "Competitive Pressures and the Emergence of Mothers' Aid Programs in the U.S." *Policy Studies Journal* 32(4): 521–44.

Allard, S., and Danziger, S. 2000. "Welfare Magnets: Myth or Reality?" *Journal of Politics* 62: 350–68.

Anderson, E. 1990. *Streetwise: Race, Class, and Change in an Urban Community.* Chicago: University of Chicago Press.

Anderson, P.M., and Levine, P.B. 2000. "Child Care and Mothers' Employment Decisions." In *Finding Jobs: Work and Welfare Reform,* eds. D. Card and R.M. Blank, 420–62. New York: Russell Sage Foundation.

Argys, L.M., Averett, S.L., and Rees, D.I. 2000. "Welfare Generosity, Pregnancies, and Abortions among Unmarried AFDC Recipients." *Journal of Population Economics* 13: 569–94.

Bachrach, C.A. 1998. "The Changing Circumstances of Marriage and Fertility in the United States." In *Welfare, the Family, and Reproductive Behavior,* ed. R.A. Moffitt, 9–32. Washington, DC: National Research Council.

Bailey, M.A., and Rom, M.C. 2004. "A Wider Race? Interstate Competition across Health and Welfare Programs." *Journal of Politics* 66(2): 326–47.

Bane, M.J., and Ellwood, D.T. 1994. *Welfare Realities: From Rhetoric to Reform.* Cambridge, MA: Harvard University Press.

————. 1983. "The Dynamics of Dependence: The Routes to Self-Sufficiency." Report prepared for the U.S. Department of Health and Human Services. Cambridge, MA: Urban Systems Research and Engineering.

Bane, M.J., and Jargowsky, P.A. 1988. "Urban Poverty Areas: Basic Questions Concerning Prevalence, Growth, and Dynamics." Center for Health and Human Resources Policy Discussion Paper Series, Harvard University.

Barber, B. 1984. *Strong Democracy.* Berkley: University of California Press.

Barrilleaux, C., Holbrook, T., and Langer, L. 2002. "Electoral Competition, Legislative Balance, and American State Welfare Policy." *American Journal of Political Science* 46(2): 415–27.

Barrilleaux, C., and Miller, M.E. 1988. "The Political Economy of State Medicaid Policy." *American Political Science Review* 82: 1089–1107.

Bartik, T.J. 2000. "Displacement and Wage Effects of Welfare Reform." In *Finding Jobs: Work and Welfare Reform,* eds. D. Card and R.M. Blank, 119–58. New York: Russell Sage Foundation.

————. 1996. *Who Benefits from State and Local Economic Development Policies?* Kalamazoo, MI: W.E. Upjohn Institute for Employment Research.

Bartik, T.J., and Eberts, R.W. 1999. "Examining the Effect of Industry Trends and Structure on Welfare Caseloads." In *Economic Conditions and Welfare Reform,* ed. S.H. Danziger, 119–58. Kalamazoo, MI: W.E. Upjohn Institute for Employment Research.

Bassi, L. 1987. "Family Structure and Poverty among Women and Children: What Accounts for Change?" Mimeo. Washington, DC: Georgetown University. June.

Beamer, G. 2005. "State Tax Credits and Making Work Pay." Forthcoming. *Review of Policy Research.*

Bell, S.H. 2001. "Why Are Welfare Caseloads Falling? Assessing the New Federalism." Discussion paper 01–02. Washington, DC: Urban Institute.

Bergman, B. 1989. "Occupational Segregation, Wages and Profits When Employers Discriminate by Race and Sex." *Eastern Economic Journal* 1 (April): 103–10.

Berinsky, A.J. 2002. "Silent Voices: Social Welfare Policy Opinions and Political Equality in America." *American Journal of Political Science* 46(2): 276–87.

Bernstein, J., and Garfinkel, I. 1997. "Welfare Reform: Fixing the System Inside and Out." In *The National Government and Social Welfare: What Should Be the Federal Role?* eds. J.E. Hansan and R. Morris, 166–81. Westport, CT: Auburn House.

Berry, W.D., Fording, R.C., and Hanson, R.L. 2003. "Reassessing the 'Race to the Bottom' Thesis: A Spatial Dependence Model of State Welfare Policy." *Journal of Politics* 659(2): 327–49.

Berry, W.D., Fording, R., and Hanson, R. 1998. "Measuring Citizen and Government Ideology in the American States, 1960–93." *American Journal of Politics* 42: 327–48.

Berry, F.S., and Berry, W. 1990. "State Lottery Adoptions as Policy Innovations: An Event History Analysis." *American Political Science Review* 84: 395–415.

Blank, R. 1997. "Why Has Economic Growth Been Such an Ineffective Tool Against Poverty in Recent Years?" In *Poverty and Inequality: The Political Economy of Redistribution,* ed. J. Neil, 188–210. Kalamazoo, MI: W.E. Upjohn Institute for Employment Research.

————. 1994. "The Employment Strategy: Public Policies to Increase Work and Earnings." In *Confronting Poverty: Prescriptions for Change,* eds. S. Danziger, G. Sandefur, and D. Weinberg, 168–204. Cambridge, MA: Harvard University Press.

Blank, R.M. 2001. "Declining Caseloads, Increased Work: What Can We Conclude About the Effects of Welfare Reform?" *Economics Policies Review* 7(2): 25–36.

Blank, R.M., Card, D., and Robins, P.K. 2000. "Financial Incentives for Increasing Work and Income among Low-Income Families." In *Finding Jobs: Work and Welfare Reform,* eds. R. Blank and D. Card, 373–419. New York: Russell Sage Foundation.

Blank, R.M., and Ellwood, D.T. 2002. "The Clinton Legacy for America's Poor." In *American Economic Policy in the 1990s,* eds. J. Frankel and P. Orszag, 749–800. Cambridge, MA: MIT Press.

Blank, R.M., and Ruggles, P. 1996. "When Do Women Use AFDC and Food Stamps? The Dynamics of Eligibility vs. Participation." *Journal of Human Resources* 31(1): 57–89.

Blank, R.M., and Schmidt, L. 2001. "Work, Wages, and Welfare." In *The New World of Welfare,* eds. R.M. Blank and R. Haskins, 70–102. Washington, DC: Brookings Institution.

Bloom, D., and Winstead, D. 2002. *Sanctions and Welfare Reform: Brookings Welfare Reform and Beyond.* Policy Brief no. 12. Washington, DC: Brookings Institution.

Bloom, D., and Michalopoulos, C. 2001. *How Welfare and Work Policies Affect Employment and Income: A Synthesis of Research.* New York: Manpower Demonstration Research Corp.

Bloom, D., et al. 2000. *Jobs First: Final Report on Connecticut's Welfare Reform Initiative.* New York: Manpower Demonstration Research Corporation.

Blum, B.B., and Berrey, E.C. 1999. *Welfare Research Perspectives: Past, Present and Future.* National Center for Children in Poverty. New York: Columbia University.

Bobo, L., and Smith, R. 1994. "Antipoverty Policy, Affirmative Action, and Racial Attitudes." In *Confronting Poverty: Prescriptions for Change,* eds. S. Danziger, G. Sandefur, and D. Weinberg, 365–95. Cambridge, MA: Harvard University Press.

Bos, H., et al. 1999. "New Hope for People with Low Incomes: Two-Year Results of a Program to Reduce Poverty and Reform Welfare." Memo. New York: Manpower Demonstration Corporation.

Bound, J., and Freeman, R. 1992. "What Went Wrong? The Erosion of Relative Earnings and Employment among Young Black Men in the 1980s." *Quarterly Journal of Economics* 107(1): 201–32.

Bound, J., and Holzer, H. 1993. "Industrial Structure, Skill Levels, and the Labor Market for White and Black Males." *Review of Economics and Statistics* 75(3): 387–96.

Bound, J., and Johnson, G. 1992. "Changes in the Structure of Wages in the 1980s: An Evaluation of Alternative Explanations." *American Economic Review* 82(3): 371–92.

Brace, P., and Jewett, A. 1995. "The State of State Politics Research." *Political Research Quarterly* 48: 643–81.

Brandon, P. 1995. "Vulnerability to Future Dependence among Former AFDC Mothers." Discussion paper no. 1055–95. Madison: Institute for Research on Poverty, University of Wisconsin.

Brauner, S., and Loprest, P. 1999. *Where Are They Now? What States' Studies of People Who Left Welfare Tell Us.* Series A, no. A-32, Assessing the New Federalism Project. Washington, DC: Urban Institute.

Brown, L., and Pollitt, E. 1996. "Malnutrition, Poverty, and Intellectual Development." *Scientific American* 274(2): 38–43.

Brown, M.K. 1999. *Race, Money, and the American Welfare State.* Ithaca, NY: Cornell University Press.

Brown, R.D. 1995. "Party Cleavages and Welfare Effort in the American States." *American Political Science Review* 89(1): 23–33.

Bryner, G. 1998. *Politics and Public Morality: The Great American Welfare Reform Debate.* New York: W.W. Norton.

Bryner, G., and Martin, R. 2005. "Innovation in Welfare Policy: Evaluating State Efforts to Encourage Work among Low-Income Families." Forthcoming. *Review of Policy Research.*

Bureau of the Census. 2004a. "Income, Poverty, and Health Insurance Coverage in the United States: 2003." *Current Population Reports,* Series P60–226. Washington, DC: U.S. Government Printing Office.

———. 2004b. "Evidence from Census 2000 about Earnings by Detailed Occupation for Men and Women." United States Census, Historical Tables. Washington, DC: U.S. Government Printing Office.

———. 2004c. www.census.gov. Historical Tables—Population. Washington, DC: U.S. Government Printing Office.

———. 2004d. *Statistical Abstract of the United States: 2003,* 117th edition. Washington, DC: U.S. Government Printing Office.

———. 2003a. "Poverty in the United States: 2002." *Current Population Reports,* Series P60–222. Washington, DC: U.S. Government Printing Office.

———. 2003b. "Income in the United States: 2002." *Current Population Reports,* Series P60–221. Washington, DC: U.S. Government Printing Office.

———. 2003c. "Children's Living Arrangements and Characteristics: March 2002." *Current Population Reports,* Series P20–547. Washington, DC: U.S. Government Printing Office.

———. 2002. "America's Families and Living Arrangements: 2000." *Current Population Reports,* Series P20–537. Washington, DC: U.S. Government Printing Office.

———. 1994. "Marital Status and Living Arrangements: March 1993." *Current Population Reports,* Series P20–478. Washington, DC: U.S. Government Printing Office.

Burke, V. 2003. *Cash and Noncash Benefits for Persons with Limited Income.* Washington, DC: Congressional Research Service.

———. 1998. *Cash and Noncash Benefits for Persons with Limited Income: Eligibility Rules, Recipient and Expenditure Data, Fiscal Years 1994–96* (98–226 EPW). Washington, DC: Congressional Research Service.

Burtless, G. 1995. "Employment Prospects of Welfare Recipients." In *The Work Alternative: Welfare Reform and the Realities of the Job Market,* eds. D.S. Nightingale and R.H. Haverman. Washington, DC: Urban Institute Press.

Burtless, G., Corbett, T., and Primus, W. 1998. "Improving the Measurement of American Poverty." *Focus* 19(2): 12–21.

Cain, G. 1987. "Negative Income Tax Experiments and the Issue of Marital Stability and Family Composition." In *Lessons from the Income Experiments,* ed. A. Munnell. Boston: Federal Reserve Bank.

Cancian, M., et al. 2003. "The Employment, Earnings, and Income of Single Mothers in Wisconsin Who Left Cash Assistance: Comparisons Among Three Co-horts." Madison: Institute for Research on Poverty, University of Wisconsin.

Cancian, M., et al. 2002. "Before and After TANF: The Economic Well-Being of Women Leaving Welfare." *Social Service Review* 76: 603–42.

———. 1998a. "Who Left Wisconsin's Welfare Rolls after 1995, and Who Stayed?" Memo. May.

———. 1998b. "Post-Exit Earnings and Benefit Receipt among Those Who Left AFDC in Wisconsin." Memo. August.

———. 1998c. "Post-Exit Earnings and Benefit Receipt among Those Who Left AFDC in Wisconsin." Memo. October.

Cancian, M., and Meyer, D.R. 1998. "Work After Welfare: Women's Work Effort, Occupation, and Economic Well-Being." Unpublished manuscript.

Casey Foundation. 1995. *Kids Count Data Book.* Baltimore: Annie E. Casey Foundation.

Centers for Disease Control and Prevention. 2003. "Births, Marriages, Divorces, and Deaths: Provisional Data for October–December 2002." Atlanta, GA.

Cheng, T. 1995. "The Chances of Recipients Leaving AFDC: A Longitudinal Study." *Social Work Research* 19(2): 67–96.

Cherlin, A., et al. 2002. "Operating within the Rules: Welfare Recipients' Experiences with Sanctions and Case Closings." *Social Service Review* 76(3): 387–405.

Citizen's Board of Inquiry into Hunger and Malnutrition in the United States. 1968. *Hunger, USA.* Boston: Beacon.

Citro, C.F., and Michael, R.T. (eds.). 1995. *Measuring Poverty: A New Approach.* Washington, DC: National Academy Press.

Colville, L., et al. 1997. "A Study of AFDC Case Closures Due to JOBS Sanctions." Michigan Family Independence Program. Available at www.mfia.state.mi.us/sanctions.

Congressional Research Service. 2004. Committee on Ways and Means. *2004 Green Book: Background Material and Data on Programs within the Jurisdiction of the Committee on Ways and Means.* Washington, DC: U.S. Government Printing Office.

———. 2000. Committee on Ways and Means. *2000 Green Book: Background Material and Data on Programs within the Jurisdiction of the Committee on Ways and Means.* Washington, DC: U.S. Government Printing Office.

———. 1998. Committee on Ways and Means. *1998 Green Book: Background Material and Data on Programs within the Jurisdiction of the Committee on Ways and Means.* Washington, DC: U.S. Government Printing Office.

Cook, J., and Martin, K.S. 1995. *Differences in Nutrient Adequacy among Poor and Nonpoor Children.* Medford, MA: Tufts University School of Nutrition, Center on Hunger, Poverty, and Nutrition Policy.

Corbett, T. 1995. "Welfare Reform in Wisconsin: The Rhetoric and the Reality." In *The Politics of Welfare Reform,* eds. D.F. Norris and L. Thompson, 216–37. Thousand Oaks, CA: Sage.

———. 1991. "Macroeconomic Performance and the Disadvantaged." *Brookings Papers on Economic Activity* 2: 1–61.

Corcoran, M. 2002. "Mobility, Persistence, and the Consequences of Poverty for Children: Child and Adult Outcomes." In *Understanding Poverty,* eds. S. Danziger and R.H. Haverman, 127–61. New York and Cambridge, MA: Russell Sage Foundation and Harvard University Press.

Corcoran, M., and Loeb, S. 1999. "Will Wages Grow with Experience for Welfare Mothers?" *Focus* 20(2): 20–21. Madison, WI: Institute for Research on Poverty.

Council of Economic Advisors. 1995. "Living Conditions of American Families." Table 1E. Annual Report, Washington, DC: U.S. Government Printing Office.

Danziger, Sandra, et al. 2000. "Barriers to the Employment of Welfare Recipients." In *Prosperity for All? The Economic Boom and African Americans,* eds. R. Cherry and W.M. Rodgers, 245–78. New York: Russell Sage Foundation.

Danziger, Sheldon, and Weinberg, D. 1994. "The Historical Record: Trends in Family Income, Inequality, and Poverty." In *Confronting Poverty: Prescriptions for Change,* eds. S.H. Danziger, G. Sandefur, and D. Weinberg, 18–50. Cambridge, MA: Harvard University Press.

Danziger, Sheldon, et al. 2002. *Does It Pay to Move from Welfare to Work?* PSC Research Report 00–449. August.

———. 1982. "Work and Welfare as Determinants of Female Poverty and Household Headship." *Quarterly Journal of Economics* 98(2): 519–34.

Darity, W.A., and Myers, S.L. 1983. "Changes in Black Family Structure: Implications for Welfare Dependency." *American Economic Review* 73 (May): 59–64.

Department of Health and Human Services. 2004a. *Temporary Assistance for Needy Families*. Fifth Annual Report to Congress, 2003. Washington, DC.

———. 2004b. *Trends in the Well-Being of America's Children & Youth: 2003*. Washington, DC: U.S. Government Printing Office.

———. 1998. *Temporary Assistance to Needy Families (TANF) Program.* First Annual Report to Congress. August. Washington, DC: Author.

Derr, M.K. 1998. "The Impact of Sanctioning on Utah's TANF Families." Paper presented at Association of Public Policy and Management Annual Research Conference, October, Los Angeles.

Devere, C. 2001. *Welfare Reform Research: What Do We Know about Those Who Leave Welfare?* CRS report for Congress. Washington, DC: Congressional Research Service.

Donovan, P. 1998. "Falling Teen Pregnancy, Birthrates: What's Behind the Declines?" *Guttmacher Report* 1(5). Available at www.agi-usa.org/pubs/journals/gr010506.html.

Downes, B.T. 1968. "Social and Political Characteristics of Riot Cities: A Comparative Study." *Social Science Quarterly* 49 (December): 509–20.

Duncan, G.J., and Chase-Lansdale, P. 2001a. "Welfare Reform and Child Well-Being." In *The New World of Welfare,* eds. R. Blank and R. Haskins, 391–417. Washington, DC: Brookings Institution.

———. 2001b. *For Better and For Worse: Welfare Reform and the Well-Being of Children and Families.* New York: Russell Sage Foundation.

Duncan, G.J., and Brooks-Gunn, J. 1998. "Making Welfare Reform Work for Our Children." National Center for Children in Poverty. *News and Issues* 8(1): 2–3.

Duncan, G.J., and Hoffman, S.D. 1988. "Welfare Dependence Within and Across Generations." *Science* 239: 467–71.

Duncan, G.J., et al. 1998. "How Much Does Poverty Affect the Life Chances of Children?" *American Sociological Review* 63(3): 406–23.

Elizar, D. 1984. *American Federalism: A View From the States.* New York: Harper & Row.

Ellwood, D., and Bane, M.J. 1985. "The Impact of AFDC on Family Structure and Living Arrangements." *Research in Labor Economics* 7(2): 137–49.

Ellwood, D.A. and Boyd, D. 2000. *Changes in State Spending on Social Services since the Implementation of Welfare Reform: A Preliminary Report.* Albany, NY: Rockefeller Institute of Government.

Ellwood, D.T. 2000. "The Impact of the Earned Income Tax Credit and Social Policy Reforms on Work, Marriage, and Living Arrangements." *National Tax Journal* 53:4 (pt. 2): 1063–105.

———. 1989. "Conclusions." In *Welfare Policy for the 1990s,* eds. P.H. Cottingham and D.T. Ellwood, 269–90. Cambridge, MA: Harvard University Press.

Ellwood, D.T., and Crane, J., 1990. "Family Change among Black Americans." *Journal of Economic Perspectives* 4(4): 65–84.

Ellwood, D.T., and Jencks, C. 2001. *The Growing Difference in Family Structure: What Do We Know? Where Do We Look for Answers?* Cambridge, MA: Kennedy School of Government, Harvard University.

Ellwood, D.T., and Rodda, D.T. 1991. "The Hazards of Work and Marriage: The Influence of Male Employment on Marriage Rates." Working paper, John F. Kennedy School of Government, Harvard University, Cambridge, MA.

Erikson, R., Wright, G., and McIver, J. 1993. *Statehouse Democracy: Public Opinion and Policy in the American States.* Cambridge, UK: Cambridge University Press.

Esping-Anderson, G. 1999. *Social Foundations of Postindustrial Economies.* New York: Oxford University Press.

European Commission. 1985. "On Specific Community Action to Combat Poverty (Council Decision of December 19, 1984)." 85/8/EEC. *Official Journal of the European Communities* 2(240).

Fagan, J. 1992. "Drug Selling and Illicit Income in Distressed Neighborhoods: The Economic Lives of Street-Level Drug Users and Sellers." In *Drugs, Crime, and Social Isolation: Barriers to Urban Opportunity,* eds. A.V. Harrell and G.E. Peterson, 292–312. Washington, DC: Urban Institute Press.

Feagin, J.R. 1975. *Subordinating the Poor: Welfare and American Beliefs.* Englewood Cliffs, NJ: Prentice Hall.

Federman, M., et al. 1996. "What Does It Mean to Be Poor in America?" *Monthly Labor Review* (May): 13–21.

Fein, D.J. 1999. *Will Welfare Reform Influence Marriage and Fertility? Early Evidence from the ABC Demonstration.* Bethesda, MD: Abt Associates.

Fein, D., and Karweit, J. 1997. *The Early Economic Impacts of Delaware's ABC Welfare Reform Program.* Cambridge, MA: Abt Associates.

Figlio, D.N., Gundersen, C., and Ziliak, J.P. 2000. "The Effects of the Macro-economy and Welfare Reform on Food Stamp Caseloads." *American Journal of Agriculture Economics* 82(3): 635–41.

Figlio, D.N., and Ziliak, J.P. 1999. "Welfare Reform, the Business Cycle, and the Decline in AFDC Caseloads." In *Economic Conditions and Welfare Reform,* ed. S. Danziger, 17–48. Kalamazoo, MI: W.E. Upjohn Institute for Employment Research.

Fisher, G.M. 1999. "Income Adequacy? The Official Poverty Line, Possible Changes, and Some Historical Lessons." *Community Action Digest* 1(1): 37–42.

———. 1998. "Setting American Standards of Poverty; A Look Back." *Focus* 19(2): 49–50.

————. 1997. "Disseminating the Administrative Version and Explaining the Administrative and Statistical Versions of the Federal Poverty Measure." *Clinical Sociology Review* 15(4): 164–68.

————. 1995 "Is There Such a Thing as an Absolute Poverty Line over Time? Evidence from the United States, Britain, Canada, and Australia on the Income Elasticity of the Poverty Line." Working paper. Washington, DC: U.S. Bureau of the Census. Available at www.census.gov/hhes/poverty/povmeasures/papers/elastap4.html.

————. 1992. "The Development and History of the Poverty Thresholds." *Social Security Bulletin* 55(4): 3–14.

Fitzgerald, J. 1995. "Local Labor Markets and the Local Area Effects on Welfare Duration." *Journal of Policy Analysis and Management* 14(1): 43–67.

Food Research and Action Center. 2004. Available at www.FRAC.org.

Fording, R. 2003. "Laboratories of Democracy or Symbolic Politics? The Racial Origins of Welfare Reform." In *Race, Welfare, and the Politics of Reform,* eds. S.F. Schram, J. Soss, and R. Fording, 116–31. Ann Arbor, MI: University of Michigan Press.

————. 2001. "The Political Response to Black Insurgency: A Critical Test of Competing Theories of the State." *American Political Science Review* 95(1): 115–30.

Foster, M. 1993. "Comparing Poverty in 13 OECD Countries: Traditional and Synthetic Approaches." *Studies in Social Policy* 10. Paris.

Freedman, S., et al. 2000. *National Evaluation of Welfare-to-Work Strategies.* New York: Manpower Demonstration Research Corporation

————. 1996. "The GAIN Evaluation: Five-Year Impacts on Employment, Earnings, and AFDC Receipt." Working paper 96.1. New York: Manpower Demonstration Research Corporation.

Freeman, R.B., and Katz, L.F. (eds.). 1995. *Differences and Changes in Wage Structures.* Chicago: University of Chicago Press.

Fremstad, S. 2004. *Recent Welfare Reform Research Findings: Implications for TANF Reauthorization and State TANF Policies.* Washington, DC: Center on Budget and Policy Priorities.

Friedlander, D., and Burtless, G. 1995. *Five Years After: The Long-Term Effects of Welfare-to-Work Programs.* New York: Russell Sage Foundation.

Fuchs, V. 1989. "Women's Quest for Economic Equality." *Journal of Economic Perspectives* 3 (Winter): 25–41.

Gabe, T. 2001. *Trends in Welfare, Work, and Economic Well-Being of Female-Headed Families with Children.* Congressional Research Service, Report for Congress. Washington, DC.

Gais, T.L., et al. 2001. "Implementation of the Personal Responsibility Act of 1996." In *The New World of Welfare,* eds. R. Blank and R. Haskins, 35–69. Washington, DC: Brookings Institution.

Garfinkel, I., Hochschild, J.L., and McLanahan, S.S. (eds.). 1996. *Social Policies for Children.* Washington, DC: Brookings Institution.

Garfinkel, I., and McLanahan, S.S. 1994. "Single-Mother Families, Economic Security, and Government Policy." In *Confronting Poverty: Prescriptions for Change,* eds. S. Danziger, G. Sandefur, and D. Weinberg, 205–25. Cambridge, MA: Harvard University Press.

———. 1986. *Single Mothers and Their Children: A New American Dilemma.* New York: Russell Sage Foundation.

General Accounting Office. 2003. *Child Care: Recent State Policy Changes Affecting the Availability of Assistance for Low-Income Families.* Washington, DC.

———. 1997. "Welfare Reform: States' Early Experiences with Benefit Termination." Available at www.gao.gov.

Gilens, M. 1999. *Why Americans Hate Welfare: Race, Media, and the Politics of Antipoverty Policy.* New Haven, CT: Yale University Press.

Gottschalk, P., and Danziger, S. 1986. "Poverty and the Underclass." Testimony before the Select Committee on Hunger, U.S. Congress. August.

Gottschalk, P., McLanahan, S., and Sandefur, G. 1994. "The Dynamics and Intergenerational Transmission of Poverty and Welfare Participation." In *Confronting Poverty: Prescriptions for Change,* eds. S. Danziger, G. Sandefur, and D. Weinberg, 85–108. Cambridge, MA: Harvard University Press.

Gottschalk, P., and Moffit, R. 1994. "The Growth of Earnings Instability in the U.S. Labor Market." *Brookings Papers on Economic Activity* 2(1): 217–72.

Gramlich, E., and Laren, D. 1991. "Geographical Mobility and Persistent Poverty." Paper presented at the Conference on Urban Labor Markets and Labor Mobility, Airlie House, VA, March 7–8.

Gray, V. 1973. "Innovation in the States: A Diffusion Study." *American Political Science Review* 67: 1174–85.

Green Book. 1994. Committee on Ways and Means, U.S. House of Representatives, U.S. Congress. Washington, DC: U.S. Government Printing Office.

Greenberg, D., Robins, P., and Walker, R. 2005. "Conducting Meta-Analysis of Evaluation of Government-Funded Training Programs." Forthcoming. *Review of Policy Research.*

Greenberg, M., Mezey, J., and Schumacher, R. 2003. *Child Care Funding: The Story Since 1996, the Challenges in Reauthorization.* Washington, DC:Center for Law and Social Policy.

Greenstein, R., and Guyer, J. 2001. "Medicaid and Food Stamps." In *The New World of Welfare,* eds. R. Blank and R. Haskins, 335–68. Washington, DC: Brookings Institution.

Gritz, R.M., and MaCurdy, T. 1991. *Patterns of Welfare Utilization and Multiple Program Participation among Young Women.* Report to the U.S. Department of Health and Human Services under Grant 88–ASPE 198A.

Groeneveld, L., Hanna, T., and Tuma, N. 1983. "Marital Stability." *Final Report of the Seattle/Denver Income Maintenance Experiment, Vol. 1: Design and Results.* Washington, DC: U.S. Government Printing Office.

Grogger, J. 2002. "The Behavioral Effects of Welfare Time Limits." *American Economics Review* 92(2): 385–89.

———. 2000. "The Effect of Time Limits, the EITC, and Other Policy Changes on Welfare Use, Work, and Income among Female-Headed Families." *Review of Economics Statistics* 4: 231–45.

Grogger, J., and Bronars, S.G. 2001. "The Effect of Welfare Payments on the Marriage and Fertility Behavior of Unwed Mothers: Results from a Twins Experiment." *Journal of Political Economy* 109(3): 529–45.

Gueron, J., and Pauly, E. 1991. *From Welfare to Work.* New York: Russell Sage Foundation.

Hacker, J.S. 2004. "Privatizing Risk without Privatizing the Welfare State: The Hidden Politics of Social Policy Retrenchment in the United States." *American Political Science Review* 98(2): 243–60.

———. 2002. *The Divided Welfare State: The Battle over Public and Private Social Benefits in the United States.* Cambridge, UK: Cambridge University press.

Hagenaars, A.K., DeVos, F., and Zaidi, A. 1994. "Patterns of Poverty in Europe." Paper presented to the 23rd General Conference of the IARIW, St. Andrews, Canada, August.

Hahn, L.H., and Feagin, J.R. 1970. "Rank-and-File Versus Congressional Perceptions of Ghetto Riots." *Social Science Quarterly* 51 (September): 361–73.

Harknett, K., and Gennetian, L.A. 2001. *How an Earnings Supplement Can Affect the Marital Behavior of Welfare Recipients: Evidence from the Self-Sufficiency Project.* Ottawa, Canada: Social Research and Demonstration Corporation.

Harris, K.M. 1996. "Life After Welfare: Women, Work and Repeat Dependency." *American Sociological Review* 61(1): 407–26.

———. 1993. "Work and Welfare among Single Mothers in Poverty." *American Journal of Sociology* 99(3): 317–52.

Haskins, R. 2001. "The Second Most Important Issue: Effects of Welfare Reform on Family Income and Poverty." In *The New World of Welfare,* eds. R. Blank and R. Haskins, 103–36. Washington, DC: Brookings Institution.

Haverman, R. 1987. *Poverty Policy and Poverty Research: The Great Society and the Social Sciences.* Madison: University of Wisconsin Press.

Haverman, R., and Wolfe, B. 1994. *Succeeding Generations: On the Effects of Investments in Children.* New York: Russell Sage Foundation.

Hill, K.Q., and Leighley, J.E. 1992. "The Policy Consequences of Class Bias in State Electorates." *American Journal of Political Science* 36: 351–65.

Hill, K.Q., Leighley, J.E., and Hinton-Andersson, A. 1995. "Lower-Class Mobilization and Policy Linkage in the U.S." *American Journal of Political Science* 39: 75–86.

Hoffman, S.D., Duncan, G.J., and Mincy, R.B. 1991. "Marriage and Welfare Use among Young Women: Do Labor Market, Welfare and Neighborhood Factors Account for Declining Rates of Marriage among Black and White Women?" Paper presented at the annual meetings of the American Economic Association, New Orleans, December.

Holcomb, P.A., et al. 1998. "Building an Employment Focused Welfare System: Work First and Other Work Oriented Strategies in Five States." Memo. Washington, DC: Urban Institute.

Holcomb, P.A., and Ratcliffe, C. 1998. "Consequences for Noncompliance in Indiana." Paper presented at the Association of Public Policy and Management Annual Research Conference. Washington, DC: Urban Institute.

Holzer, H.J. 1991. "The Spatial Mismatch Hypothesis: What Has the Evidence Shown?" *Urban Studies* 28(4): 104–22.

Holzer, H.J., and Stoll, M.A. 2001. *Employers and Welfare Recipients: The Effects of Welfare Reform in the Workplace.* San Francisco: Public Policy Institute.

Holzer, H.J., Stoll, M.A., and Wissoker, D. 2001. "Job Performance and Retention among Welfare Recipients." Discussion paper no. 1237–01, Institute Research on Poverty, University of Wisconsin, Madison.

Horvath-Rose, A., and Peters, H.E. 2001. "Welfare Waivers and Non-Marital Child-bearing." In *For Better and For Worse: Welfare Reform and the Well-Being of Children and Families,* eds. G.J. Duncan and P.L. Chase-Lansdale, 222–44. New York: Russell Sage Foundation.

Howard, C. 2003. "Is the American Welfare State Unusually Small?" APSA OnLine, July, 411–16. Available at www.apsanet.org/content_18086.cfm

———. 1999. "The American Welfare State, or States?" *Political Research Quarterly* 52: 421–42.

Hoynes, HW. 2000. "The Employment, Earnings and Income of Less Skilled Workers over the Business Cycle." In *Finding Jobs: Work and Welfare Reform,* eds. R. Blank and D. Card, 23–71. New York: Russell Sage Foundation.

———. 1996. "Local Labor Markets and Welfare Spells: Do Demand Conditions Matter?" Institute for Research on Poverty, Discussion paper no. 1104–96. Madison, WI.

Hoynes, H.W., and MaCurdy, T. 1994. "Has the Decline in Benefits Shortened Welfare Spells?" *American Economic Review* 84(2): 43–48.

Hughes, M.A. 1989. "Misspeaking Truth to Power: A Geographical Perspective on the Urban Fallacy." *Economic Geography* 65(1): 185–207.

Israel, F.I. (ed.). 1966. *State of the Union Messages of the Presidents 1790–1966,* vol. 3. New York: Chelsea House.

ISSP. 2001. International Social Survey Programme. Available at www.issp.org.

Jencks, C. 1992. *Rethinking Social Policy: Race, Poverty and the Underclass.* New York: Harper-Perennial.

Jencks, C., and Mayer, S. 1990. "Residential Segregation, Job Proximity, and Black Job Opportunities." In *Inner-City Poverty in the United States,* eds. L.E. Lynn, Jr. and M.G. McGeary, 319–37. Washington, DC: National Academy Press.

Johnson, J.H., and Oliver, M.L. 1991. "Economic Restructuring and Black Male Joblessness in U.S. Metropolitan Areas." *Urban Geography* 12(6): 542–62.

Johnson, R., and Cochrane, M.E. 2003. "The Road to Economic Self-Sufficiency: Job Quality and Job Transition Patterns After Welfare Reform." Working paper. Washington, DC: Center on Budget and Policy Priorities.

Jones, B. 2001. *Politics and the Architecture of Choice: Bounded Rationality and Governance.* Chicago: University of Chicago Press.

Juhn, C., Murphy, K.M., and Pierce, B. 1993. "Wage Inequality and the Rise in Returns to Skill." *Journal of Political Economy* 101(3): 410–42.

Kalil, A., et al. 2003. "Sanctions and Material Hardship under TANF." *Social Service Review* 76(4): 642–62.

Kamerman, S.B. 1988. *Mothers Alone: Strategies for a Time of Change.* Dover, MA: Auburn House.

Kaplan, J. 1999. "The Use of Sanctions Under TANF." Welfare Information Network. Available at www.welfareinfo.org/sanctionissue.

Kasarda, J.D. 1992. "The Severely Distressed in Economically Transforming Cities." In *Drugs, Crime, and Social Isolation: Barriers to Urban Opportunity,* eds. A.V. Harrell and G.E. Peterson, 61–84. Washington, DC: Urban Institute Press.

———. 1990. "Structural Factors Affecting the Location and Timing of Urban Underclass Growth." *Urban Geography* 11(1): 234–64.

———. 1989. "Urban Industrial Transition and the Underclass." *Annals of the American Academy of Political and Social Science* 501 (January): 26–47.

―――. 1988. "Jobs, Migration, and Emerging Urban Mismatches." In *Urban Change and Poverty,* eds. M.G. McGeary and L.L. Lynn Jr., 98–109. Washington, DC: National Academy Press.

Katz, M.B. 2001. *The Price of Citizenship: Redefining the American Welfare State.* New York: Metropolitan.

―――. 1986. *In the Shadow of the Poorhouse: A Social History of Welfare in America.* New York: Basic Books.

Kaus, M. 1995. *The End of Equality.* New York: Basic Books.

Kaushal, N., and Kaestner, R. 2001. "From Welfare to Work: Has Welfare Reform Worked?" *Journal of Political Analysis* 20(4): 699–719.

Key, V.O. 1949. *Southern Politics in State and Nation.* New York: Knopf.

Kinder, D., and Sanders, L. 1996. *Divided by Color: Racial Politics and Democratic Ideals.* Chicago: University of Chicago Press.

Korenman, S., and Miller, J. 1997. "Effects of Long-Term Poverty on Physical Health of Children in the National Longitudinal Survey of Youth." In *Consequences of Growing Up Poor,* eds. G.J. Duncan and J. Brook-Gunn, 213–43. New York: Russell Sage Foundation.

Kotz, N. 1979. *Hunger in America: The Federal Response.* New York: Field Foundation.

―――. 1971. *Let Them Eat Promises: The Politics of Hunger in America.* New York: Doubleday.

Ku, L., and Broaddus, M. 2003. "Why Are States' Medicaid Expenditures Rising?" Center on Budget and Policy Priorities, January. Available at www.cbpp.org

Lemann, N. 1991. *The Promised Land: The Great Black Migration and How It Changed America.* New York: Alfred A. Knopf.

Lemke, R.J., Witt, R., and Witte, A.D. 2001. "Child Care and the Welfare to Work Transition." Working paper, Economics Department, Wellesley College.

Lerman, R.I. 1989. "Employment Opportunities of Young Men and Family Formation." *American Economic Review* 79 (May): 62–66.

Leuchtenburg, W.E. 1963. *Franklin D. Roosevelt and the New Deal, 1932–1940.* New York: Harper & Row.

Lichter, D.T., et al. 1992. "Race and the Retreat from Marriage: A Shortage of Marriageable Men?" *American Sociological Review* 56(2): 15–32.

Lieberman, R. 1998. *Shifting the Color Line: Race and the American Welfare State.* Cambridge, MA: Harvard University Press.

Lieberman, R.C., and Shaw, G.M. 2000. "Looking Inward, Looking Outward: The Politics of State Welfare Innovation Under Devolution." *Political Research Quarterly* 53: 215–40.

Llobrera, J., and Zahradnik, B. 2004. "How State Earned Income Tax Credits Help Working Families Escape Poverty in 2004." Center on Budget and Policy Priorities, May. Available at: www.cbpp.org

Loprest, P. 2003. "Disconnected Welfare Leavers Face Serious Risks." Washington, DC: Urban Institute, August 21.

Loprest, P. 2001. *How Are Families that Left Welfare Doing? A Comparison of Early and Recent Welfare Leavers.* Series B, no. B-36, Assessing the New Federalism Project. Washington, DC: Urban Institute.

―――.1999. "Families Who Left Welfare: Who Are They and How Are They Doing?" Discussion paper, Assessing the New Federalism, An Urban Institute Program to Assess Changing Social Policies. Washington, DC.

Magnet, M. 1993. *The Dream and the Nightmare: The Sixties' Legacy to the Underclass*. New York: William Morrow.

Mare, R., and Winship, C. 1991. "Socioeconomic Change and the Decline of Marriage for Blacks and Whites." In *The Urban Underclass*, eds. C. Jencks and P. Peterson, 112–34. Washington, DC: Brookings Institution.

Martinson, K. 2000. *The National Evaluation of Welfare-to-Work Strategies Evaluation: The Experience of Welfare Recipients Who Find Jobs*. Washington, DC: MDRC for U.S. Department of Health and Human Services.

Massey, D.S. 1990. "American Apartheid: Segregation and the Making of the Underclass." *American Journal of Sociology* 96(2): 329–357.

Mead, L.M. 2004. *Government Matters: Welfare Reform in Wisconsin*. Princeton, NJ: Princeton University Press.

———. 2000. "Caseload Change: An Exploratory Study." *Journal of Political Analysis* 19(3): 465–72.

———. 1997. *The New Paternalism: Supervisory Approaches to Poverty*. Washington, DC: Brookings Institution.

———. 1992. *The New Politics of Poverty: The Nonworking Poor in America*. New York: Basic Books.

———. 1986. *Beyond Entitlement: The Social Obligations of Citizenship*. New York: Free Press.

Mettler, S. 2000. "States Rights, Women's Obligations: Contemporary Welfare Reform in Historical Perspective." *Women and Politics* 21(1): 1–34.

Mettler, S., and Soss, J. 2004. "The Consequences of Public Policy for Democratic Citizenship: Bridging Policy Studies and Mass Politics." *Perspectives on Politics* 2(1): 55–73.

Meyer, B.D. and Rossenbaum, D.T. 2001. "Welfare, the Earned Income Tax Credit, and the Labor Supply of Single Mothers." *The Quarterly Journal of Economics* August: 1063–1112.

Meyer, D., and Cancian, M. 1999. "Work after Welfare: Work Effort, Occupational and Economic Well-Being." *Social Work Research* 24: 69–86.

Meyer, D.R., and Cancian, M. 1998. "Economic Well-Being Following an Exit from AFDC." *Journal of Marriage and the Family* 60: 479–92.

Meyers, M., Gornick, J., and Peck, L. 2001. "More? Less? Or More of the Same? Trends in State-Level Social Policy after the Devolution Revolution." Paper presented at the American Political Science Association meetings, San Francisco, August.

Meyers, M.K., Glaser, B., and MacDonald, K. 1998. "On the Front Lines of Welfare Delivery: Are Workers Implementing Policy Reforms?" *Journal of Political Analysis* 17(1): 1–22.

Mezey, J., Greenberg, M., and Schumacher, R. 2002. *Welfare Reform Research: What Do We Know about Those Who Leave Welfare?* Washington, DC: Center for Law and Social Policy.

Mezey, J., et al. 2004. *Reversing Direction on Welfare*. Washington, DC: Center for Law and Social Policy.

Miller, C., et al. 2000. *Reforming Welfare and Rewarding Work: Final Report on the Minnesota Family Investment Program. Vol. 1: Effects on Adults*. New York: MDRC.

Moffit, R., and Roff, J. 2000. "The Diversity of Welfare Leavers: The Three-City Study." Working paper. Baltimore, MD: Johns Hopkins.

Moffitt, Robert A. 1992. "Incentive Effects of the U.S. Welfare System: A Review." *Journal of Economic Literature* 30(1): 1–61.

———. 1987. "Historical Growth in Participation in Aid to Families with Dependent Children: Was There a Structural Shift?" *Journal of Post-Keynesian Economics* 9(3) 347–63.

Moller, S., et al. 2003. "Determinants of Relative Poverty in Advanced Capitalist Democracies." American Sociological Review 68: 22–51.

Morris, P., et al. 2001. *How Welfare and Work Policies Affect Children: A Synthesis of Research.* New York: MDRC.

Moynihan, D.P. 1992. "How the Great Society Destroyed the American Family." *Public Interest* 108 (Summer): 53–64.

———. 1970. *Maximum Feasible Misunderstanding: Community Action in the War on Poverty.* New York: Free Press.

Murphy, K.M., and Welch, A. 1993. "Industrial Change and the Rising Importance of Skill." In *Uneven Tides: Rising Inequality in America,* eds. S. Danziger and P. Gottschalk, 81–107. New York: Russell Sage Foundation.

Murray, C. 1994. "Does Welfare Bring More Babies?" *Public Interest* 115: 17–30.

———. 1984. *Losing Ground: American Social Policy 1950–1980.* New York: Basic Books.

Nathan, R.P. 1986. "The Underclass: Will It Always Be With Us?" Paper presented to a symposium at the New School for Social Research, New York, November.

Nord, M., Andrews, M., and Carlson, S. 2003. *Household Food Security in the United States, 2002.* Washington, DC: Economic Research Service, USDA.

OECD. 1976. *Public Expenditures on Income Maintenance Programmes.* Paris: OECD.

O'Hare, W.P., and Curry-White, B. 1992. "The Rural Underclass: Examination of Multiple-Problem Populations in Urban and Rural Settings." Mimeo. Washington, DC: Population Reference Bureau. January.

Olson, K., and Pavetti, L. 1996. "Personal and Family Challenges to the Successful Transition from Welfare to Work." Memo. Washington, DC: Urban Institute.

Orshansky, M. 1988. "Commentary: The Poverty Measure," *Social Security Bulletin* 51(10): 22.

———. 1965. "Counting the Poor: Another Look at the Poverty Profile." *Social Security Bulletin* 28(1): 3–29.

Patterson, J. 1986. *America's Struggle against Poverty, 1900–1985.* Cambridge, MA: Harvard University Press. Revised edition.

Pauly, E., and DiMeo, C. 1996. *Adult Education for People on AFDC: A Synthesis of Research.* Washington, DC: U.S. Department of Health and Human Services and U.S. Department of Education.

Pavetti, L. 1999. "State Use of Sanctions." Memo. Prepared for AEI/Brookings Seminar on Welfare Reform. Washington, DC: Mathematica. January.

———. 1993. "The Dynamics of Welfare and Work: Exploring the Process by Which Women Work Their Way Off Welfare." Ph.D. dissertation, Harvard University.

Pavetti, L., and Acs, G. 1997. "Moving Up, Moving Out or Going Nowhere? A Study of the Employment Patterns of Young Women and the Implications for Welfare Mothers." Unpublished manuscript.

Pavetti, L., and Bloom, D. 2001. "Sanctions and Time Limits: State Policies, Their

Implementation and Outcomes for Families." In *The New World of Welfare,* eds. R. Blank and R. Haskins, 245–69. Washington, DC: Brookings Institution.

Pavetti, L., Derr, M.K., and Hesketh, H. 2003. *Review of Sanction Policies and Research Studies: Final Literature Review.* Report submitted to U.S. Department of Health and Human Services. Washington, DC: Mathematica.

Pavetti, L., et al. 1997. "Welfare to Work Options for Families Facing Personal and Family Challenges: Rationale and Program Strategies." Memo. Washington, DC: Urban Institute.

———.1996. "Designing Welfare-to-Work Programs for Families Facing Personal or Family Challenges: Lessons from the Field." Memo. Washington, DC: Urban Institute. December.

Payne, J.L. 1998. *Overcoming Welfare: Expecting More From the Poor and Ourselves.* New York: Basic Books.

Peterson, P.E., and Rom, M.C. 1989. "American Federalism, Welfare Policy, and Residential Choices." *American Political Science Review* 83: 711–29.

———. 1990. *Welfare Magnets: A New Case for a National Welfare Standard.* Washington, DC: Brookings Institution.

Pierson, Paul (ed.). 2001. *The New Politics of the Welfare State.* Oxford: Oxford University Press.

Piven, F.F., and Cloward, R.A. 1971. *Regulating the Poor: The Functions of Public Welfare.* New York: Vintage.

———. 1988. *Why Americans Don't Vote.* New York: Pantheon.

Plotnick, R.D. 1989. "Welfare and Out-of-Wedlock Childbearing: Evidence from the 1980s." Discussion paper no. 876–89. Madison, WI: Institute for Research on Poverty.

Plotnick, R.D., and Winters, R.F. 1985. "A Politico-Economic Theory of Income Redistribution." *American Political Science Review* 79: 458–73.

Poglinco, J.B., Brash, J., and Granger, R. 1998. *An Early Look at Community Service Jobs in the New Hope Demonstration.* New York: Manpower Demonstration Research Corporation.

Primus, W., et al. 1999. *The Initial Impacts of Welfare Reform on the Incomes of Single-Mother Families.* Washington, DC: Center Budget Policy Priorities.

Rainwater, L., and Smeeding, T.M. 2003. *Poor Kids in a Rich Country: America's Children in Comparative Perspective.* New York: Russell Sage Foundation.

Rangarajan, A., Schochet, P., and Chu, D. 1998. "Employment Experiences of Welfare Recipients Who Find Jobs: Is Targeting Possible?" Memo. Washington, DC: Mathematica.

Ravitch, D. 1996. "Somebody's Children: Educational Opportunity for All American Children." In *Social Policies for Children,* eds. I. Garfinkel and S. McLanahan, 83–112. Washington, DC: Brookings Institution.

Rector, R. 1998. *The Myth of Widespread American Poverty.* Heritage Foundation Backgrounder no. 1221. Washington, DC: Heritage Foundation.

Reischauer, R.D. 1989. "The Size and Characteristics of the Underclass." Paper presented at the Annual Meeting of the Association for Public Policy Analysis and Management, Bethesda, MD, October.

Richer, E., Savner, P., and Greenberg, M. 2001. "Frequently Asked Questions About Welfare Leavers." Pub. No. 01-30. Washington, DC: Center for Law and Social Policy.

Ricketts, E.R., and Sawhill, I.V. 1988. "Defining and Measuring the Underclass." *Journal of Policy Analysis and Management* 7(2): 316–25.

Rodgers, H.R. 1996. *Poor Women, Poor Children: American Poverty in the 1990s,* 3rd ed. Armonk, NY: M.E. Sharpe.

———. 1979. *Poverty Amid Plenty: A Political and Economic Analysis.* Reading, MA: Addison-Wesley.

Rom, M. 1999. "Transforming State Health and Welfare Programs." In *Politics in the American States,* eds. V. Gray and H. Jacobs, 117–31. Washington, DC: CQ Press.

Rom, M., Peterson, P., and Scheve, K. 1998. "Interstate Competition and Welfare Policy." *Publius* 28: 17–37.

Roosevelt, Franklin D. 1938. "Annual Message to the Congress, January 4, 1935." In *The Public Papers and Addresses of Franklin D. Roosevelt,* vol. 4. New York: Random House.

Rosenblatt, R. 1982. "Legal Entitlement and Welfare Benefits." In *The Politics of Law: A Progressive Critique,* ed. D. Kairys, 71–92. New York: Pantheon.

Ruggles, P. 1990. *Drawing the Line: Alternative Poverty Measures and Their Implications for Public Policy.* Washington, DC: Urban Institute Press.

Saavedra, L.A. 2000. "A Model of Welfare Competition with Evidence from AFDC." *Journal of Urban Economics* 47 (March): 248–79.

Sandefur, G., and Wells, T. 1997. "Using Siblings to Investigate the Effects of Family Structure on Educational Attainment." Discussion paper no. 1144–97. Madison, WI: Institute for Research on Poverty.

Schneider, A., and Ingram, H. 1993. "Social Construction of Target Populations: Implications for Politics and Policy." *American Political Science Review* 87(2): 334–47.

Schram, S. 1999. "Welfare Reform: A Race to the Bottom?" In *Welfare Reform: A Race to the Bottom?* eds. S.F. Schram and S.H. Beer, 165–87. Baltimore: Johns Hopkins University Press.

Schram, S.F., Soss, J., and Fording, R.C. (eds.). 2003. *Race and the Politics of Welfare Reform.* Ann Arbor, MI: University of Michigan Press.

Scrivener, S., et al. 1998. "National Evaluation of Welfare-to-Work Strategies: Implementation, Participation Patterns, Costs, and Two-Year Impacts of the Portland (Oregon) Welfare-to-Work Program." Executive summary taken from http://aspe.os.dhhs.gov/hsp/isp/portland/xsportld.htm.

Sears, D.O., Sidanius, J., and Bobo, L. (eds.). 2000. *Racialized Politics: The Debate about Racism in America.* Chicago: University of Chicago Press.

Sen, A. 1992. *Inequality Reexamined.* Cambridge, MA: Harvard University Press.

Shapiro, R.Y., et al. 1987. "The Polls: Public Assistance." *Public Opinion Quarterly* 51 (Spring): 120–30.

Sherman, A. 1997. *Poverty Matters: The Cost of Child Poverty in America.* Washington, DC: Children's Defense Fund.

Sherman, A., et al. 1998. *Welfare to What? Early Findings on Family Hardship and Well-Being.* Washington, DC: Children's Defense Fund, National Coalition for the Homeless. Available at www.childrensdefense.org/family.

Sherraden, M. 1991. *Assets and the Poor: A New American Welfare Policy.* Armonk, NY: M.E. Sharpe.

Shore, R. 1997. *Rethinking the Brain: New Insights into Early Development.* New York: Families and Work Institute.

Skocpol, T. 2000. *The Missing Middle: Working Families and the Future of American Social Policy.* New York: W.W. Norton.

———. 1996. *Boomerang: Clinton's Health Security Effort and the Turn against Government in U.S. Politics.* New York: W.W. Norton.

Skocpol, T., et al. 1993. "Women's Associations and the Enactment of Mother's Pensions." *American Political Science Review* 87: 686–701.

Smeeding, T.M. 2004. "Public Policy, Economic Inequality, and Poverty: The United States in Comparative Perspective." Memo. Maxwell School, Syracuse University.

———.2002. *Globalization, Inequality and the Rich Countries of the G-20: Evidence from the Luxembourg Income Study (LIS).* Syracuse, NY: Maxwell School of Citizenship and Public Affairs, Syracuse University.

———. 1992a. "U.S. Poverty and Income Security in a Cross-National Perspective: The War on Poverty, What Worked?" *Challenge* 35 (Jan.–Feb.): 16–23.

———. 1992b. "Why the U.S. Antipoverty System Doesn't Work Very Well." *Challenge* 35 (Jan.–Feb.): 30–35.

Smeeding, T., et al. 1993. "Noncash Income, Living Standards and Inequality: Evidence from the Luxembourg Income Study." *Review of Income and Wealth* Sept.: 229–56.

Smeeding, T., Rainwater, L., and O'Higgins, M. (eds.). 1990. *Poverty, Inequality and Income Distribution in Comparative Perspective: The Luxembourg Income Study.* London: Harvester Wheatsheaf and Washington, DC: Urban Institute Press.

Smeeding, T.M., Rainwater, L., and Burtless, G. 2001. "United States Poverty in a Cross-national Context." In *Understanding Poverty,* eds. S.H. Danziger and R.H. Haverman, 213–55. New York and Cambridge, MA: Russell Sage Foundation and Harvard University Press.

Soss, J. 2000. *Unwanted Claims: The Politics of Participation in the U.S. Welfare System.* Ann Arbor, MI: University of Michigan Press.

———. 1999. "Lesson of Welfare: Policy Design, Political Learning, and Political Action." *American Political Science Review* 93(2): 363–80.

Soss, J., et al. 2001. "Setting the Terms of Relief: Explaining State Policy Choices in the Devolution Revolution." *American Journal of Political Science* 45(2): 378–95.

Strawn, J. 1999. *Welfare-to-Work Programs: The Critical Role of Skills.* Center for Law and Social Policy. Available at www.clasp.org/pubs/jobseducation/skillspapere.htm.

Strawn, J., Greenberg, M., and Savner, S. 2001. "From Welfare-to-Work to Workforce Development." In *The New World of Welfare,* eds. R. Blank and R. Haskins, 223–44. Washington, DC: Brookings Institution.

Testa, M. 1991. "Male Joblessness, Nonmarital Parenthood, and Marriage." Paper presented at the Urban Poverty and Family Life Conference, University of Chicago, October 10–12.

Tobin, J. 1994. "Poverty in Relation to Macroeconomic Trends, Cycles, and Policies." In *Confronting Poverty: Prescriptions for Change,* eds. S.H. Danziger, G.D. Sandefur, and D.H. Weinberg, 147–67. Cambridge, MA: Harvard University Press.

Townsend, P. 1979. *Poverty in the United Kingdom.* Harmondsworth: Penguin.

U.S. Department of Agriculture. 2004. *Food and Action Center: State of the States.* Washington, DC.

U.S. Department of Housing and Urban Development. 1995. American Housing

Survey for the United States in 1995. *Current Housing Reports,* o. H150/95RV. Tables 2.9 and 4.9. Washington, DC.

U.S. National Center for Health Statistics, *Vital Statistics of the United States,* annual; and *National Vital Statistics Reports (NVSR),* formerly *Monthly Vital Statistics Report;* and unpublished data. See also www.cdc.gov/nchs.

Venti, S.F. 1984. "The Effects of Income Maintenance on Work, Schooling, and Nonmarket Activities of Youth." *Review of Economics and Statistics* 66(1): 16–25.

Ventry, D.J. 2000. "The Collision of Tax and Welfare Politics: The Political History of the Earned Income Tax Credit, 1969–99." *National Tax Journal* 53(4) (pt. 2): 983–1026.

Volden, C. 2003. "The Politics of Competitive Federalism: A Race to the Bottom in Welfare Benefits?" *American Journal of Political Science* 46(20): 352–64.

Walker, J.L. 1969. "The Diffusion of Innovations among the American States." *American Political Science Review* 63: 880–99.

Weaver, R.K. 2000. *Ending Welfare As We Know It.* Washington, DC: Brookings Institution.

West, C. 1993. *Race Matters.* Boston: Beacon Press.

Wilensky, H. 1975. *The Welfare State and Equality.* Berkeley: University of California Press.

Wilson, J.Q. 1973. *Political Organizations.* New York: Basic Books.

Wilson, W.J. 1987. *The Truly Disadvantaged: The Inner City, the Underclass, and Public Policy.* Chicago: University of Chicago Press.

———. 1980. *The Declining Significance of Race: Blacks and Changing American Institutions,* 2nd ed. Chicago: University of Chicago Press.

Wilson, W.J., and Mead, L.M. 1987. "The Obligation to Work and the Availability of Jobs: A Dialogue Between L.M. Mead and W.J. Wilson." *Focus* 10(2): 11–19.

Wilson, W.J., and Neckerman, K.M. 1986. "Poverty and Family Structure: The Widening Gap Between Evidence and Public Policy Issues." In *Fighting Poverty: What Works and What Doesn't,* eds. S.H. Danziger and D.H. Weinberg, 232–83. Cambridge, MA: Harvard University Press.

Wiseman, M. 1996. "State Strategies for Welfare Reform: The Wisconsin Story." *Journal of Policy and Management* 15(4): 515–46.

Wong, Y.I., Garfinkel, I., and McLanahan, S. 1993. "Understanding Cross-National Variation in Occupational Mobility." *American Sociological Review* 55(2): 560–73.

World Bank. 2004. *World Development Indicators 2004.* Oxford,UK: Oxford University Press.

Wright, G. 1976. "Racism and Welfare Policy in America." *Social Science Quarterly* 57: 718–30.

Wu, Chi-Fang, et al. 2004. "How Do Welfare Sanctions Work?" Discussion paper no. 1282–04. Madison, WI: Institute for Research on Poverty.

Zedlewski, S.R., and Loprest, P. 2001. "Will TANF Work for the Most Disadvantaged Families?" In *The New World of Welfare,* eds. R. Blank and R. Haskins, 311–34. Washington, DC: Brookings Institution.

Ziliak, J.E., et al. 2000. "Accounting for the Decline in AFDC Caseloads: Welfare Reform or the Economy?" *Journal of Human Resources* 35(3): 570–86.

Index

241

About the Author

Harrell R. Rodgers Jr., is a professor of political science and chair of the department of political science at the University of Houston. He is a policy specialist who has published ten books and over three dozen articles in peer-reviewed journals on American poverty. Rodgers has made over sixty presentations at American, European, and Asian universities on public finance, income distribution, and poverty in the Western world. He is International President-elect of Phi Beta Delta, the honor society for international scholars.